Ireland and the Home Rule Movement

Michael F. J. McDonnell

Contents

PREFACE 7
INTRODUCTION 10
CHAPTER I THE EXECUTIVE IN IRELAND..13
CHAPTER II THE FINANCIAL RELATIONS BETWEEN GREAT ....
    BRITAIN AND IRELAND..28
CHAPTER III THE ECONOMIC CONDITION OF IRELAND.....................41
CHAPTER IV THE LAND QUESTION..55
CHAPTER V THE RELIGIOUS QUESTION 86
CHAPTER VI THE EDUCATIONAL PROBLEM 110
CHAPTER VII UNIONISM IN IRELAND...131
CHAPTER VIII IRELAND AND DEMOCRACY 150
CHAPTER IX IRELAND AND GREAT BRITAIN 164
CHAPTER X CONCLUSION 187
NOTES 197

IRELAND AND THE HOME RULE MOVEMENT

BY

Michael F. J. McDonnell

PREFACE

Without agreeing with every expression of opinion contained in the following pages I heartily recommend this book, especially to Englishmen and Scotchmen, as a thoughtful, well-informed, and scholarly study of several of the more important features of the Irish question.

It has always been my conviction that one of the chief causes of the difficulty of persuading the British people of the justice and expediency of conceding a full measure of National autonomy to Ireland was to be found in the deep and almost universal ignorance in Great Britain regarding Irish affairs present and past--an ignorance which has enabled every unscrupulous opponent of Irish demands to appeal with more or less success to inherited and anti-Irish prejudice as his chief bulwark against reform. It was this conviction that led Mr. Parnell and his leading colleagues, after the defeat of the first Home Rule Bill in 1886, to establish an agency in England for the express purpose of removing the ignorance and combating its effects, and no advocate of Irish claims in England or Scotland has failed to find traces down to this day of the good effects of the propaganda thus set on foot, the discontinuance of which was one of the lamentable results of the dissensions in the Irish National Party between 1890 and 1900.

This book carries on the work of combating British ignorance of Irish affairs and the effects of that ignorance in a manner which seems to me singularly effective. The writer is no mere rhetorician or dealer in generalities. On the contrary, he deals in particular facts and gives his authorities. Nothing is more striking than the care he has obviously taken to ascertain the details of the subjects with which he has concerned himself and the inexorable logic of his method. It is perfectly safe to say that he neglected few sources of information which promised any valuable results, and that he has condensed into a few pages the more vital points of many volumes. It is not necessary to say anything of his style except that the cultured reader will most appreciate and enjoy it.

I shall not anticipate what the author has to say except in respect of one particular matter to which it seems to me expedient that particular public attention should be directed, especially by English and Scotch readers. The study of Irish history throws an inglorious light on the character of many British statesmen, and one of the salient facts brought into prominence in this little volume is that, even since the conversion of Mr. Gladstone to Home Rule, more than one leader of each of the two great political parties in Great Britain have displayed an utter lack of political principle in their dealings with Ireland, and especially with the Irish National question. I cannot but think that if the facts, as told by the author of this volume, were universally, or even widely, known amongst Englishmen and Scotchmen there would be much less heard in the future regarding Home Rule eventuating in Rome Rule or endangering the existence of the Empire.

This volume will, I hope, have a wide circulation not only in Great Britain, where such works are specially needed but in Ireland itself, where also it is well calculated to strengthen the faith of convinced Home Rulers and to bring light to the few who are still opposed to the Irish National demand for self-government, and to other important, though minor, reforms.

J. E. REDMOND.
December, 1907.

"You desire my thoughts on the affairs of Ireland, a subject little considered, and consequently not understood in England."

--JOHN HELY HUTCHINSON, Provost of Trinity College, Dublin, in a letter written in 1779 to the Lord Lieutenant of Ireland.

INTRODUCTION

A decree of Pope Adrian IV., the only Englishman who has sat in the chair of St. Peter, in virtue of the professed jurisdiction of the Papacy over all islands, by a strange irony, sanctioned the invasion of Ireland by Strongbow in the reign of Henry II. Three years ago I stood in the crypt of St. Peter's in Rome, and the Englishman who was with me expatiated on the appropriate nature of the massive sarcophagus of red granite, adorned only with a carved bull's head at each of the four corners, which seemed to him to stand as a type of British might and British simplicity, and in which the sacristan had told us lay all that was mortal of Nicholas Breakspeare. Seeing that I took no part in this panegyric, he took me on one side and said that he had observed that all the English Protestants to whom he showed that tomb, situated as it is literally **ad limina Apostolorum**, waxed eloquent, but, on the other hand, the Irish Catholics whom he told that it contained the bones of the dead Pontiff invariably shook their fists at the ashes of the unwitting, but none the less actual, source of their country's ills. To this I replied by quoting to him a saying of Robert Louis Stevenson, who as a Scot viewed the matter impartially, and who declared "that the Irishman should not love the Englishman is not disgraceful, rather, indeed, honourable, since it depends on wrongs ancient like the race and not personal to him who cherishes the indignation."

* * * * *

The great tendency which has been so marked a feature of Irish life in the course of the last decade to turn the attention of the people towards efforts at self-improvement and the development of self-reliance without regard to English aid, English neglect, or English opinion, excellent though it has been in every other respect, has had this one drawback--that there has grown up a generation of Englishmen, well-intentioned towards our country, to whom the problems of Irish Government are an unknown quantity. The ignorance of Irish affairs in England is due partly to ourselves, but also to a natural heedlessness arising from distance and preoccupation with problems with which Englishmen are more intimately concerned.

In view of the awakening of the democratic forces of Great Britain it is vital that Irish questions should be set before the eyes of the electorate of Great Britain, in order that, when for the first time the constitutional questions involved are placed before voters unprejudiced by class interests or a fellow-feeling for the pretensions of property wherever situate, there may be a body of electors who realise the gravity of the problems in question, and who have a full appreciation of the history of the case.

The Irish question has at no time been brought before the English public less than at the present day. Fenianism in the seventies and the various agrarian agitations in the eighties served to keep it constantly before the English eyes, and after the acquittal of Mr. Parnell and his colleagues of the charges brought against them by the *Times* much educative work was done for a short time by Irish Members of Parliament on English platforms.

The demands of Ireland have always been met by an unjust dilemma. When she has been disturbed the reply has been that till quiet is restored nothing can be done, and when a peaceful Ireland has demanded legislation the absence of agitation has been adduced as a reason for the retort that the request is not widespread, and can, in consequence, be ignored.

The remedy against such inaction proving successful in the future lies in the existence of a strong body of public opinion in Great Britain, educated to such a degree in the facts of the case as to brook no delay in the application of remedies. As for us, we cannot expect to be believed on our mere *ipse dixit*, and must state our case frankly and fully. The present moment seems timely, before the smoke of conflict has once again obscured the broad principles at issue. I propose to deal with reform in a plea of urgency, endeavouring at the same time to trace the evolution of things as they are to-day, quoting history as I go, with one aim only in view, to point a moral and adorn a tale. It will serve, I hope, to explain the past, to illustrate the present and to provide a warning for the future.

The Irish question, as Lord Rosebery has said, has never passed into history, because it has never passed out of politics.

M.F.J. McD.
Goldsmith Building, Temple.

CHAPTER I
THE EXECUTIVE IN IRELAND

"La 'Garnison' a occupee le pays sans le 'gouverner,' ou en ne le gouvernant que de son propre interet de classe: son hegemonie a ete toute sa politique."

--L. PAUL-DUBOIS, _L'Irlande Contemporaine_, 1907.

"A regarder de pres on percoit pourtant que cette imitation Irlandaise de la justice brittanique n'en est sur bien des points qu'une assez grossiere caricature, ce qui prouve une fois de plus que les meilleures institutions ne vaient que ce que valent les hommes qui les appliquent, et que les lois sent pen de choses quand elles ne sont pas soutenus par les moeurs."--Ibid.

What does Ireland want now; what would she have more?" asked Pitt of Grattan at the dinner table of the Duke of Portland in 1794, and Englishmen have echoed and re-echoed the question throughout the century which has elapsed. The mode in which it is asked reminds me, I must confess, of that first sentence in Bacon's Essays--"What is truth? said jesting Pilate, and would not wait for an answer."

When, at the end of the nineteenth century, the nations of Europe devoted themselves to a retrospective study of the progress which the passing of a hundred years had brought in its train, Ireland alone was unable to join in the chorus of self-congratulation which arose on every side.

To her it was the centenary of the great betrayal to which, as a distinguished writer has said, the whole of her unbribed intellect was opposed, and which formed the climax to a century of suffering. The ancients who held that when ill-fortune befell their country the gods must be asleep would have said so, I have no doubt, of Ireland at the end of the eighteenth century. The people, in a phrase which has become historic, had put their money on the wrong horse in their devotion to the Stuart cause, but, more than this, while they thereby earned the detestation of the Whigs, they were not compensated for it by the sympathy of the Tories, who feared their Catholicism even more than they liked their Jacobitism. In this way the country fell between two stools, and was not governed, even as English Statesmen professed to govern it, as a dependency, but rather it was exploited in the interest of the ruling caste with an eye to the commercial interests of Great Britain in so far as its competition was injurious. Religious persecution, aiming frankly at proselytism, and restrictions imposed so as to choke every industry which in any way hit English manufactures were the keynotes of the whole policy, and in the pages of Edmund Burke one may find a more searching indictment of English rule in Ireland in the eighteenth century than any which has since been drawn up.

The concession of Parliamentary independence in 1782 was, as the whole world knows, yielded as a counsel of prudence in the panic fright resulting from the American war and the French revolution. Under Grattan's Parliament the country began to enjoy a degree of prosperity such as she had never known before, and the destruction of that Parliament was effected, as Castlereagh, the Chief Secretary, himself expressed it, by "buying up the fee-simple of Irish corruption"; in other words, by the creation of twenty-six peerages and the expenditure of one and a half million in bribing borough-mongers.

In very truth, the Act of Union was one which, by uniting the legislatures, divided the peoples; and it has been pointed out as significant that when the legislatures of England and Scotland were amalgamated a common name was found for the whole island, but that no such name has been adopted for the three kingdoms which were united in 1800.

The new epoch began in such a way as might have been expected from its conception. The bigotry of George III., undismayed by what he used to call Pitt's "damned long obstinate face," delayed for more than a quarter of a century the grant of Emancipation to the Catholics, by promises of which a certain amount of their hostility had been disarmed. The tenantry asked in vain for nearly three-quarters of the century for some alleviation of the land system under which they groaned, and for an equal length of time three-quarters of the population were forced to endure the tyranny of being bound to support a Church to which they did not belong. The cause of struggling nationality on the Continent of Europe, in Italy, in Hungary, in Poland, in the Slav provinces, has in each case gained sympathy in Great Britain, but the cause of Irish nationality has received far other treatment. That charity should begin at home may be a counsel of perfection, but in point of fact one rarely sees it applied. Sympathy for the poor relation at one's door is a rare thing indeed. Increasing prosperity makes nations, as it makes men, more intolerant of growing adversity, and the poor man is apt to get more kicks than half-pence from the rich kinsmen under the shadow of whose palace he spends his life, and to whom his poverty, his relationship, and his dependence are a standing reproach. When I hear surprise expressed by Englishmen at the fact that England is not loved in Ireland I wonder at the deep-seated ignorance of the mutual feelings which have so long subsisted, one side of which one may find expressed in the literature of England, from Shakespeare's references to the "rough, uncivil kernes of Ireland" down to the contemptuous sneers of Charles Kingsley, that most English of all writers in the language, each of whom provides, as I think, a sure index to the feelings of his contemporaries and serves to illustrate the inveterate sentiment of hostility, flavoured with contempt, which, as Mr. Gladstone once said, has from time immemorial formed the basis of English tradition, and in regard to which the *locus classicus* was the statement of his great opponent, Lord Salisbury, that as to Home Rule the Irish were not fit for it, for, he went on to say, "nations like the Hottentots, and even the Hindoos, are incapable of self-government."

A cynical Irish Secretary once asked whether the Irish people blamed the Government for the weather; but it must be conceded that the mode of government made the Irish people more dependent than otherwise they would have been on climatic conditions, for this reason, that the margin between their means and a starvation wage was extremely small, and thus it was that in the middle of the century an act of God brought sufferings in its train, the results of which have not yet been effaced. Through it all the country was governed not in the interests of the majority, but according to the fiat of a small minority kept in power by armed force, not by the use of the common law, but of a specially enacted coercive code applicable to the whole or any part of the country at the mere caprice of the chief of the Executive. The record, it must be admitted, is not edifying. Irish history, one may well say, is not of such a nature as to put one "on the side of the angels." Lecky's "History of the Eighteenth Century" has made many converts to Home Rule, and I venture to think that when another Lecky comes to write of the history of the nineteenth century the converts which he will make will be even more numerous.

Among the anomalies of Irish government there is none greater than that of the Executive, the head of which is the Viceroy. The position of this official is very different from that of the governor of a self-governing colony. If the Viceroy is in the Cabinet his Chief Secretary is not; but the more common practice of recent years has been for the Chief Secretary to have a seat in the Cabinet to the exclusion of the Lord Lieutenant. Whether the latter be in the Cabinet or not he has no ministers as has a colonial governor, to whose advice he must listen because they possess the confidence of a representative body, and moreover, although the Lord Lieutenant is a Minister of the Crown, his salary is charged on the Consolidated Fund, with the result that his acts do not come before the House of Commons on Committee of Supply as do those of the Chief Secretary on the occasion of the annual vote for his salary.

As early as 1823 Joseph Hume ventilated the question of the abolition of the Lord Lieutenancy, and a motion introduced by him to that effect in 1830 received a considerable measure of support. Lord Clarendon, who in 1847 succeeded Lord Bessborough as Viceroy, accepted the office on the express condition that the Government should take the first opportunity of removing the anomaly. In pursuance of this agreement Lord John Russell, in 1850, introduced a Bill, which was supported by Peel, with the abolition of the office for its object. On its second reading it was passed by the House of Commons by 295 votes to 70. In spite of this enormous majority in its favour the Bill was dropped in an unprecedented manner, and never reached the Committee stage owing, it is said, to the opposition of Wellington, who objected to the fact that it would deprive the Crown of its direct control over the forces in Ireland and to the fact that it would leave the Lord Mayor of Dublin, a person who was elected by a more or less popular vote, as the chief authority in that city.

In 1857 the question was mooted once more, but no action ensued; and again, on the resignation of Lord Londonderry in 1889, a number of Irish Unionists, headed by the Marquis of Waterford, urged Lord Salisbury to consider the advisability of abolishing the office, together with the Viceregal Court, which a recent French observer has stigmatised as "peuple de snobs, de parasites et de parvenus."[1] In the event Lord Salisbury, so far from acceding to the request, nominated the Marquis of Zetland to the vacant post, and the proposal to abolish it has not since been raised in public. Men like Archbishop Whately, in the middle of the nineteenth century, whose ambition it was to see what they called the consolidation of Great Britain and Ireland effected, were strongly in favour of the proposal, and its rejection on so many occasions has been doubtless due to the fact that to mix and confound the administration of Ireland with that of Great Britain would necessitate the abandonment of the extreme centralisation of Irish Government, and those who were most anxious, as the phrase went, to make Cork like York were the very people who were most opposed to any abdication of Executive powers which an assimilation of methods of government would have inevitably brought in its train.

The government of Ireland is effected by more than forty boards--the forty thieves the late Mr. Davitt used to call them--and it will be for the reader, after he has studied the account which I propose to give of them, to say whether or not they deserve the name.

It is nearly twenty years since Mr. Chamberlain, in a celebrated speech at Islington, made the following remarkable declaration:--"I say the time has come to reform altogether the absurd and irritating anachronism which is known as Dublin Castle, to sweep away altogether the alien boards of foreign officials and to substitute for them a genuine Irish administration for purely Irish business." Change of opinions, no one can refuse to admit, in a statesman any more than in other men, and as regards the latter part of the extract which I have quoted Mr. Chamberlain may have changed his views, but it is to the earlier part of the sentence that I would refer. There is in it a definite statement of facts which no change in opinion on the part of the speaker could alter, and which express, as well as they can be expressed, the views of the Nationalists as to the Castle, the alien boards of foreign officials in which remained undisturbed during the course of the seven years after the coalition of Unionists and Tories, in which Mr. Chamberlain was the most powerful Minister of the Crown.

Of the purely domestic branches of the Civil Service in Great Britain, the Treasury, the Home Office, the Boards of Education, of Trade, and of Agriculture, the Post Office, the Local Government Board, and the Office of Works, are all responsible to the public directly, through representative Ministers with seats in the House of Commons, the liability of whom to be examined by private members as to minutiae of their departmental policy is one of the most valuable checks against official incompetence or scandals, and is the only protection under the constitution against arbitrary rule. The whole administrative machinery of the forty-three boards in Ireland has been represented in Parliament by one member, the Chief Secretary to the Lord Lieutenant, but he is supported since a few months ago by the Vice-president of the Department of Agriculture. The result is that, while in Great Britain a watchful eye can be kept on extravagance or mismanagement of the public services, the maintenance of a diametrically opposite system of government in Ireland, under which it is impossible to let in the same amount of light, leads to the bureaucratic conditions of which Mr. Chamberlain spoke in the speech from which I have quoted.

In answer to these complaints it is usual to point to the case of Scotland as analogous, and to ask why Ireland should complain when the Scottish form of government arouses no resentment in that country. The parallel in no sense holds good, for Scotland has not a separate Executive as has Ireland, although she has, like Ireland, a separate Secretary in the House of Commons. Scottish legislation generally follows that of England and Wales, and in any case Scotland has not passed through a period of travail as has Ireland, nor have exceptional remedies at recurring periods in her history been demanded by the social conditions of the country; and last, but by no means least, one has only to look at a list of Ministers of the Crown in the case of this Government, or of that which preceded it, to see that the interests of Scotland are well represented by the occupants of the Treasury Bench, whichever party is in power, so that it is no matter for surprise that she is precluded by her long acquiescence from demanding constitutional change.

More than half a century ago Lord John Russell promised O'Connell to substitute County Boards for the Grand Jury, in its capacity of Local Authority, but the latter survived until ten years ago. The members of the Grand Jury were nominated by the High Sheriffs of the Counties, and as was natural, seeing that they were the nominees of a great landlord, they were almost entirely composed of landlords, and the score of gentlemen who served on these bodies in many instances imposed taxation, as is now freely admitted, for the benefit of their own property on a rack-rented tenantry. A reform of this system of local government was promised by the Liberals in the Queen's Speech of 1881, but so far was the powerful Government at that time in office from fulfilling its pledges that not only was no Bill to that effect introduced, but, further, in April, 1883, a Bill to establish elective County Councils, which was introduced by the Irish Party, was thrown out in the House of Commons by 231 votes to 58. In his famous speech at Newport in 1885, when the Tories were, as all the world thought, coquetting with Home Rule, Lord Salisbury declared that of the two, popular local government would be even more dangerous than Home Rule. He based his view partly on the difficulty of finding thirty or forty suitable persons in each of the thirty-two counties to sit on local bodies, which would be greater than that of finding three or four suitable M.P.s for the same divisions of the country; but, even more than this, he insisted on the fact that a local body has more opportunity for inflicting injustice on minorities than has an authority deriving its sanction and extending its jurisdiction over a wider area, where, as he declared, "the wisdom of the several parts of the country will correct the folly or mistakes of one." In spite of this explicit declaration, when, in the following year, the Tories had definitely ranged themselves on the side of Unionism, the alternative policy to the proposals of Mr. Gladstone was nothing less than the establishment of a system of popular local government. Speaking with all the premeditation which a full sense of the importance of the occasion must have demanded, Lord Randolph Churchill, on a motion for an Address in reply to the Queen's Speech after the general election of 1886 had resulted in a Unionist victory, made use of these words in his capacity of leader in the House of Commons:--

"The great sign posts of our policy are equality, similarity, and, if I may use such a word, simultaneity of treatment, so far as is practicable in the development of a genuinely popular system of local government in all the four countries which form the United Kingdom."

In 1888 this pledge was fulfilled so far as the counties of England and Wales were concerned, and in regard to those of Scotland in the following year. When the Irish members, in 1888, introduced an Irish Local Government Bill, Mr. Arthur Balfour, as Chief Secretary, opposed it on behalf of the Government, and Lord Randolph Churchill, who at that time, having "forgotten Goschen," was a private member, gave further effect to the solemnity of the declaration, which, as leader of the party, he had made two years before, by his strong condemnation of the line adopted by the Chief Secretary in respect of a measure, to which, as he said, "the Tories were pledged, and which formed the foundation of the Unionist Party." In 1892 the Unionist Government introduced, under the care of Mr. Arthur Balfour, a Bill purporting to redeem these pledges. By one clause, which became known as the "put them in the dock clause," on the petition of any twenty ratepayers a whole Council might be charged with "misconduct," and, after trial by two judges, was to be disbanded, the Lord Lieutenant being empowered to nominate, without any form of election, a Council which would succeed the members who were removed in this manner. The criticism which this provision aroused was, as was natural, acute. The *Times* at this juncture declared that to attempt to legislate would be to court danger. The Local Government Bill was abandoned, and in this connection a sidelight is shed on the sincerity of the promises which had been made, in a letter from Lord Randolph Churchill to Lord Justice FitzGibbon on this question, dated January 13th, 1892, at the time when the Government of 1886 was drawing to a close, and Mr. Balfour was about to introduce the unworkable Bill which was clearly not intended to pass into law.

"My information," writes Lord Randolph, "is that a large, influential, and to some extent independent, section of Tories kick awfully against Irish Local Government, and do not mean to vote for it. This comes from a very knowledgable member of the Government outside the Cabinet. If the Government proceed with their project they will either split or seriously dishearten the party, and to do either on the verge of a general election would be suicidal. This is what they ought to do. They ought to say that Irish Local Government is far too large a question to be dealt with by a moribund Parliament; they ought to say that there is not sufficient agreement among their supporters as to the nature and extent of such a measure such as would favour the chances of successful legislation, and that they have determined to reserve the matter for a new Parliament when the mind of the country upon

Irish administration has been fully ascertained."[2]

The reflections suggested by this account of the evolution of a measure of party policy cannot be edifying to an Englishman or calculated to appeal as wise statesmanship to an Irishman. For what were the facts? A policy denounced as dangerous in the extreme in 1886 by the leader of the party was propounded as part of the policy of the same party in the following year with the acquiescence and, one must suppose, the imprimatur of its chief. Two years later pledges were thrown to the winds, and the excluded minister was provoked to criticism by the dropping of that line of action, of which he himself four years later is found in a private letter to be advising the abandonment on the most frankly avowed grounds of pure partisan tactics.

Twelve years were allowed to elapse before the promises made by Unionist leaders in the campaign of 1886 were fulfilled by the Local Government Act of 1898, which, for the first time in the history of Ireland, established by law democratic bodies in the country. One feels inclined to quote, in reference to the history of this question, that phrase of the largest master of civil wisdom in our tongue, as some one has called Edmund Burke, "that there is a way of so withholding as to excite desire, and of so giving as to excite contempt."

Under the provisions of the Act, County Councils, Urban District Councils, and Rural Councils were set up, and some notion of the revolution which it effected may be gathered from the fact that in a country which had hitherto been governed by the Grand Jury in local affairs the new Act at a sweep established a Nationalist authority in twenty-seven out of thirty-two counties.

Under the old *regime* the landlord used to pay one-half of the poor rate and the occupier the other half. The outcry of the landed interest, that under the County Councils they would be liable to be robbed by excessive poor rates, resulted in their share being made a charge on the Imperial Treasury, by which means they secured a dole of L350,000 a year out of the L725,000 concerned in the financial arrangements under the Act. Of the recipients of this *solatium* it was pointed out by an observer that the family motto of the Marquis of Downshire, who was relieved under the Act of liabilities to the extent of more than L2,000, is--"By God and my sword have I obtained"; while that of Earl Fitzwilliam, who had to be content with one-half of that amount, is--"Let the appetite be obedient to reason." The best answer to the pessimists in whom one suspects the wish was father to the thought, who prophesied disaster from an Act which they declared would open the door to peculation and jobbery, is to be found in the Local Government Board Report for 1903, issued on the expiry of the first term of office of the County Councils. It expressly declares that in no matter have the Councils been more successful than in their financial administration, and goes on to say that the introduction of political differences in the giving of contracts and the appointment of officers has occurred only in quite exceptional cases, and it concludes by declaring its opinion that the conduct of their affairs by the various local authorities will continue to justify the delegation to them of large powers transferred to their control by the Local Government Acts.

So much for the working of an Act, of which Lord Londonderry spoke as one "which the Loyalists view with apprehension and dismay." So far as certain loss of their supremacy was concerned they might indeed do so, but it is not for Englishmen to throw stones, since events have proved that it is not in the Irish local bodies, but in some of those of London itself, that financial scandals have been rife.

The one important respect in which the system of local government in Ireland differs from that established in England, Scotland, and Wales is that in the first named country the control of the constabulary is ruled out of the functions of the local bodies, and is still maintained under the central executive. The plethora of police in the country is one of the most striking features that meet the eye of anyone visiting it for the first time. The observant foreigner who, after travelling in England, crosses to Ireland and there sees on every wayside station at least two policemen varying the *ennui* of their unoccupied days by watching the few trains that pass through, feels homely pleasure at the thought that the *octroi* system which he has missed in England is in force in Ireland, and supposes that the men in uniform whom he cannot fail to see are the officials of the municipal customs. The tradition in Ireland is that half a century ago Smith O'Brien, who was under warrant for arrest, was detained at the station at Thurles by a railway guard, and that atonement has been made ever since for the absence of police on that occasion.

The Royal Irish Constabulary, than whom it would be difficult to find a physically finer lot of men, is a semi-military force living in barracks, armed with rifles, bayonets, swords, and revolvers. Well may a French writer exclaim--"Combien differents du legendaire et corpulent 'bobby,' cette 'institution populaire' de la Grande Bretagne," who goes without even a truncheon as a weapon of offence. The numbers of the Royal Irish Constabulary, which were largely increased in the days of widespread agitation, are still maintained with scarcely any diminution. The force, when established just seventy years ago, at a time when the population of the country was nearly eight millions, numbered only 7,400 men; the population of the island is to-day only half what it was then, but there are now on the force of the constabulary 12,000 men, and 8,000 pensioners are maintained out of the taxes. In addition to this, there is a separate body of Dublin Metropolitan Police, and smaller bodies in Belfast and Derry are also maintained. The Dublin police force costs nearly six times as much per head of population as does that of London. It comprises 1,200 men, and there has been a remarkable increase in cost in the last twenty years, rising to its present charge of L160,950, with no apparent corresponding increase in numbers or in pay. The total cost of the police system of Ireland is one and a half million pounds per annum; that of Scotland, with an almost equal population, is half a million sterling. To appreciate the point of this it must be realised that the indictable offences committed in Ireland in a year are in the proportion of 18 as compared with 26 committed in Scotland, while criminal convicts are in the ratio of 13 in Ireland to 22 in Scotland.

Such a state of things as this, by which the cost of police per head of population is no less than 7s., has only been maintained by the busy efforts, which Lord Dunraven denounced a couple of years ago, of those who paint a grossly exaggerated picture of Ireland, so as "to suggest to Englishmen that the country is in a state of extreme unrest and seething with crime." The columns of the English Unionist Press show the manner in which these impressions are disseminated, and there is in London a bureau for the supply of details of examples of violence in Ireland for the consumption of English readers. The Chief Secretary, in the House of Commons last session, spoke of the fact that he received large numbers of letters of complaint, purporting to come from different sufferers from violence and intimidation in Ireland, but which, on close examination, turned out to be signed by one man. The recent disgraceful attempt to beat up prejudice on the part of the ***Daily Graphic***, which reproduced what purported to be not the photograph of an actual moonlighting scene, but a photograph of "the real moonlighters, who obligingly re-enacted their drama for the benefit of our photographer," incurred the disgust which it deserved; but it was only one instance of an organised campaign of bruiting abroad invented stories of lawlessness in Ireland which constitutes the deliberate policy of the "carrion crows," whose action Mr. Birrell so justly reprobated, and of which the most flagrant instances were the purely fictitious plots to blow up the Exhibition in Dublin; an outrage at Drumdoe, which on investigation proved to be the work of residents in the house which was supposed to be attacked, and the allegation of a dynamite outrage at Clonroe, in County Cork, which the police reported had never occurred. One would have thought that the experience which the *Times* and the Loyal Irish and Patriotic Union gained at the hands of Richard Pigott would at least have made people chary of this form of propaganda. The comparison of the criminal statistics of Ireland with those of Scotland which I have made shows how much truth there is in the imputations of widespread lawlessness, as does also the number of times on which in each year the Judges of Assize comment favourably on the presentment of the Grand Jury; and, moreover, the closing of unnecessary prisons which is going on throughout the country is a further proof, if any be needed, of the falsity of the charges which are so industriously spread abroad. The only gaol in the County of Wexford was closed a few years ago; that at Lifford, the only one in the County of Donegal, has since been closed as superfluous. Of the two which existed till recently in County Tipperary, that at Nenagh is now occupied as a convent, in which the Sisters give classes in technical instruction to the girls of the neighbourhood; but perhaps the most piquant instance is to be found in Westmeath, where an unnecessary gaol at Mullingar, having been for some time closed, is now used for the executive meetings of the local branch of the United Irish League. All these, it should be noted, are to be found in districts which are inhabited not by "loyal and law-abiding" Unionists, but by a strongly Nationalist population.

Enough insistence has not been laid on one important fact in the administration of the criminal law in Ireland. In England anyone who alleges that he has been wronged can institute a criminal process, and this is a frequent mode of effecting prosecutions. In Ireland the social conditions in the past have brought it about that the investigation and prosecution of crime is left to the police, who, as a result, have attained something of the protection which *droit administratif* throws over police and magistrates in France and other Continental countries, by which State officials are to a large extent protected from the ordinary law of the land, are exempted from the jurisdiction of the ordinary tribunals, and are subject instead to official law administered by official bodies.

The principles on which it is based in countries where it forms an actual doctrine of the constitution are the privilege of the State over and above those of the private citizen, and, secondly, the *separation des pouvoirs* by which, while ordinary judges ought to be irremovable and independent of the Executive, Government officials ought, *qua* officials, to be independent to a great extent of the jurisdiction of the ordinary courts, and their *actes administratifs* ought not to be amenable to the ordinary tribunals and judges. The absorption by the constabulary of the conduct of prosecutions has tended towards such a state of things as this; but a far more potent factor in the same direction has been the confusion of administrative and judicial functions which the relations of the resident magistrates to the police have engendered, and to an even greater degree has this tendency been accentuated in the case of the special "removable" magistrates appointed in proclaimed districts under the Coercion Acts, for they are officials in whom the judicial and the constabulary functions are inextricably confounded. That this suspicion of officialism detracts from the authority of the police force in popular esteem is undoubted. Their complete dissociation from popular control, the fact that they receive extra pay for any work performed for local bodies, in addition to rewards received from the Inland Revenue for the detection of illicit stills, and the fact the only connection of police administration with local bodies occurs when any county is called upon to pay for the additional force drafted into it on account of local disturbance, all exert their influence in the same direction.

That the same curse of extravagance extends to the judiciary in Ireland one would expect from the fact that the number of the High Court Judges is greater than in Scotland, though, as we have seen, the population is smaller and the crime is less. According to a statement made by the Financial Secretary to the Treasury a few months ago the salaries of the judges of the Superior Courts charged on the Consolidated Fund amount to 1s. 1d. per head of population in England and Wales, to 2s. 8d. per head in Scotland, to no less a sum than 3s. 3d. per head in Ireland. And this discrepancy in cost occurs at a time when the complaint in England is that there are not enough judges of the King's Bench, while in Ireland their numbers are excessive.

The difference between the attitude of the judiciary in England and in Ireland is to be seen from the fact that M. Paul-Dubois, after quoting with approval the Comte de Franqueville's tribute to the fact that the summing up of a judge in England is a model of impartiality, goes on to say that in Ireland, "c'est trop souvent un acte d'accusation."

The fact is that in Ireland, where the salaries of judges are higher than the incomes earned by even the most successful barristers, the judiciary has become to an extent far greater than in England a place of political recompense for Unionist Members of Parliament, who, unlike their English brethren, carry their political prejudices with them on appointment to the Bench. As recently as 1890 Mr. Justice Harrison, at Galway Assizes, asked why the garrison did not have recourse to Lynch law, and until his death Judge O'Connor Morris, unchecked by either party when in power, month by month contributed articles to the reviews, in which he denounced in unmeasured terms the provisions of Acts of Parliament which, in his capacity of Judge of a Civil Bill or County Court, he was called upon to apply.

The jury system is discredited in Ireland by every possible means. Many crimes, which in England are classed as felonies, have been statutorily reduced to misdemeanours in Ireland so as to limit the right of challenge possessed by the accused from twenty jurors to six, and at the same time, after Lord O'Hagan's Act had withdrawn from the sheriff the power of preparing jury lists, which he used for political purposes; by resuscitating a common law right of the Crown which has not been used in England for fifty years, arbitrarily to order jurors to "stand aside," the provisions of O'Hagan's Act have been evaded, and a panel hostile to the accused is most frequently secured.

The natural protection by which the balance is artificially redressed when the application of the laws has not the sympathy of those who are subject to them is a common symptom in every country and every age. When all felonies were capital offences in England, the wit of juries, by what Blackstone called "a kind of pious perjury," was engaged in devising means by which those who were legally guilty could escape from the penalty; and if it be true that an unpacked jury would possibly in many instances of political offences in Ireland have a prejudice in favour of the accused, the inference is not consequently to be drawn that the ends of justice can only be secured by substituting, as is done, a jury which has a prejudice against him. It is not by methods like these that are inspired sentiments, such as those which prompted Victor Hugo eloquently to describe a tribunal:--"Ou dans l'obscurite, la laideur, et la tristesse, se degageait une impression austere et auguste. Car on y sentait cette grande chose humaine qu'on appelle la loi, et cette grande chose divine qu'on appelle la justice."

CHAPTER II
THE FINANCIAL RELATIONS BETWEEN GREAT BRITAIN AND IRELAND

"It will not do to deny the obligation. The case (of Ireland's alleged over-taxation) has been heard before a competent tribunal, established and set up by England. The verdict has been delivered; it is against England and in favour of Ireland's contention. Until this verdict is set aside by a higher court, and a more competent tribunal, the obligation of England to Ireland stands proved."

--T.W. RUSSELL, *Ireland and the Empire*.

The contrast between the history of Great Britain and that of Ireland during the last century--in the one case showing progress and prosperity, advancing, it is not too much to say, by leaps and bounds, and in the other a stagnation which was relatively, if not absolutely, retrograde--is one of the most dismal factors in English politics. Those who would explain it by natural, racial, or religious considerations are probing too deep for an explanation which is in reality much closer at hand. If the external forces in the two countries throughout that period had been the same it would be right and proper to search for an explanation in such directions as have been named, but that these forces have not been so distributed it is my contention to prove.

The closing years of the eighteenth century in Ireland, coinciding as they did with the achievement of Parliamentary independence, witnessed in that country a remarkable growth of national prosperity. Up to the year 1795 the taxation of the country never exceeded one and a half millions of pounds, and the National Debt was not more than one million. In the succeeding years the French war and the rebellion of '98 swelled the expenditure, as did the maintenance of an armed force in the country, which was the corollary of the rebellion, and that process which Lord Cornwallis, the Lord Lieutenant, described as "courting those whom he longed to kick," by which the Act of Union was passed, added another million and a half to the national expenditure.

The result of the various causes was that in the year 1799-1800 the taxation of the country had risen to three millions, and the National Debt amounted to just under four millions of pounds.

It is necessary to enter into these details, because it was on the basis of the years 1799-1800, and not on that of a year of normal expenditure, such as was 1795, that Pitt and Castlereagh framed the financial clauses of the Act of Union, which were to establish the taxable relations between Great Britain and Ireland.

Having said so much we need not pause to consider how far the financial clauses were justified. It will suffice to say that they provided that Ireland should pay two-seventeenths of the joint expenditure of the United Kingdom, together with the annual charge upon her pre-union debt. One should add, however, that the Irish House of Lords protested that the relative taxable capacities of Ireland and England did not bear to each other the ratio which the Act enunciated of 1 to 7-1/2, but in reality of 1 to 18.

It was no part of Pitt's scheme that there should be fiscal union. A separate Irish Chancellor of the Exchequer, drawing up an Irish budget and regulating an Irish debt, remained after the union of the legislatures. Speaking in 1800 on this very point Lord Castlereagh declared that:--

"It must be evident to every man that if our manufactures keep pace in advancement for the next twenty years with the progress they have made in the last twenty, they may at the expiration of it be fully able to cope with the British, and that the two kingdoms may be safely left like any two countries of the same kingdom to a free competition."

The seventh article of the Act of Union, which comprised the financial proposals of the Act, has been summarised as follows in the report of a Royal Commission, to which we shall have occasion to refer later:--

"Ireland and Great Britain had entered into legislative partnership on the clear understanding that they were still, for the purposes of taxation, to be regarded as separate and distinct entities. Ireland was to contribute to the common expenditure in proportion to her resources, so far as the same could be ascertained, and even after the imposition of indiscriminate taxation, if circumstances permitted, she might claim special exemptions and abatements."

We have seen how the taxation of Ireland at the time of the Union was three millions. Five years later the figure had risen to four millions, and it went on increasing at this rate until in 1815 it amounted to no less than six and a half millions, having more than doubled in amount in a space of fifteen years, while during the same time the National Debt had risen from four and a half to ten and a half millions.

To understand the significance of these figures it must be realised that the Napoleonic war was in progress, and that the supply, on the part of Ireland, of provisions at enhanced war prices was the only means by which she was able to cope with her increasing liabilities. The conclusion of the war and the consequent fall in prices accelerated a crisis in Irish finance. Even in the years of plenty not more than one-half of what the Act of Union proposed could be squeezed out of the country, and the balance, which was added to her debt, raised the ratio which it bore to that of Great Britain from the proportion of 1 to 15-1/2 in 1800 to that of 2 to 17 in 1817. One would have thought that such an increase of debt would have made Ireland less fitted to bear equal taxation with Great Britain, but the statesmen of the day thought otherwise, and in 1817 the Exchequers were amalgamated. Even then the fiscal systems of the two countries were not in all respects assimilated, though in regard to some taxes an equalisation was effected, as, for example, in the case of tobacco, the duty on the unmanufactured variety of which was raised from 1s. to 3s. per lb., while that on cigars and manufactured tobacco was raised from 1s. to 16s. per lb. The manner in which the change affected social conditions in Ireland at this time may best be illustrated by the fact that the taxes on commodities, which necessarily hit the poorest classes hardest, rose from 4s. a head per annum in 1790 to 11s. a head per annum in 1820. After the Consolidating Act of 1817 the annual taxation fell to about five millions, abatements and exemptions being made every year. The tobacco tax and the Stamp Duty of 1842, which realised about L120,000 a year, were, it is true, equalised in the two countries, but for many years the system of special treatment was pursued. To Sir Robert Peel credit is due for having refused in 1842 to extend to Ireland the Income Tax, which he re-imposed in England, and for reducing the duty on Irish whiskey to its original figure by the remission of an additional 1s. per gallon which he had imposed.

Soon after this the country supped full of horrors in the famine of 1846-1847. In the decade from 1845 to 1855 more than a quarter of Ireland's population was lost. No sooner did she begin to recover from the effects of this visitation than the Repeal of the Corn Laws dealt her an almost equally disastrous blow. The absence of an industrial side which she might develop, as did England, the almost complete dependence on agriculture, joined to the enfeebled condition in which the lean years had left her, made the adoption at this moment of the principle of Free Trade--in her case--deplorable. Nor was this all. It was at this moment that the opportunity was taken by Mr. Gladstone, at that time Chancellor of the Exchequer, to reverse the discriminative policy upon which Peel had so strongly insisted.

The Income Tax was applied to Ireland in 1853 at the rate of seven pence in the pound. Ten years later it had risen to seventeen pence. At the same time an additional duty of eight pence a gallon on Irish whiskey was exacted, which in two years was multiplied fourfold, while in 1858 Disraeli assimilated for the first time the whiskey duty in the two islands by raising it in Ireland to 8s. a gallon. The result of this new departure in taxation may be summarised by saying that the Irish revenue was raised from just under five millions in 1850 to nearly eight millions in 1860, and that, too, at a time when, of all others, her distress demanded special treatment and care.

Although the process of assimilation was carried far in 1853 and the subsequent years, fiscal unity has never been completely effected. To this day Ireland secures exemption from the Land Tax, the Inhabited House Duty, the Railway Passenger Duty, and the tax on horses, carriages, patent medicines, and armorial bearings. It will be said, no doubt, that Ireland ought to show due gratitude for these exemptions, but though they raise collectively a sum of L4,000,000 by their incidence in England, Scotland, and Wales, it is calculated that if applied to Ireland they would bring in not more than L150,000 a year, a sum so small that one may ask whether it would bear the cost of collecting.

By way of set-off to the imposition of income tax, which it should be noted was at the time said to be "temporary," Mr. Gladstone wiped out a capital debt of four millions, but it must be pointed out that, in the fifty years which have ensued, a sum of between twenty millions and thirty millions has been collected in Ireland as income tax. Objection cannot--beyond a certain point--be taken to the incidence of this tax, seeing that it does not fall upon the poorest classes, and that no country benefits more than does Ireland from the substitution of direct for indirect taxation. But what does call for censure is that its application was not made an occasion for the remission of other taxes.

In 1864 the Conservative Government recognised the serious problem of the unequal incidence of taxation in the two islands, and appointed a committee to consider their financial relations. Sir Stafford Northcote, the chairman of this committee, declared that, notwithstanding the fact that they were both subject to the same taxation, "Ireland was the most heavily taxed and England the most lightly taxed country in Europe." Twenty-five years later Mr. Goschen, the Conservative Chancellor of the Exchequer, consented to the appointment of another Committee on the same subject, but no report was ever issued. In 1895 a Royal Commission was appointed, comprising representatives of all political parties, and presided over by a man of commanding ability in the person of Mr. Childers, a former Liberal Chancellor of the Exchequer. The terms of reference were "to inquire into the financial relations between Great Britain and Ireland and their relative taxable capacity." The following extract will serve to show the conclusions of the Commissioners:--

"In carrying out the inquiry we have ascertained that there are certain questions upon which we are practically unanimous, and we think it expedient to set them out in this report. Our joint conclusions on these questions are as follows:--

"(1) That Great Britain and Ireland must, for the purposes of this inquiry, be considered as separate entities.

"(2) That the Act of Union imposed upon Ireland a burden which, as events showed, she was unable to bear.

"(3) That the increase of taxation laid upon Ireland between 1853 and 1860 was not justified by the then existing circumstances.

"(4) That identity of rates of taxation does not necessarily involve equality of burden.

"(5) That whilst the actual tax revenue of Ireland is about one-eleventh of that of Great Britain, the relative taxable capacity of Ireland is very much smaller, and is not estimated by any of us as exceeding one-twentieth."

It is difficult to conceive a more damning indictment of English rule in Ireland. One cannot help recalling the glowing promises of Pitt in 1800:--

"But it has been said, 'What security can you give to Ireland for the performance of the conditions?' If I were asked what security was necessary, without hesitation I should answer 'None.' The liberality, the justice, the honour of the people of England have never yet been found deficient."

One is reminded of Dr. Johnson's remark to an Irishman who discussed with him the possibility of the union of the Parliaments:--

"Do not make a union with us, sir; we should unite with you only to rob you."

It is a striking testimony to the fact that the approach to some men's hearts is through their pockets; that the report of the Commissioners brought all Ulster into line with the Nationalists. Such a vision of the Protestant lion lying down with the Catholic lamb had not been seen since the Volunteers had mustered in 1778, and then, too, curiously enough, the common cause was financial, being the demand for the removal of the commercial restraints on the island.

A conference was held in 1896, presided over by Col. Saunderson, the leader of the Orangemen, and was attended by all the Irish members, irrespective of party. The outcome was a resolution in the House of Commons, proposed by Mr. John Redmond, and seconded by Mr. Lecky. The rejoinder of the Government to the demands made was to the effect that the postulate of the Commissioners that Ireland and Great Britain must, for the purposes of the inquiry, be considered as separate entities stultified the report.

One cannot characterise this attitude otherwise than as a piece of special pleading. The appointment, not merely of the Royal Commission, but of the Select Committees of 1865 and 1890, presupposed a disparity between the conditions in the two countries which not only existed in fact but were recognised by law.

In regard to the Church, the kind, the police, education, and even marriage, the laws are different in the two countries; and we have seen how, in respect of such widely separate things as land, railway passengers, and armorial bearings, the systems of taxation are distinct.

The position of the official Conservatives was well stigmatised by one of the most distinguished among their own body--Mr. Lecky--when he declared that--

"Some people seem to consider Ireland as a kind of intermittent personality--something like Mr. Hyde and Dr. Jekyll--an integral part when it was a question of taxation, and, therefore, entitled to no exemptions, a separate entity when it was a question of rating, and, therefore, entitled to no relief."

To the argument that Ireland has no greater claim to relief, on the score of her poverty, than have the more backward agricultural counties of England, the answer is that Wiltshire or Somersetshire--shall we say--have always received equal treatment with the rest of the country, and have never entered into a mutual partnership as did Ireland when she trusted to the pledges made to her by England, and expressed in these terms by Castlereagh:--

"Ireland has the utmost possible security that she cannot be taxed beyond the measure of her comparative ability, and that the ratio of her contribution must ever correspond with her relative wealth and prosperity."

The attitude of Ireland in this matter is perfectly plain. While deprecating in the strongest terms the means by which the Union was carried, she is prepared, so long as it remains in force, to abide by its terms. It partakes of the nature of what lawyers call a bilateral contract, imposing duties and obligations on both sides, and these liabilities can only be removed--as in the case of the Disestablished Irish Church--by the consent of both the contracting parties to the treaty.

The spectacle of the richest country in Europe haggling over shekels with the poorest is a sight to give pause, while Great Britain's insistence upon her pound of flesh is the more unpardonable because Ireland declares that it is not in the bond. That the highest estimate of the taxable capacity of Ireland arrived at by the Commissioners was one-twentieth, while the actual revenue contribution of Ireland was one-eleventh of the total for the United Kingdom, throws much light upon the social conditions of the smaller island. The rate of taxation per head per annum went up in the second half of the nineteenth century more than 250 per cent.--rising from about L1 in 1850 to more than L2 10s. in 1900. This occurred simultaneously with a diminution of population in the same period from seven millions to four and a half millions, a change which is in glaring contrast with the concurrent increase in Great Britain from twenty millions in 1850 to more than thirty-eight millions at the present day. Whatever may be the other causes which have led to the stream of emigration from Ireland it may certainly be claimed that not least among them is the ever-increasing incidence of taxation which is year by year laying a greater burden upon the privilege of living in that country.

A recent Report, issued by the Labour Department of the Board of Trade, gives statistics with reference to the earnings of agricultural labourers throughout the three kingdoms. It concludes that on an average a labourer in England obtains 18s. 3d. a week, in Wales 17s. 3d., in Scotland 19s. 3d., and in Ireland 10s. 11d. It may be noted that in no English county is the average lower than 14s. 6d., while in Ireland in seven counties it is less than 10s., Mayo being the lowest with an average wage of 8s. 9d. The present writer has had occasion in the course of the last few months to hear old men on political platforms in a typical English agricultural constituency pointing a moral from their own or their fathers' recollections of the days before the Corn Laws when wages ran from 8s. to 9s. a week. What is recalled with horror in England as the state of affairs in the "hungry forties" is the present condition in several of the Irish counties. It would be idle to multiply proofs to show the desperate condition of the country. Even in the ten years which have elapsed since the issue of the Report of the Royal Commission the taxation of the country has increased by more than two and a half million pounds, while the population, it is estimated, has in the same period diminished by no less than 200,000. On the assumption arrived at by the Commissioners, that the proper share which Ireland should pay was one-twentieth of the contribution of Great Britain, the country was overtaxed ten years ago to the extent of two and three-quarter millions; yet in spite of that fact in the course of those ten years two millions of additional taxation has been imposed. Two years ago the Chancellor of the Exchequer, in answer to an inquiry, announced to the House of Commons that in the year 1903-4, the latest for which figures were available, the proportions of tax revenue derived from direct and indirect taxes were:--

	Great Britain	Ireland
Direct Taxes	50.6 per cent.	27.8 per cent.
Indirect Taxes	49.4 per cent.	72.2 per cent.

These figures show very clearly to what an extent in Ireland taxation falls, not on the luxuries of the rich, but on the commodities which are to a great extent the necessaries of the poor. The manner in which this state of things is maintained was expressed by Sir Robert Giffen in his evidence before the Royal Commission:--

"It is only evident that in matters of taxation Ireland is virtually discriminated against by the character of the direct taxes which happen to be on articles of Irish consumption."

The heavy duties on tea, tobacco, and alcohol--articles which form a larger part of the family budget of the Irish peasant than of the English labourer--are the causes of this burden. The reasons for the larger consumption of what may be roughly called stimulants by the Irishman is undoubtedly to be found in climatic conditions, and also in the smaller amount of nourishing food which he is able to afford. With regard to alcohol, the form in which it is most used in England--namely, beer--is subjected to a special exemption at the expense of the whiskey-drinking people of Ireland and Scotland. Cider is not taxed. The tax on whiskey is between two-thirds and three-fourths its price, while that on beer is one-sixth of its price; so that sixty gallons of beer bear the same weight of taxation as does one gallon of whiskey. The usual standard of taxation of liquor is its alcoholic strength, but the special treatment accorded to the Englishman's principal drink reduced--according to the Royal Commissioners--the taxation to which, in proportion to its alcohol it should be subjected, from 1s. to 2d. per gallon. Even in respect of tea and tobacco, the inequitable treatment of Ireland is obvious to any one who considers that what is spoken of as equality of taxation is, in reality, identical taxation on articles consumed in vastly different proportions in Great Britain and Ireland.

The argument by which the charge that Ireland is overtaxed was rebutted by the late Unionist Government was that the balance is restored by the amount of money spent in the administration of that country. When the complaint is heard that she is contributing at this day no less a sum than,L9,750,000 to revenue, the answer is made that she has no grievance since the cost of Irish services amounts to more than L7,500,000, the balance, a paltry two and a quarter millions, forming her Imperial contribution.

Ireland is being bled to death, and to her complaints the answer is that she is being expensively administered. To fleece a poor man of his pittance and to justify the action by telling him that it is on every appurtenance of a spendthrift to which he objects that it is being spent is scarcely to provide a satisfactory justification. The two cases are exactly parallel, and it is a weak position which has to entrench itself behind the fact that the cost of government per head is in Ireland double what it is in England.

The country is against its will saddled with a Viceregal Court, of which the Lord Lieutenant enjoys a salary twice as great as that of the President of the United States. The government is conducted by more than forty boards, only one of which is responsible, through a Minister in the House of Commons, to the country. Official returns show that Scotland, with a population slightly larger than that of Ireland, possesses 942 Government officials as against 2,691 in Ireland. In Scotland the salaries of these public servants amount to less than L300,000, while in Ireland the corresponding cost is more than L1,000,000 per annum, showing that the average salaries in the poorer country are considerably higher than in the richer. Of the L7,500,000 devoted to Irish services, L1,500,000 goes to the Post Office and Customs, while one half of the remainder is consumed by the salaries and pensions of policemen and officials.

To take a single example--the Prison Boards of Scotland and Ireland work under identical Acts, dating from 1877. It is instructive, therefore, to compare the conditions of the two. The estimates for the year 1905 were calculated on the assumption that there were 120 fewer prisoners a day in Irish prisons than in Scotland. In spite of this the cost of the Irish Board for the last year of which I have seen the figures was L144,597, and that of the Scottish Board was only L105,588. The ratio between these figures is as 1.3 to 1, which is in nearly the same proportion as is the number of the officials on the two boards--namely, 622 in Ireland and in Scotland 467, and this, too, in spite of the fact that further statistics show, namely, that there are five convicted criminals in Scotland for every three in Ireland.

These are a few facts which show the value of the case for the present state of affairs, based on the assumption that over-taxation is balanced by profligate expenditure. The maintenance--to take only one point--of a police force about half the size of the United States army, when at the present time white gloves--the symbol of a crimeless charge--are being given to the judges on every circuit, is a state of affairs which is intolerable, while the small proportion which in the returns Ireland is shown to bear of the Imperial contribution is the result of the inclusion of the Viceregal and Civil Service charges, not, as should be the case, in the Imperial account, but in the separate Irish account.

As an instance showing how exorbitant exactions defeat their own end by diminishing, and not raising, the available revenue, it should be noted that in 1853 an income tax of 7d. in the pound raised L200,000 more than did an income tax of 8d. in the pound at the date of the Royal Commission. Of the remedies which are suggested, the alteration of the Fiscal system, by making abatements in the Irish Excise and Customs, is not likely to be attempted. Reduction of expenditure, liberating money which may be made to serve a useful purpose, is obviously the first step, but any scheme of allocation of large sums for Irish development, without full and proper financial control, will undoubtedly fail to meet the case. The multiplication of irresponsible boards must be stopped, and to what extent anything, save economies in expenditure, can be effected without far larger changes remains a moot point. Of one thing, at any rate, one may be certain--the present Liberal Government when in Opposition joined forces with the Irish members in driving home the tremendous admissions of the Royal Commissioners, and it is impossible to think that, now they are in power, they will repudiate their obligations, the more so as the present Chancellor of the Exchequer last year announced the intention of the Government to see how far it is possible to adjust the financial relations between the two kingdoms on a fairer basis.

Sir Hercules Langrishe, the friend and correspondent of Edmund Burke, is said to have accounted for the swampy condition of the Phoenix Park by saying--"The English Government are too much engaged in *draining* the rest of the kingdom to find time to attend to it."

Enough has been said to show that the process of which Sir Hercules spoke is still going on. One would have thought that counsels of prudence would have made an end of it. It remains to be seen whether the uncontestable facts to which they themselves have subscribed will prevail with the Government. "The liberality, the justice, the honour of the people of England" are concerned in it now, as truly as when Pitt spoke. Moreover, it is one of the instances in which the claims of justice and of expediency coincide. The findings of the Financial Relations' Commission fully justified the attitude of the Irish Party to the proposal, under Mr. Gladstone's

Bill, that the Irish contribution to the Imperial Treasury should be one-fourteenth of that of Great Britain, while Mr. Parnell declared that it ought to have been one-twentieth. The population, since the publication of the Report of the Commission, has decreased by a quarter of a million, but taxation has increased from,L7,500,000 to L10,500,000. If Ireland had secured the fixed contribution, against the height of which she protested, she would nevertheless have been guarded from such a disproportionate rise of taxation.

Whatever test be taken, be it population, a comparison of exports and of imports, the consumption of certain dutiable articles, relative assessments to death duties, income tax, or the estimated value of commodities of primary importance consumed, every one of them shows the relative backwardness of Ireland as compared with Great Britain, in view of which the fact that the cost of government per head of population is double in Ireland what it is in England, shows the extent to which the one is liable in damages to the other. The increased expenditure on the navy obviously does not benefit equally the two countries, of which the one only has dockyards and manufactories, and this is especially the case seeing that the country which lacks these things is also without a commerce needing defence; while any advantage resulting from a portion of the army being quartered in Ireland is minimised when it is found that arms and accoutrements are purchased in England.

The attempt to stultify the findings of the Commission on the ground that its report was based on a fallacy, since Ireland has no more right to be considered as a separate entity than an English county, is remarkably disingenuous in view of the acknowledgment of this in the separate treatment which she received in the matter of grants made in relief of local taxation and for the establishment of free education in the years 1888 and 1890 and 1891. Moreover, it was impliedly admitted that she was a separate entity in the appointment of a Select Committee on taxation in 1864, and again by Lord Goschen in 1890, and the whole history of her separate legislation bears the same construction. One cannot give a better commentary on what has been seen of the economic condition of the island than by quoting the peroration of the speech of John Fitzgibbon, Earl of Clare, the "great father of the Union," speaking in the Irish House of Parliament:--"It is with a cordial sincerity and a full conviction that it will give to this, my native country, lasting peace and security for her religion, her laws, her liberty, and her property, an increase of strength, riches, and trade, and the final extinction of national jealousy and animosity, that I now propose to this grave assembly for their adoption an entire and perfect Union of the Kingdom of Ireland with Great Britain. If I live to see it completed, to my latest hour I shall feel an honourable pride in reflecting on the little share I may have in contributing to effect it."

CHAPTER III
THE ECONOMIC CONDITION OF IRELAND

"When the inhabitants of a country leave it in crowds because the government does not leave them room in which to live, that government is judged and condemned."
--JOHN STUART MILL, *Political Economy*.

I have shown something of the incubus of taxation which overpowers Ireland from the fact that she--the poorest country in Western Europe--is bound to the richest in such a manner that the latter has not the common prudence to recognise the flagitious injustice which she is inflicting, while, by a refinement of cruelty, she repeats her assurances that Ireland is a spoilt child, and for this reason alone does not appreciate the blessings of British rule. In the light of the facts before us one may well ask whether it was an extreme hyperbole of which Grattan made use when he declared that "Ireland, like every enslaved country, will be compelled to pay for her own subjugation."

When we are urged to put into practice the counsels of perfection and study the virtue of patience while we wait for the opportune moment for reform, from the point of view of English party politics, our reply is that things have reached so desperate a pass that to submit to the delays entailed by the exigencies of political strategy is a suicidal policy which we cannot afford to endure without protest.

The inhabitants of Great Britain had their Imperial taxation cut down in the nineteenth century by one-half, that of the Irish people was doubled. Every year that passes without radical change in the relations between the two countries makes it more serious, and makes the changes more drastic which will be required when the need for them is at last fully realised.

At the present day more than ten millions per annum are raised by taxation in Ireland. Of these seven and a half are spent on the *home* government of the country, which in 1890 cost only just over five millions, while that of Scotland at this moment costs a little more--namely, five and a half millions.

If one looks at the case of Denmark one finds a rich agricultural country with a population of six and a half millions, which is able to maintain her home and foreign government, a Royal Family, a debt, an army with a war strength of 70,000, a fleet, and the expense of three colonies, on an expenditure of four and a half millions.

Sweden, to take another case, with a population of six and a half millions, a large commerce, and many industries, is able to support her whole government, army, navy, diplomatic and consular service on a budget of little more than five millions; and the cost of civil government of Belgium, with a greater population and four times the trade, is one-half that of Ireland. The relative cost of *home* government per head of population, which amounts in Ireland to L1 14s. 3d., in England and Wales to L1 3s., and in Scotland to L1 3s. 3d., illustrates in a striking manner the ruinous condition of the present incidence in Ireland.

If this administrative waste is palliated by the statement that it retains money in Ireland, the reply is that the excess of administrative expenditure which is included in this sum is enough to effect large measures of social reform in the country, the benefit of which is not to be named in the same breath with the present mode of maintaining an extravagant staff of highly-paid officials. As things are, however, all motives to secure economies in the Irish services are vitiated by the existing system by which any economies in Irish administration go, not to Ireland, but to the Imperial Treasury, and in this way economical government is not merely not encouraged but actually discouraged, and hence it is that one has such contrasts as that to be seen in each year's Civil Service Estimates, where, under the item of stationery and postage in respect of public departments, the amount for the last year which I have seen is, for Scotland L24,000, and for Ireland, L43,000, and that the Department of Agriculture, out of a total income from Parliamentary Grant of L190,000, spends no less than L80,000 on salaries and wages, and another L10,000 on travelling expenses.

Sir Robert Giffen has calculated that the incomes of the wage-earning classes in Ireland are, man for man, one-half those of the members of the same classes in

England. Statistics of every kind bear out the striking difference in the conditions of the two countries. The average poor law valuation in Ireland is about equal to that of the poorest East London Unions, where it is L3. Though the population is between one-seventh and one-eighth of that of England, the number of railway passengers is one-thirty-seventh, the tons of railway freight is one-seventeenth, the telegrams are one-eighteenth, the postal and money orders are one-nineteenth of those of England.

Ireland, to take another test of prosperity, is the fourth meat-producing country in the world and the sixteenth meat-eating, while England, by a curious coincidence, is the sixteenth meat-producing, but the fourth meat-eating, country in the world. The one direction in which the extension of the powers and duties of the Executive has often been urged has not been pursued. I mean the matter of railways. Though in 1834 a Royal Commission recommended that Irish railways should be built with money from the British Treasury, and should be subject to State control, nothing was done in the matter. Lord Salisbury and Lord Randolph Churchill were in 1886 in favour of the nationalisation of Irish railways, but at that date again no steps were taken. Mr. Balfour, it is true, when Chief Secretary, secured the passing of the Light Railways Act, under which powers were obtained to open up the Congested Districts by means of light railways, such as those which have been built to Clifden, in County Galway, and to Burtonport, in County Donegal. But the policy which was followed in this Act was to build the railway out of a Treasury grant, and after it had been built to hand it over to one of the existing railway companies.

There are to-day 3,000 odd miles of railway in Ireland--a mileage scarcely exceeding that of a single company, the Great Western Railway, in England. They are owned by nearly thirty companies, each with a separate staff of directors and salaried officials, the directors alone being over 130 in number. The railways of the country are, without exception, notoriously bad, the delay and dislocation incident to the transfer of goods from one line to another, and the high rates which prevail, inevitably serve to impede any traffic in goods, especially if they are of a perishable character.

It is not traffic that makes communications, but cheap communications that make traffic. The Belgian Government, fifty years ago, took over the railways of that country, and reduced the freights to such a degree that in eight years the quantity of goods carried was doubled, the receipts of the railways were increased fifty per cent., and the profits of the producers were multiplied five-fold. I am not quoting this instance by way of plea that the present remedy for the grave economic problems of Ireland lies in nationalisation of railways. I have said enough to show the extravagance and irresponsibility of the present Executive system, and in view of that no sane man would propose to endow it with further powers than those which it already possesses; but let me say this, that if the present state of diffusive impotence which rules in the matter of transit in the country continues, some very drastic remedies may before long have to be devised.

The cheapest freights for grain in the world are those between Chicago and New York, and the reason why this is so is that there exists keen competition on the part of the inland waterways. Of the 580 miles of canals in Ireland a considerable part are owned by the railway companies, and their weed-choked condition shows the use to which they are put in the national economy.

Whoever it was that said the carriers of freight hold the keys of trade was stating what appears almost an axiom, and an illustration is afforded of the results of reduced rates in an analogous business in the way in which the establishment of penny postage sent up the receipts of the General Post Office.

The difference in the freights in the three kingdoms may be seen by a comparison of the average rate per ton of merchandise in the year 1900--

In England	In Scotland	In Ireland
4s. 10.26d.	4s. 11.64d.	6s. 7.90d.

In the decade from 1890-1900 the figure in England and Wales decreased 8.79d., in Scotland 1.7d., and in Ireland increased by 1.92d.

Again, the control of the great English railway corporations over the small companies in Ireland has led to a state of things by which freights for imported goods are relatively lower than are those for purely internal carriage, and by this means the railways of Great Britain maintain their grip of the carrying trade, and incidentally destroy the industry of Ireland.

The trade of Ireland is not two per cent. of that of the three kingdoms, and this policy of swamping the Irish market with English-made goods at low rates to such an extent that over twelve million pounds' worth of imported goods are sold annually in Ireland shows the manner in which the principles of free trade are applied to that country; and so it has come to pass that the opening up of the country by railways has often tended to destroy local industries and to substitute for their products articles manufactured in England and Continental Europe at a cheaper cost, carried in either case by English railways, which, in consequence, reap the benefit of the freight. The carriage per ton paid by eggs to London, to take one example, is 16s. 8d. from Normandy, 24s. from Denmark, and no less that 94s. from Galway.

The bearing of the transit question on the agricultural problem is seen by a consideration of the rates for every form of farm produce, which in Ireland are fifteen to twenty per cent. of their value. On the Continent the average is five to six per cent., and in the United States and Canada it is three per cent. The discouragement of such a tariff to agricultural enterprise has had a great bearing on the transformation of plough land into cattle ranches, and the extent to which this has occurred may be seen from the fact that there are to-day twelve million acres of pasture to three millions of arable land in the island, and fertile land, like that of the plains of Meath, is to be seen growing, not corn for men, but grass for cattle. The success of the country in stock-raising may very easily be rendered nugatory if the exclusion of Argentine and Canadian cattle from the English market be ended by the passing of an Act giving the Board of Agriculture a discretionary power to maintain or remove the embargo on their importation, according as the danger of an introduction of cattle disease exists or disappears. The enormous import trade which is done in Danish butter, Italian cheese, and even Siberian eggs, shows the commercial possibilities of farm produce when freights are low. As a tangible example of the discrimination which the railways pursue may be mentioned the fact that the freight for goods per ton from Liverpool to Cavan is 10s. 8d., while that from Cavan to Liverpool is 16s. 8d. The numbers employed on agriculture have diminished, not only in proportion to the population but also relatively to its decrease. According to Mr. Charles Booth land employs as many people to-day in England as it did in 1841, and it probably supports nearly as many, and though in that country, building and manufacture employ a vast number more, in Ireland there has been in the same time a decrease of nearly eleven per cent. of those so employed--the total decrease being 626,000.

The population of England has in the last century been multiplied by four, that of Scotland has increased threefold, while that of Ireland has decreased by one-fourth. If we take the last sixty years it will be seen that the people of England have doubled their numbers, but those of Ireland have divided by two. It would be idle to pretend that the great exodus which took place after the famine was in all respects to be regretted. The abnormal increase in population which took place in the first forty years of the nineteenth century was in itself out of all proportion to the increase of productive capacity in the country, and was closely related to the unnatural inflation of prices, and consequent spurious appearance of prosperity, due to the great war. When the climax came this was rapidly followed by a reaction, and when emigration reduced the numbers of eight million people who were in the island in 1841, the modified competition in the labour market and in the land market tended to restore prices to a normal figure.

Emigration was at one time a well-recognised remedy with English statesmen for Irish ills. Did not Michael Davitt once say that manacles and Manitoba were the two cures for Ireland which they could propose? Even then, no attempt was made to regulate emigration by the State. The ball which was thus set rolling at that date has been in motion ever since, and that which half a century ago was regarded as the hand of the ***deus ex machina*** setting right a grave economic problem has continued, so that it has become at this day a problem no less grave, which to an equal degree presses for solution.

Four million people in the last sixty-five years fled from the country, and though the figures, as they are published, seem to show a slight decrease each year, the apparent diminution is to a large extent fallacious, since the residue of population from which emigrants are drawn becomes each year less, and an apparent decrease may in truth be a relative increase.

We heard much a few years ago in England of the evils of immigration into the British Isles of aliens, whom the Board of Trade returns show amount to eight thousand per annum--a figure which appears paltry when compared with the forty thousand people who leave Ireland every year. It is a cry which one is told should make the thirty-seven million inhabitants of England and Scotland burn with indignation that this number of foreigners land on their shores every year. Surely we

Irishmen have a far greater cause of complaint in the fact that out of a population of four and a half millions, less than is that of London, a number greater than those of a town of the size of Limerick emigrate every year. Most of these emigrants are in the prime of life. Their average age is from twenty to twenty-five, and more than ninety per cent. are between the ages of ten and forty-five years. Here is the crucial fact, that it is the young, the active, and the plucky who are being tempted by promises of success abroad, to which they see no likelihood of attaining at home, and in this way is established a system of the survival of the unfittest, an artificial selection of the most malignant kind, which is leaving the old, the infirm, the poor, and the unadventurous behind to swell the figures of pauperism and to propagate the race. All the authorities are agreed in attributing to this cause the lamentable increase of lunacy, which is one of the most terrible factors in the economy of modern Ireland. The last Census report shows the total number of lunatics and idiots to have been in 1851 equal to a ratio of 1 in 637 of the population, and to be in 1901 equal to a ratio of 1 in 178. The proportion is, as one would expect, highest in the purely agricultural districts and lowest in the neighbourhood of cities, such as Dublin and Belfast, where industrial conditions imply better wages and food, and a less monotonous existence.

It should be remembered that the proportion of imbeciles in Great Britain has risen in the period of fifty years as it has in Ireland--partly, no doubt, owing to a better system of registration of lunacy--but, at the same time, the fact remains that the average in Ireland is very much greater than in England and Wales, rising in some Irish counties to a proportion twice, and in another to a ratio thrice, as high as that of the average of the whole of England and Wales.

If urban industrial conditions militate against an increase of lunacy, on the other hand it must be remembered that in most Irish towns there is an appalling amount of overcrowding. The death-rate of Dublin--the highest of any city in Europe--is, in consequence, no less than 25 per 1,000, as against 16 per 1,000 in Paris and New York, and 17 per 1,000 in London. The percentage of families, consisting on an average of four persons, living in one room is in London 14.6, in Edinburgh 16.9, in Glasgow 26.1, in Cork 10.6, in Limerick, 15.8, while in Dublin it reaches the appalling percentage of 36. In Belfast, which, unlike any other of the cities which I have mentioned, is for the most part modern, the percentage is not higher than 1, and this fact has a very great bearing on the industrial conditions in that city. Side by side with these figures may be placed those of the death-rate from tuberculosis, which from 1864 to 1906 in England decreased from 3.3 per 1,000 to 1.6, in Scotland decreased from 3.6 per 1,000 to 2.1, and in Ireland *increased* from 2.4 to 2.7 per 1,000.

The rate war of the steamship companies, which reduced the cost of passage across the Atlantic in 1904, caused the emigration returns to rise from 45,000 to 58,000 in a single year, and at the same time there were employed in Ireland two hundred emigration agents of one company alone--the Cunard--each of whom received six shillings a head for each banished Irishman and Irishwoman whom he got safely out of the country. It is easy for the Irishman to wax eloquent about the exiles who, from the time when O'Neil and O'Donnell weighed anchor in Lough Swilly at the very beginning of the seventeenth century, sailed from their country to seek their fortunes abroad in Church or State or camp, since proscription deprived them of the *carriere ouverte aux talents* at home. The history of the "wild geese" in the service of France, Spain, Italy, Austria, Prussia, and of Russia; of the Irishmen who were respectively the first Quartermaster-General of the United States Army and the first Commodore of the United States Navy, or of the seven Irish Field Marshals of Austria, or of those who served as Viceroys to Chili, Peru, and Mexico, is the story of the citizens of no mean city. Catholic Europe is flecked with the white graves of the Irish exiles of the seventeenth and eighteenth centuries; from Rome to Valladolid, from Douai to Prague, from Salamanca to Louvain, and from Tournai to Paris you will find their bones. But the pathos of this is, to my mind, as nothing compared with the pathos of what is occurring now. For one thing, it was only men in those days that went in any large numbers, while to-day it is both men and women. From the point of view of England the result has been in no small degree serious. Of the four million people who have emigrated since the great tidal wave began with the famine, nearly ninety per cent. have gone, not to British Colonies, but to the United States. Of the fifty thousand who emigrated in 1905 more than forty-four thousand went to the North-American Republic.

Coelum non animum mutant qui trans mare currunt; the Ulster Protestants who were driven from their country by the commercial restrictions of the eighteenth century formed the nucleus of the most implacable enemies of Great Britain in the War of Independence--half Washington's army was recruited from Irishmen in America; and in the same way the exiles of the nineteenth century became, and have remained even to the second generation, irreconcilable adversaries of the system of government which, by affording for too long no relief to the conditions in Ireland, was responsible for the flight from their home to a land which was, by comparison, flowing with milk and honey.

Side by side with emigration goes on another factor in the social life of the country which is very significant of the stress under which, in some districts, the Irish peasant ekes out an existence. I am referring to the migratory labourers, of whom nearly 18,000 leave their homes in Ireland every year to work in the harvest fields of England and Scotland, that they may there secure a wage by which they are able to make both ends meet in a manner which the uneconomic nature of their holdings does not permit. How small is the diminution in this annual migration is seen by the fact that the highest figures in connection with it recorded in the last quarter of a century are those of 1880, in which year nearly 23,000 migrated, while within the last six years--in 1901--the figures were as high as 19,700. More than three-quarters of these labourers come from Connacht, and of the total number more than one-half from County Mayo, from which every year 47.8 per thousand of the population migrate, and if one takes the adult male population--*i.e.*, that of men over twenty years of age--one finds that the number of migratory labourers represents a proportion of 177.4 per thousand. Nearly three-quarters of them go to England, and the harvest fields of Lincolnshire and Yorkshire are in a large measure reaped by their hands. From February till June the migration occurs, and the labourers return in the late autumn to their homes. The fact that the sum brought back by them is, at the highest estimate, said to be about L18 after nine months of labour, and that the wages which they earn amount to an average of 17s. a week, while, in addition to the cost of living for three-quarters of the year, about L2 is spent on their railway fare, all serve to show the nature of the economic conditions in the West of Ireland which make such a migration for such a wage worth while on the part of nearly twenty thousand people. One factor in this connection which should be noted is that the number of girls who migrate every year is said to be increasing, and is estimated to amount to nearly half the total throughout the country. The precariousness of a dependence on such a means of subsistence as this, is seen from the fact that a bad harvest in England or a development in agricultural machinery would put an end to the source of livelihood which it provides. If from no other point of view the problem should be regarded seriously by Englishmen in the light of the depopulation of the English countryside, with its direct bearing upon the material for recruiting the army and navy, and the problem of unemployment in general.

It is a surprising thing that the support of home industries, which was one of the foibles of Dean Swift, who advised Irishmen to burn everything that came from England except its coal, has only of very recent years been resuscitated. So much is this the case that the action of the South Dublin Board of Guardians, who in 1881 insisted that the workhouse inmates should be clothed in Irish produce, was conspicuous by its exceptional nature. At this day all are agreed, whatever be their religious or political opinions, on the advocacy of this form of exclusive dealing at which economists may scowl as at a deliberate attempt to fly in the face of the regular play of the forces of supply and demand, but the success which has so far attended the concerted policy of insisting upon being supplied with Irish produce, and the fact that it is, after all, the only mode of restoring to their natural functions the economic forces in a country where industrial conditions were, by artificial means, thrown out of their natural course, is the justification for its employment.

If for no other reason, the activity displayed by "religious" in Ireland in the encouragement and development of local industries as a check on emigration should protect them from the attacks which have been made upon them, as tending to encourage the uneconomic aspect of the situation in Ireland. To name only a few that come into one's mind, the nuns' co-operative factories, which have revived Irish point lace at Youghal, Kenmare, Gort, Carrick-on-Suir, Carrickmacross, and Galway, are instances. Father Dooley, in Galway, has started a woollen factory, with a capital of L10,000, in which nearly two hundred girls are employed, of whom many earn L1 10s. a week. Father Quin, at Ballina, has founded a co-operative shoe factory, and at Castlebar Father Lyons has established an electric power station. The work of the Sisters of Charity at Foxford is well known, and stands in need of no praise, and at Kiltimagh, in Mayo, they employ a hundred and twenty girls at dress and lace making; while Father Maguire, at Dromore, in Tyrone, has established a lace and crochet factory on co-operative principles, which has over a hundred employees; and at Lough Glynn, in Connacht, a carpet and cheese making industry has been built up solely through the efforts of a religious order of nuns. These are random examples, and I do not claim that they are typical. They are, on the other hand, not exceptional.

It is impossible to exaggerate the effect of the English commercial policy towards Ireland in the seventeenth and eighteenth centuries. Wool, cotton, sailcloth, sugar refining, shipping, glass, the cattle and provision trade, were all deliberately strangled. And besides the loss of wealth to Ireland which was the consequence, one must take into account the fact that traditions of commercial enterprise perished through desuetude, so that in the industrial revolution at the beginning of the nineteenth century Ireland was too severely crippled to derive any benefit from the new order, as to which she was still further handicapped by the poverty of her coal fields.

The land system, which is only now disappearing, served, moreover, not to inculcate habits of thrift, but positively as a discouragement of economic virtues. Until the legal recognition of tenant-right had been secured, the tenant who made improvements was liable to have his rent raised, and was aware that he had no legal right to compensation for them on his removal from the holding. Further, the judicial fixing of rents, which, as the time for rent revision has approached, has presented to the tenant the temptation not to make the best of his land, and so run the risk of an augmentation of rent, has been a source of insidious demoralisation to the occupant of the soil.

The social upheaval resulting from land purchase will nowhere be more marked than in this respect in the stability which it will produce in the financial conditions of the country, and it may be expected to do something to remedy the lamentable state of things which so far has but little altered from that of twenty years ago, when it was estimated that five-sixths of the total capital of the country was invested abroad. A great opportunity presents itself at the present moment. It was stated a few years ago that eleven millions of rent were spent out of the island. At this day when, under the Land Purchase Act, an immense amount of property is being realised, the patriotic Irish landlord seeking an investment for his money can, by starting industries in Ireland, at one and the same time do a patriotic work by providing against the stream of emigration, and can secure a safe and profitable investment for his purchase-money. There are very nearly eighty million pounds of capital to be set free under the Act, and it is scarcely too much to expect that a large proportion of it will be invested by the expropriated landlords in their own country. The possibility of an industrial revival in Ireland is well illustrated by the increase in the number of co-operative societies, in which there are at the present day 100,000 members, while less than twenty years ago there were only fifty.

The effect of the Dairy, Agricultural, and Poultry Societies is very important, but perhaps of still greater importance are the Raffeisin banks, which aim at the promotion of farming by means of co-operative credit. The loans which they make, at an interest of five per cent. or six per cent., are dealing a death-blow at that curse of Irish life--the gombeen man, whose usury used to mount up to thirty per cent. The extremely rare cases of default in the repayment of these loans for agricultural purposes will not be surprising to those who recall the tribute paid by Mr. Wyndham, in connection with land purchase annuities, to the Irish peasant as a debtor whose reliability is unimpeachable. More than twenty years ago the Baroness Burdett Coutts made a loan of L10,000 to the fishermen of Baltimore, with a view to the development of their industry, and the unfailing punctuality with which payments were made afforded another instance of the reliability which is a characteristic of the Irish peasant. This brings one to note in passing that of all others the fishing industry has probably suffered most from the lack of proper means of transit. The 2,500 miles of coast line offer great scope, but the catch of fish off the Irish coast is only one-eighth of that off Scotland, and one-sixteenth of that off England and Wales, and Irish waters are to a very large extent fished by boats from the coasts of Scotland, the Isle of Man, France, and Norway. Oyster fisheries used to abound-- the celebrated beds at Arcachon in the Landes were stocked from Ireland--but they have fallen into disuse, and with their disappearance a very remunerative business has been lost. The need for extensive and scientific forestry one may also note is obvious, from the fact that there are seven million acres of former woodland which are now reduced to a waste. The results of planting a shelter bed of pines on the north and west coasts, as a protection from the Atlantic winds, would be very great, while the industrial effect of systematised forestry would be immense. Bark for tanning, charcoal, moss, resin, manure from fallen leaves, litter, fuel, and mushrooms are some of the bye-products of this reproductive industry, while by planting willows, which yield a rapid return, along bogs a basket weaving industry might very rapidly be developed. The need, however, for planting on an extensive scale and the inevitable delay before any returns for expenditure accrue, make forestry essentially an object not for private but for public enterprise.

It is not generally known that in 1831 Ireland grew one-fifth of the tobacco consumed in the three kingdoms, but that in that year the first Liberal Government which was in power for a generation put down a profitable industry for which the turfy soil of the country was particularly well adapted. With the help of a shilling rebate it is being shown, on an experimental area, that tobacco can be grown successfully in Ireland. At present the Treasury has refused to allow any extension of the area under cultivation, and it remains to be seen whether the united demands of Irish members--Unionist as well as Nationalist--will secure the removal of the prohibition against its growth, and so possibly lead to a re-establishment of its cultivation on a similar scale to that of three-quarters of a century ago.

Perhaps the most important and, one may surmise, far-reaching step which has been taken in respect of Irish industries in the last few years is to be found in the registration, under the Merchandise Marks Act of 1905, of a national trade-mark, the property in which is vested in an association, which, on payment of a fee, grants the right to use it to manufacturers of the nature of whose credentials it is satisfied. The value of this is obvious as giving a guarantee of the country of origin of goods at a time when the increased demand for Irish produce has added to the number of unscrupulous traders who sell as "made in Ireland" goods which are not of Irish manufacture. It is said that twenty years ago most of the tweed which was placed upon the market which had been made in Ireland was sold as Cheviot, and that today the *roles* are reversed, and it is certain that for many years the great bulk of Irish butter masqueraded in English provision shops as Danish. The income of the association is devoted to the taking of legal action against traders who fraudulently sell as Irish, foreign including English made goods. If an instance is needed of the results which the protection of a national trade-mark gives in the encouragement of industry, by the guarantee of origin which it entails, it is to be found in the success of similar action in the cases of the butter industries of Sweden and Austria. It is a great tribute to the Trade-Mark Association that within two years of its incorporation the Congested Districts Board has applied for the use of the trade-mark for the products of its lace classes and for its homespuns.

The task proposed by Henry Grattan to the Irish Parliament may well be taken to heart by the Irish people to-day:--"In the arts that polish life, the manufactures that adorn it, you will for many years be inferior to some other parts of Europe, but to nurse a growing people, to mature a struggling, though hardy, community, to mould, to multiply, to consolidate, to inspire, and to exalt a young nation, be these your barbarous accomplishments."

CHAPTER IV
THE LAND QUESTION

"I can imagine no fault attaching to any land system which does not attach to the Irish system. It has all the faults of a peasant proprietary, it has all the faults of feudal landlordism, it has all the faults incident to a system under which the landlords spend no money on their property, and under which a large part of the land is managed by a Court; it has all the faults incident to the fact that it is to the tenant's interest to let his farm run out of cultivation as the term for revising the judicial rent approaches."
--A.J. BALFOUR, on the Second Reading of the Land Bill, May 4th, 1903.

The reason for the importance of the system of land tenure in the social conditions of Ireland is to be found in the manner in which the restrictions on Irish commerce in the seventeenth and eighteenth centuries drove the population to secure a livelihood in the only direction left open to them--namely, agriculture. The results of this are to be seen to-day in the fact that there are 590,000 holdings in the island, and that out of a total population of four and a half million people it is well within the mark to say that three and a half million are dependent, directly or indirectly, on the land for their means of existence.

The system of tenure in Ireland was as different as possible from that existing in Great Britain. The gist of the difference lay in this, that in England and Scotland landlords let farms, while in Ireland they let land. "In Ireland," wrote an English observer more than a hundred years ago, "landlords never erect buildings on their property, nor expend anything in repairs." This feature, which was the result of historical reasons, was due to the fact that Irish land-owners were the descendants of settlers intruded on Irish land, who brought with them English notions of tenure, but had not the capital to render economic the numerous small holdings situated on their estates. Hence it came about that the provision of capital by an English landlord for the equipment of farms with cottages, outhouses, fencing, and a drainage system, which results in a sort of partnership between landlord and tenant, was, to a large extent, a thing unknown in Ireland, where, as was aptly said, tenants' improvements were landlords' perquisites, and where point was lent to the differences by the fact that the few properties on which the equipment of the holdings was provided by the landlord were known as "English-managed estates," and the number of these, Lord Cowper told the House of Lords in 1887, could be counted on one's fingers.

Irish landlords have been compared, not to English squires, but to the ground landlords of London, bound to the occupiers only in so far as they received from their tenants a rent-charge liable to increase as the tenant improved the holding, or as competition arose with the growth of population.

The reasons for this state of things are to be found in the number and the small size of the Irish holdings, but more than this in the fact that from the first landlords came there in a business capacity.

"Les uns comme les autres," says a French writer, M. Paul-Dubois, "ils n'ont vu dans la terre Irlandaise qu'une affaire, et non une patrie. Ils sont restes conquerants en pays de conquete. De la cette consequence que, conscients d'etre des etrangers, des intrus, ils se sont crus libres et quittes de toute dette envers le pays, de tous les devoirs de la propriete."[3]

Planted on land which was confiscated, and, as a result, insecurely held, to risk the expenditure of money would have been unnatural, the more so since the expenditure which, in the circumstances, fell upon the tenant in the matter of improvements, provided the best possible security to the landlord by making the tenant all the more anxious to remain on the holding on which he had sunk what little capital he possessed, and in consequence virtually obliged, at risk of ejection, to submit unwillingly to periodical enhancements of rent.

In addition to the few English-managed estates it was only in Ulster that matters were otherwise, owing to the existence of the custom--an embryo copyhold, Lord Devon called it--known as tenant-right. On the various confiscations of land, grants of which had been made to the "undertakers," many of the latter were either public bodies, such as the great City Companies, others were landlords who, even if not resident at a distance, had neither the means nor the inclination to spend the necessary money on their estates. This was provided by the tenant, who, without aid from the landlord, made improvements on his holding by his own labour; and in Ulster, where the tenants were settlers from England and Scotland, there arose an equitable proprietorship vested in the occupier, by which, on quitting the farm, he was entitled to claim from the new tenant a sum of money partly in compensation for the money and labour he had invested in the holding and partly as a price paid for the goodwill or possession, which the new tenant would have no other means of acquiring. The nature of this "Ulster Custom," which, until 1870, had no sanction or protection from the law, was clearly defined by the Master of the Rolls, in the case of M'Elroy *v.* Brooke, in the following words:--"The essentials of the custom are the right to sell, to have the incoming tenant, if there be no reasonable objection to him, recognised by the landlord, and to have a sum of money paid for the interest in the tenancy transferred." The English system we see then, with its competitive rent fixed by contract, and subject to the laws of supply and demand, did not exist; the social and prescriptive ties which in England bound the owner and the occupier to each other never arose under this state of things, and in their absence did not arise one of the strongest inducements to a landed gentry to live on their estates and to concern themselves in the welfare of their tenants, a social system which, by the interchange of kindly offices wherever in England the proprietors live on their property, does much to make the countryside attractive to the poorer classes and to check migration.

There is no more erroneous idea than to suppose, as do some people, that there was a large body of resident landed proprietors in Ireland until the land war drove them to seek safety across the Channel. As a matter of fact, long before this had begun there existed an absentee aristocracy dependent on middlemen or agents--"the vermin of the country," Arthur Young called them--who constituted a mere mechanical medium for the collection of rent, and as such were the worst exponents of the amenities which, in happier circumstances, are supposed to subsist between owners and occupiers of agrarian land. At the beginning of the nineteenth century the increase of population in the island and the high prices resulting from the war led to a very great sub-division of holdings, while the exercise of the franchise by the forty shillings freeholder until the year 1829 provided an additional inducement to the landlord to multiply the number of tenants on his land, since by doing so he increased the number of votes under his control, and, **_pari passu_**, his political influence.

After the famine, when it was found that one-third of the Irish landlords were bankrupt, the Encumbered Estates Court Act was passed to cope with the situation which had arisen of a country full of numerous landlords saddled with land which, owing to mortgages, debts, and incumbrances, was inalienable. Under the Act the Court was empowered, on the petition of any person sufficiently interested, to sell the encumbered estate and give an indefeasible title, so that persons who before had a claim on the estate should now have a claim only on the purchase-money. It was a piece of strong legislation in its disregard of vested rights and in the manner in which it set aside express contracts under which creditors had a claim on the land which could only be disturbed by paying off that claim.

In the event the rush of creditors to this Court--created to afford relief from the delays of Chancery in effecting alienation--was so great that, as a result of the consequent fall in prices, land became a drug in the market, and properties in many instances did not realise enough to meet the mortgages. To the landlords ruined in this manner succeeded a new class, who bought up bankrupt estates, often with borrowed money, as a commercial speculation, and caring nothing for the tenant or his welfare, looking only on the business side of the transaction, raised rents arbitrarily to such a pitch that the tenantry were unable to meet their liabilities. Wholesale evictions ensued, and in this wise arose the condition of things in which the **_Times_**--never an unfriendly critic of the landed interest--was constrained to admit in 1852 that "the name of an Irish landlord stinks in the nostrils of Christendom."

By an Act of 1858 the Encumbered Estates Court was replaced by the Landed Estates Court, which had power to carry out the sale of, and give an indefeasible title to, any interests in land, whether hypothecated or not, and after the passing of the Judicature Act of 1877 the name of the Court became the Land Judges' Court.

The disfranchising clauses of the Emancipation Act, and the consequent disappearance of the advantages accruing to the landlords from a multiplication of holdings on their estates, the miserable poverty resulting from the famine, the anxiety of the proprietors to escape the burdens of the remodeled Poor Law, and the demand by the new class of land speculators for large grazing or tillage farms, to form which the consolidation of existing holdings was demanded, were the factors which resulted in the clearances of 1849 and the subsequent years. "Notices to quit," in a historic phrase, "fell like snowflakes," at a time when it was truly said that an eviction was equal to a sentence of death. In a few months whole counties, such as those of Meath and Tipperary, were converted into prairies; cabins were thrown down, fences removed, and peasants swept off, and in ten years nearly 300,000 families were evicted from their homes, and a million and a half of the population fled across the Atlantic. "I do not think," said Sir Robert Peel--and his verdict has been endorsed by the judgment of history--"I do not think that any country, civilised or uncivilised, can offer similar scenes of horror."

The Devon Commission, the Report of which was issued in 1845, recommended that in future compensation should be given to Irish tenants for permanent improvements effected by them. Bills to carry out the recommendation of the Commission were introduced in 1845 by Lord Stanley, in 1846 by Lord Lincoln, and in 1852 by Mr. Napier, the Attorney-General for Ireland. But it was not until the Act of 1870 was passed--a quarter of a century after the Report of the Commissioners had been issued--that its recommendations were embodied in an Act of Parliament. So far was this from being the case with the next statute dealing with Irish land--Deasy's Act, passed in 1860--that it aimed at the substitution of the commercial principles of contract for the equitable principles of custom in the relations between landlord and tenant, in this respect that it refused to allow compensation to the tenant for improvements other than those made with the landlord's consent. The object of this Act--the last word of the Manchester School on the Irish Land Question--was, therefore, to destroy any claim by a tenant in respect of future improvements, unless under the terms of some contract, express or implied. In point of fact, the Act proved almost a dead letter, and the one result which ensued from its passing into law was to make the position of the tenant less secure, in so far as it made the process of ejectment less costly and more simple, and enabled the landlord in many instances to confiscate improvements.

Twenty-three Bills in favour of the tenants were thrown out in the forty years which followed Emancipation. The struggle between landlord and tenant was occupied with the attempts of the latter to enforce the custom of tenant-right in Ulster, and secure its application in the other provinces. The Land Act of 1870, for the first time, gave legal sanction to this principle by giving the tenant a claim to compensation for disturbance. It gave its imprimatur to the doctrine that an Irish tenant does not contract for the occupation of a farm, that Irish land is not the subject of an undivided ownership, but of a simple partnership. The pecuniary damages to which a landlord was liable under its provisions was a blow aimed at wanton evictions, and with the curtailment of the power arbitrarily to effect these, the threats by which landlords had been able unjustly to raise rents were robbed of much of their force.

The tenant under the Act secured a recognition of his property in the land and of his right to occupy it, provided he complied with certain conditions, and, in addition, he obtained compensation, albeit inadequate, for disturbance for non-payment of rent, in cases in which the Court considered the rent exorbitant, and in which failure to pay was due to bad seasons. Thus tenant-right, which Lord Palmerston had dismissed with epigrammatic flippancy as landlord wrong only a few years before, received the sanction of law from his own party.

In actual practice under the Act the landlords recouped themselves for the compensation which they had to pay to an evicted tenant by raising the rent on his successor in the tenancy in the comparatively few cases in which the evicted tenant could afford the legal costs which the filing of a claim for compensation entailed, but this much at least had been secured, that the virtual confiscation of the tenants' improvements had been stopped. The Act of 1870 had been passed to prevent arbitrary evictions and to secure to the tenant compensation for improvements, and in certain cases for disturbance. It succeeded only in making arbitrary evictions more costly for the landlord, it gave the tenant no fixity of tenure since the compensation for disturbance was inadequate. To remedy this Isaac Butt in 1876 introduced a Bill based on the "three F.s"--fair rent, free sale, and fixity of tenure--but it was rejected by 290 votes to 56, and several other amending Bills were thrown out by the House of Commons between 1876 and 1879. In 1880 the Government were at last stirred to action in the introduction of the Compensation for Disturbance Bill, which caused the retirement of Lord Lansdowne from the Cabinet, and was followed by threats of resignation on the part of the Duke of Argyll. Under the Act of 1870 only those occupiers were entitled to claim compensation for disturbance whose rents were not in arrear. By this Bill it was proposed to extend the right to that claim to all those who were unable to pay as a result of bad harvests, and who were willing to hold their farms on just and reasonable terms, which the landlord refused.

After passing through the House of Commons, in spite of Lord Randolph Churchill's denunciation of it as the first step in a social war, the Bill, although there had been a large majority in its favour in the lower House, was thrown out by the House of Lords at a time when the need for remedial legislation was illustrated by the presence in Ireland of 30,000 soldiers and 12,000 policemen for the protection of life and property.

The Royal Commission, under the chairmanship of Lord Bessborough, which was then appointed, reported in the following year that the Land Act of 1870 afforded no protection to the tenant who remained in his holding, since compensation for improvements could only be claimed on giving up a tenancy. The Commissioners, by a majority of four to one, declared themselves in favour of the "three F.s," which the leader of the Opposition denounced as "Force, Fraud, and Folly," and the Commissioners justified their attitude by this statement, which was echoed by the Richmond Commission, which reported soon after,--"freedom of contract, in the case of the majority of Irish tenants, large and small, does not really exist," the reason being that tenants in occupation were ready to pay any rent rather than sacrifice the capital and labour they had sunk in their holdings. The good seasons after 1870 had made this rise in rent possible, but with the bad winter of 1880 the results became disastrous.

In this manner the "three F.s," which the Land League demanded, and which were secured by the Act of 1881, were conceded against the will of the Government by sheer force of circumstances. A rumour which gained currency early in 1880, that the Bessborough Commission would report in their favour, was stigmatised by Mr. Gladstone as incredible, and the adoption of the principle enunciated by the Commissioners resulted in the resignation from the Cabinet of the Duke of Argyll. The demands which had been made in 1850 by the Tenant League, the first concerted action of North and South since the Union, were repeated. They included a fair valuation of rent, the right of a tenant to sell his interest at the highest market value, and security from eviction so long as he paid his rent. Their claims were scouted in 1870, and it was not till eleven years had passed that in 1881 these "three F.s"--fair rent, free sale, and fixity of tenure, the notion of which had so recently been repudiated by Mr. Gladstone--were secured by the Land Act of that year, which recognised to the full the dual ownership of Irish land by occupier and landlord. Under this Act also was created a Court to fix fair rents for judicial periods of fifteen years.

Mr. Gladstone himself had admitted that the Land Act of 1870, which a Conservative member, destined to be a future Chief Secretary--Mr. James Lowther--described as "pure Communism," together with the Church Act of 1869, was the outcome of the Fenian agitation of the sixties, which drew the attention of English statesmen to the Irish question. In the same way the passing of the Act of 1881, which made a far more active assault upon their prerogatives, secured from a house of landlords through fear that which they denied on grounds of equity. "In view of the prevailing agitation in Ireland," said Lord Salisbury of this measure which assailed every Tory principle as to the sacredness of property, "I cannot recommend my followers to vote against the second reading of the Bill." What Fenianism had effected in 1870 the Land League secured in 1881. "I must record my firm opinion," said Mr. Gladstone ten years later, "that the Land Act of 1881 would not have become the law of the land if it had not been for the agitation with which Irish society was convulsed."

The Bill was denounced by the Tories as one of the most unquestionable and, indeed, extreme violations of the rights of property in the whole history of English legislation.[4] Lord Salisbury declared that it would not bring peace, and that henceforth the Irish landowner would look upon Parliament and the Imperial Government as their worst enemies. The Earl of Lytton declared that it was revolutionary, dangerous, and unjust; that it would organise pauperism and paralyse capital; yet for all that he warned their lordships that its rejection might be the signal for an insurrection, of which the whole responsibility would be thrown on the House of Lords. But perhaps Lord Elcho expressed the feeling which predominated in the Gilded Chamber when he expressed the opinion that the Bill was the product of "Brummagem girondists." In the event, as we have seen, Lord Lytton's warning bore fruit, and the Bill was passed. "There is scarcely a less dignified entity," as Disraeli had said in Coningsby thirty years before, "than a patrician in a panic."

Under the Act, let me repeat, for the first time was frankly recognised the legal partnership between the tenant who provided the working gear and the landlord who provided the bare soil. The latter could only evict the tenant on default, the tenant was at liberty to sell his occupancy interest at will without the leave of the landlord, and the rent payable by the tenant to the landlord was to be fixed by a judicial tribunal--the Land Commission--the establishment of which was but the carrying out of a suggestion made three years before by Parnell. The results of the agitation which had brought about the passing of the Act were seen when the Court decreed an average reduction of Irish rents by 20 per cent., knocking off no less than L1,500,000 at one stroke from the rack-rentals of the country.

The Act was not applicable to tenants whose rent was in arrear--those, that is to say, who were in the poorest circumstances--and a Bill introduced by Parnell in 1882 to wipe out these arrears by a grant of public money, was thrown out, being denounced by Lord Salisbury as a dangerous precedent of public plunder to mislead future generations.

As ballast to lighten the Act of 1881 the leaseholders were thrown overboard. For this exclusion from the benefits of the Act there was, on principle, no excuse. A Bill of Parnell's to remedy it was thrown out in 1883 by a majority of four to one, and the 35,000 tenants who suffered from it were not entirely accorded the privileges of the other tenants until the passing of the Rent Redemption Act of 1890. The average reduction in rent effected for this class of tenant has amounted to 35 per cent.

One further fact in connection with the Act of 1881 deserves mention as showing that though Parliament may propose a remedy for an admitted grievance, the Courts of law are able to dispose its application by their interpretation in direct contravention of the intentions of the legislature.

Section 8, sub-section 9, of the Act of 1881 provided:--"No rent shall be allowed or made payable in any proceedings under this Act in respect of improvements made by the tenant or his predecessors in title, and for which, in the opinion of the Court, the tenant or his predecessors in title shall not have been paid or otherwise compensated by the landlord or his predecessors in title." In the case of

Adams *v*. Dunseath, in February, 1882, it was held by the Court of Appeal, in the teeth of the obvious intention of Parliament, that the fact that a tenant had for a longer or shorter period of time enjoyed the benefit of his improvements might be taken into consideration by the judge as being an equivalent for compensation and as serving to limit the reductions in rent effected by the Commission on land which had been subjected to these improvements. By this interpretation many thousands of pounds were put into the landlords' pockets during the years which intervened before 1896, when it was superseded by a provision in the Act of that year which re-affirmed and established the principle, the enactment of which had been intended in 1881.

We must now turn to the introduction of land purchase. In 1847 Lord John Russell, in a project which was subsequently dropped, advocated, as did J.S. Mill in later years, the solution of the land question by the establishment of a peasant proprietary. The nidus, however, out of which this policy germinated was the right of pre-emption which John Bright secured for the tenants of ecclesiastical land under the Church Act of 1869. A further step in the same direction was taken in the Land Act of 1870--not more than two-thirds of the purchase-money being advanced to the tenant under its provisions. Under the Church Act 6,000, and under the Act of 1870 1,000, tenants purchased their farms.

In 1878 Parnell urged the establishment of peasant proprietorship, and under the Act of 1881 three-quarters of the purchase-money was to be advanced on such terms as to be repayable by instalments of five per cent, per annum for thirty-five years, but only 1,000 tenants took advantage of the facilities thereby offered.

Four years later was passed the Ashbourne Act, so called from the Irish Lord Chancellor responsible for its introduction, and in it we have the first Act--purely for land purchase--which has been applied to Ireland. By it the Treasury found the whole of the purchase-money up to a total of five millions sterling out of the Irish Church Surplus Fund, and forty-nine years were allowed for repayment of the purchase-money to the State at 4 per cent., of which L2 15s. was interest on the advance and L1 5s. went to a sinking fund for the liquidation of the loan.

Only 2,000 tenants took advantage of the terms of this Act, but it is nevertheless of importance as marking the point at which the principle of peasant proprietorship was recognised as the solution by both English parties. In this way was realised, not much more than twenty years ago, the importance of that change of ownership which, in Arthur Young's well-known phrase, turns sand into gold, and which has progressed ever since. A shrewd French observer--Gustave de Beaumont--saw in 1837 that this was the way out of the *impasse* of the Irish land system, and half a century ago a great opportunity presented itself at the time of the Encumbered Estates Act of establishing a peasant proprietary, when more than two million acres--one-sixth of the whole soil of Ireland--were sold in ten years, and were bought in lots of 200 to 250 acres by some 8,000 to 10,000 land-jobbers.

The Land Bill which Mr. Gladstone introduced as a pendant to the Home Rule Bill of 1886 offered to every Irish landlord the option of selling his estate to his tenants, who would thereby become occupying owners at once, paying an interest of 4 per cent. for forty-nine years on the price, which would be twenty years' purchase of the judicial rents, paid by the State issue of fifty million pounds of Consols with the revenues of Ireland as security. After the Unionist victory of 1886 Mr. Parnell brought in a Bill which also was destined never to receive the Royal Assent, but which again is of importance in view of subsequent legislation.

He based his demand upon the fall in prices which prevented tenants from paying judicial rents. By this Bill it was proposed that the Land Court should have power to abate rents fixed prior to 1885 if it were proved that the tenants could not pay the whole amount, and would pay one half and arrears, and further, if these amounts were paid evictions and proceedings for the recovery of rent should be suspended, and, lastly, the Bill aimed at the inclusion of leaseholders under the Act of 1881.

It was roundly denounced by the landlords.[5] Lord Hartington declared that were it to pass it would have the effect of stopping the payment of rent all over Ireland, and Sir Michael Hicks Beach spoke of it as "one which, though purporting to be a mere instalment of justice to the poor Irish tenant, is an act of gross injustice and confiscation to the landlords of Ireland." The Bill was thrown out by a majority of ninety-five, and the Plan of Campaign on the part of tenants against the payment of impossible rents was the result.

A Royal Commission, under the chairmanship of Lord Cowper, was appointed to inquire into the administration of the Land Laws. The Commission reported in January, 1887, and bore out the grounds on which Parnell had based his Bill of the previous year. It felt "constrained to recommend an earlier revision of judicial rents on account of the straitened circumstances of Irish farmers." It recommended that the term of judicial rents should be lowered from fifteen years to five, that those rents already fixed should be revised, and that leaseholders should be brought under the Act of 1881. In reference to the Bill of the year before Lord Salisbury had said that the revision of judicial rents would not be honest and would be exceedingly inexpedient.[6] The Bill, which is known as Lord Cadogan's, which was introduced on the last day of March, 1887, and which purported to carry out the recommendations of the Cowper Commission, opened the Land Court to leaseholders, setting aside in this way the more solemn forms of agrarian contract. As regards authorising the reduction of judicial rents on the ground of the fall in prices, it did nothing, and the Prime Minister repeated his opinion that "to do so would be to lay your axe at the root of the fabric of civilised society."[7]

Mr. Balfour, who, in the month of March, had become Chief Secretary, proclaimed with equal force that it would be folly and madness to break these solemn contracts.[8] In the Bill, as at first brought in, the Court had, in fact, power to vary contracts by fixing a composition for outstanding debts and determining the period over which payment should extend. In May the Government accepted the principle that the Court should not only do this (settle the sum due by an applicant for relief for outstanding debt), but also should fix a reasonable rent for the rest of the term. The Ulster tenants insisted on this, but, at the bidding of the landlords, it was subsequently withdrawn, and, finally, in July the Premier summoned his party and, telling them that if the Bill were not altered Ulster would be lost to the Unionist cause, passed into law a Bill sanctioning a general revision of judicial rents for three years, and in this way did the Tories lower rents in breach of a clause in the Act of 1881 that guaranteed rents fixed under its provisions for a term of fifteen years.

As a speaker of the day put it--"You have the Prime Minister rejecting in April the policy which in May he accepts, rejecting in June the policy which he had accepted in May, and then in July accepting the policy which he had rejected in June, and which had been within a few weeks declared by himself and his colleagues to be inexpedient and dishonest, to be madness and folly, and to be laying an axe to the very root of the fabric of civilised society."

When the advance of five millions for land purchase under the Act of 1885 was nearly exhausted, a further sum of equal amount was earmarked for the same purpose in 1888. Lord Randolph Churchill in 1889 expressed the opinion that something like L100,000,000 of credit should be pledged to effect purchase. In 1891 Mr. Balfour authorised the devotion of a further sum of L33,000,000 for this purpose. The whole of the purchase-money was to be advanced by the State by the issue of guaranteed land stock, limited to the amount stated, and giving a dividend at two and three-quarters per cent., repayment being effected in forty-nine years by the purchaser by the payment of an annuity on his holding of four per cent. The Act was too complicated to work well, but under its provisions 30,000 sales occurred, in comparison with 25,000 which had been effected under the Acts of 1885 and 1888. The passing of this Act marks the close of the experimental stage in land purchase. Under the Land Act of 1896 was asserted the principle of compulsory sale in the case of estates in the Landed Estates Court, whose duty it was to sell bankrupt property, if they came under certain specified conditions, and if a receiver had been appointed to them.

This roused the fury of the landlords to the highest pitch. "You would suppose," said Sir Edward Carson, "the Government were revolutionists verging on socialism.... I ask myself whether they are mad or I am mad? I am quite sure one of us must be mad." In spite of denunciations of this order the clause respecting compulsory sale of the estates mentioned was passed, occupying tenants having in those cases the right of pre-emption. Under its provisions the period for the repayment of the money advanced was extended to sixty-eight years. The annuity payable by the tenant during the first decade was to be calculated and made payable upon the total purchase-money advanced, but at the end of each of the first three decennial periods, as the debt was reduced by the accumulation of sinking fund, the annuity was to be re-calculated and made payable on the portions of the advance remaining unpaid. Under the Act every purchaser was to start with a reduction of not less than 25 per cent. on the rent which he had hitherto paid, and this amount was to be still further reduced by not less than 10 per cent. at the end of each of the first three periods of ten years. This Act effected the sale of 37,000 holdings. The applications for sale under it numbered 8,000 in 1898, and in the succeeding years the number steadily diminished, so that they amounted in 1899 to 6,000, in 1900 to 5,000, and in 1901 to only 3,000. The reasons for this are not difficult to find. The payment in

Consols was profitable so long as securities stood at a high figure, but the expenses arising from the South African war resulted in a fall of Stocks from 112 to 85, and as a result new terms for land purchase became imperatively needed. In consequence Mr. Wyndham brought in a Bill in 1902, which was, however, stillborn, but its withdrawal was accompanied with a promise of legislation in the following session. The situation in the winter of 1902 was critical. An Irish Land Trust had been formed by the landlords to oppose the United Irish League, and on the 1st of September there was issued a Viceregal proclamation, putting the Coercion Act in force in Dublin and Limerick. By a curious coincidence, the papers published the same day a letter from Captain Shaw Taylor, an Irish landlord, inviting representatives of tenants and landlords to meet in conference in Dublin and discuss a way out of the agrarian *impasse*. The proposal was scouted by the ***Times***, the ***Daily Express***, and the Dublin ***Daily Express***, but was favourably received by the Press in other quarters. A motion by Lord Mayo at the Landowners' Convention, in favour of the conference, was rejected by 77 votes to 14. A poll on the question being demanded, 4,000 landlords, each with an estate of more than 500 acres, received voting papers, and of these 1,706 replied, 1,128 in favour and 578 against a conference, while the small landlords were almost unanimously in its favour. A second appeal was then made to the Landowners' Convention through its president, Lord Abercorn, but an answer in the negative was received, for it went on to say--"It would be merely to give long-discredited politicians a certificate of good sense and of just views, we might almost say of legislative capacity to sit in an Irish Parliament in Dublin, were we to accept Captain Shaw Taylor's invitation to join them."

  The criticism of an unbiassed foreign observer on this attitude of rigid cast-iron ***non possumus*** is instructive. "Rappelons nous," writes M. Bechaux, "que le parti irlandais au Parlement, si grossierement insulte represente 4/5 du peuple irlandais, nous avons un specimen de l'esprit reactionnaire et irreconciliable du landlordisme irlandais." In spite of this the Conference met at the end of the year. The landlords' representatives were:--Lord Dunraven, Lord Mayo, Col. Hutcheson Poee, and Col. Nugent Everard; and those of the tenants were:--Mr. John Redmond, Mr. W. O'Brien, Mr. T.W. Russell, and Mr. T.C. Harrington. On the 3rd January, 1903, a joint report to serve as the basis of the new Bill was issued.

  The Report was in favour of purchase as the only possible policy to be carried out on such terms that the yearly payments of the tenants should be 15 to 25 per cent. lower than second term rents, while the sum received by the landlords was to be such as at 3 or 3-1/4 per cent. interest would yield them the same income as second term rents, less 10 per cent. deduction, as an equivalent for the cost of collection under the old system. The difference between these two sums was to be bridged by a bonus from the Treasury to the landlords in the interests of agrarian peace. The Report was further in favour of enlarging small holdings by dividing up grazing lands, and under it evicted tenants who, as such, were not entitled to have judicial rents fixed were to be given the option to purchase.

Second term rents are those fixed for the second judicial period of fifteen years under the Act of 1881, and they were on an average 37 per cent. less than those before the passing of that Act.

Under the Act which Mr. Wyndham introduced on March 25th, 1903, the Treasury may advance a sum up to one hundred millions at 2-3/4 per cent. interest, with another 1/2 per cent. sinking fund. The advances to the tenants, which are limited to L5,000 or, in exceptional circumstances, L7,000, are made in cash by the Land Commissioners, of whom three, serving as the Estates Commissioners, are expressly responsible for the working of the Act. A Treasury loan at 2-3/4 per cent. provides the necessary funds. Under the Act the issue of this Stock was limited to five million pounds a year for the first three years, but in January, 1905, this was changed to a sum of six million. By adding to the 2-3/4 per cent. interest which the tenants pay on the loan the further sum of 1/2 per cent. which they contribute to sinking fund for repayment, we arrive at 3-1/4 per cent. which they have to pay for sixty-eight and a half years to obtain the fee-simple of their land. The security which Mr. Wyndham produced for the repayment of interest was the credit of the Irish peasantry, of whom, out of more than seventy thousand purchasers owing an eighth of a million to the State under previous Purchase Acts, only two had incurred bad debts, which, as being irrecoverable, had fallen on the taxpayer. As a further safeguard the payment is secured by the annual grants-in-aid paid by the Treasury to the County Councils, which can be withheld on default to pay interest on purchase advances. In order to facilitate sales the system of "zones," which has been so much canvassed, was devised. Under it the Estates Commissioners are bound to make advances of purchase-money in all cases in which the total annuity paid by the tenant ranges from 10 to 40 per cent. less than the rent which he has hitherto paid. If it be a first term rent the reduction must be at least 20 and not more than 40 per cent. less, and if it be a second term rent there must be a reduction of not less than 10 and not more than 30 per cent. It will be, perhaps, clearer if put in this way. If a first term rent amounts to L100, then the tenant-purchaser has to pay at least L60, and at most L80, as annuity, while if the L100 represent second term rent the yearly payment varies from a minimum of L70 to a maximum of L90.

If purchases are proposed outside the zones, in which, that is to say, the annuity proposed is under 10 or over 40 per cent. of the judicial rent, the estate must, before sales are effected, be surveyed by the Estates Commissioners in order that they may see whether the security is sound, and whether the equitable rights of all parties concerned seem to be safeguarded, and without this sanction advances will not be made in the case of sales in these circumstances. The amount received by the landlord, of course, does not, if invested in Trust Securities at 3-1/4 per cent., provide the same income as did his rent roll, even when one takes into account the 10 per cent. for collection to which we have referred. On the other hand, he is secured from the possibility of further reductions in rent in the future, and there is a likelihood that the securities in which he invests may rise, but, in addition to this, a sum of twelve millions of bonus is to be devoted to bridge the gap between his former rent from the tenant and his present income from his investments.

Under this provision every landlord gets 12 per cent. bonus on his sale, and this sum is part of his life estate, and need not, therefore, be invested in trust securities, but may be invested in stock yielding a higher rate of interest. This point was not clear in the Act of 1903, but was explicitly enacted in an amending Act of 1904.

In order further to accelerate sale an investigation of title deeds, documents which a great English lawyer--Lord Westbury--once described as "difficult to decipher, disgusting to touch, and impossible to understand," is not necessary prior to sale; for an enjoyment for six years of the rents of an estate brings with it the right to sell, and proof of title is needed only after purchase has been completed in order that the vendor may establish his right of disposal of the proceeds, and as further inducement he gets a sum not exceeding one full year's arrears of rent, or at most 5 per cent. of the purchase price.

The good results which have accrued where a peasant proprietary has arisen are admitted on all sides. Mr. Long himself, in words which form an illuminating commentary on landlordism, confessed that the blessings and advantages of a change of ownership are obvious. Everyone is agreed that the happiness, bred of security on the part of the occupying owner, brings in its train sobriety and industry. The business of the gombeen man is going, and one may well hope to see arise before long that thrift and energy characteristic of the peasant proprietor, whether in France, Belgium, or Lombardy.

It must not be forgotten, however, that land purchase to bring peace must be universal. In 1901 the De Freyne tenants rebelled against the payment to their landlord of a rent which was 25 to 30 per cent. higher than the purchase annuities paid by the neighbouring tenants on the Dillon estate, which had been bought up by the Congested Districts Board. Under the Wyndham Act there are in progress reductions of annual charges, ranging from 10 to 40 per cent., on holdings adjacent to those where either the landlord is recalcitrant and refuses to sell or where the slowness of administration has delayed progress and secured no sale, and, as a result, dissatisfaction reigns among the less fortunate tenants.

According to the last report of the Estates Commissioners nearly 90,000 holdings had been sold in the period of the application of the Act, from November 1st, 1903, to March 31st, 1906. The total price of all the sales agreed upon was nearly forty millions, but the amount advanced by the Commission was less than ten millions. There is little doubt that the number of agreements for sale would have been half as many again but for the lack of money and administrative powers. One of the Estates Commissioners, in his evidence before the Arterial Drainage Commission, stated that under the Land Purchase Acts passed before that of 1903 in twenty-five years 75,000 tenants had purchased at a price of twenty-five millions, and if to these are added the ninety thousand purchasers under the Act of Mr. Wyndham the result is seen that nearly a third of the tenants have in the last quarter of a century become occupying owners.

The immense acceleration in the rate of sale which these figures indicate, leads one to ask how far the sales under the Wyndham Act have been as advantageous to the tenants as those concluded under former statutes. In the first place, it must be noted that more than four-fifths of the direct sales which have occurred have taken place under the zones. When the price proposed is above the zones the reason why inspection is demanded is obviously that the solvency of the purchaser, with which the State, as creditor, is concerned, is in question. The minimum limit of the zones was said to be necessary to protect those with rights superior to those of the landlord, but, as was observed, the value of land does not depend on the mortgages with which it is charged. In view of the modern methods by which, on purchase, there is a Treasury guarantee, inspection before sale tends to reduce the price, and the absence of inspection under the zones has tended to enhance prices. It must be further noticed that the minimum price fixed by the zones is higher than the mean price of sales effected under Purchase Acts from 1885 to 1903, and by this method in the case of every sale brought about without the delay of inspection, the provisions of the Act have secured an artificial inflation of price for the benefit of the landlord, amounting to a minimum of one year's rent. The reduction of the annuity payable by the tenants from 4 per cent. to 3-1/4 per cent, of the capital has served to obscure the amount of purchase price paid by tenants who are apt to fail to appreciate the fact that the annuity is payable over a more extended period of years, and the provisions as to the sale and re-purchase of demesnes have at the same time secured for the landlords themselves facilities for obtaining advances of ready money on reasonable terms. These are the factors in the Wyndham Act which have made M. Paul-Dubois declare of it that--"Emanee d'un gouvernment, ami des landlords, elle cache mal, sous un apparence d'impartialite d'adroits efforts pour faire aux landlords de la part belle pour hausser en leur faveur le prix de la terre."

The average price per acre for the five years before 1903 was L8 9s.; since the Act it has been L13 4s., or taking into account the bonus L15. The prices before the Wyndham Act rarely exceeded eighteen years' purchase, and were, moreover, paid in Land Stock and without a bonus. Under this Act the reasons which I have tried to outline have brought it to pass that twenty-five years of second term rents are being paid in cash, which, with the bonus, makes the total purchase price amount to twenty-eight years. Hence it is that there is widespread anxiety in Ireland lest land is being sold under the zones at prices which the Land Commission, had it been entitled to inspect, would have been unable to sanction as offering a safe security, seeing that the purchaser must pay his annuity for sixty-eight years without hope of reduction--a danger, in the event of bad seasons, which might have been diminished if the sinking fund had been fixed at a higher rate and the decadal reductions of earlier Acts retained, so as to reduce the incidence of the burden in its later stages. This, be it noted, is one of the points in which the provisions of the Act differ from the recommendations of the Land Conference.

I have referred already to the block in sales under the Act owing to the scarcity of money which is forthcoming to meet sales already effected. By the financial provisions of the statute, so as not to demoralise the market, a definite check was put upon the issue of the land stock, and just before the late Government resigned Mr. Long, as Chief Secretary, made a proposal, which was not received with enthusiasm by the parties concerned, that the landlords should in future be paid partly in stock at a nominal value and partly in cash. Nothing has since been done, and the only step taken so far has been the appointment of a judge in addition to those formerly so engaged, to accelerate the judicial inquiries necessitated by the process of transfer. The whole cost of the finance of the Act falls on the Irish taxpayer, and before the introduction of Mr. Wyndham's proposal the idea was mooted--only to be abandoned--of reviving a proposal made by Sir Robert Giffen in the *Economist* twenty years ago, which would have made the annuities paid on purchase the basis of the funds from which the local bodies in Ireland would draw their revenue, while the Imperial Exchequer would be relieved to an equivalent amount by deductions from its grants to local services.

The cost of the flotation of the Land Stock is borne by the Irish Development Fund of L185,000 per annum, which is the share of Ireland, equivalent to the grant for the increased cost of education in England under the Act of 1902. More than one-half of this fund has already been hypothecated for the costs of flotation of the twenty millions of Land Stock which have already been issued, and under the present system of finance, after a further issue of another twenty millions of stock, the whole loss will be thrown on the County Councils, and through them on the ratepayers, who have already been called upon to pay L70,000 to meet certain of the losses in this connection, which amount to twelve per cent. of the value of the stock floated.

The breaking up of the grazing lands, which in many instances the landlords are keeping back from the market, has not met with much success under the Act, and it is difficult to see how compulsion is to be avoided if the country is to be saved from the economically disastrous position of having established in it a number of occupying owners on tenancies which are not large enough to secure to them a living wage.

Under the Land Act of 1891 was created the Congested Districts Board, with an annual income of L55,000, for the purpose of promoting the permanent improvement of the backward districts of the West. The districts which come under its control are those which answer the following test, that more than twenty per cent. of the population of a county live in electoral divisions, of which the total rateable value gives a sum of less than 30s. per head of population. Such electoral divisions occur in the nine counties of Kerry, Cork, Galway, Mayo, Clare, Roscommon, Leitrim, Sligo, Donegal. In these counties there are 1,264 electoral divisions, of which 429 are congested. The setting up of particular districts as "congested" is, of course, quite arbitrary. There may be places outside the congested areas the condition of which is much worse than that of some of the congested districts, but if the population of these districts does not form one-fifth of that of the whole county they are ruled out of the scope of the Board's activities.

The conditions which subsist in them have been ably described by M. Bechaux from personal observation, and he declares that the standard of living is lower than in any other country of Western Europe. Their inhabitants number more than half a million--that is to say, 10 per cent. of the total population of the island. Most of them have farms of two to four acres, and they pay from a few shillings to several pounds for rent. In many instances the rent which they pay is rather for a roof than for the soil. They eke out a precarious livelihood by migration to England, for there is but little demand for agricultural labour owing to the prevalence of pasture in the West. Fishing has served as a secondary source of income, and kelp burning was a profitable addition to their means until the discovery of iodine in Peru sent down the price to a marked extent.

The right of turbary, which nearly every tenancy possesses, is the one thing which has kept this population from starvation, and in the case of seaside tenancies a further gain accrues from the use made of seaweed as manure, which, owing to the absence of stall-feeding, is only to be obtained in this way. Home industries, such as weaving, form another source of profit, and last, but not least, must be reckoned the money sent home by relatives who have emigrated to America. Calves, pigs, and poultry are maintained in these circumstances, and, owing to the sale of the best of the stock, the breed has steadily deteriorated. In the winter months potatoes, milk, and tea are the main articles of diet, and after the potato harvest is used up American meal, ground from maize, and American bacon of the worst possible kind take their place. The bacon of their own pigs is far too expensive for them to eat. The maize flour serves also as fodder for the live stock, and the oats which are grown are-eaten as gruel by the people as well as by the animals which they rear. The Congested Districts Board was established to remedy, as far as possible, this state of things--primarily by reorganising tenancies and amalgamating them into economic holdings, and at the same time enlarging them by the purchase of untenanted land, followed by its addition to existing tenancies. The slowness of its operations is seen from the fact that after fourteen years it had purchased less than 240,000 acres, of which three-quarters were untenanted land, while the whole extent of the congested districts is more than three and a half million acres. In justice to the Board, however, one must add that it has concerned itself with many other branches of rural economy--notably the improvement of the breed of horses, cattle, and pigs, the sale at cost price of chemical manures and seed, the making of harbours and roads, and the sale on instalment terms of fishing boats.

It is impossible to exaggerate the work done by the Board on the Dillon estate in Counties Mayo and Roscommon and in Clare Island. But when one reads in the Report for 1906--the fifteenth annual report of the Board--that since its establishment the Board has enlarged 1,220 tenures, re-arranged 537, and created 220, and realises, further, that there are in Ireland 200,000 uneconomic holdings, one may well ask what are these among so many?

Under the Act of 1903 the Board's purchases are financed by the Land Commission, and the results are to be seen in an acceleration of purchases, for while in the twelve years 1891 to 1903 the Board had bought about 200,000 acres, of which less than 45,000 were unlet land, in the three years from November, 1903, to the end of March, 1905, the acreage bought was over 160,000 acres, of which 48,000 were unlet, and negotiations were in progress for the transfer of another 100,000 acres, of which 20,500 were unlet.

Under the Act, however, in the case of "Congested Estates," which are defined as those in which one-half at least of the holdings are of valuation of L5 or under, or which consist of mountain or bog, the Land Commission is empowered to purchase and re-sell to the tenants, even at a loss, so long as the total loss on the purchase and improvements of these holdings does not exceed 10 per cent. of the cost of the total sales effected in the course of the same year. The amendments of the House of Lords, however, made the part of the Act dealing with this question a dead letter, and the Land Commissioners have given up the attempt to put it in force. The landlords, having a choice between sale direct to their tenants and to the Land Commission, have refused to give their consent to the declaration of their estate as a congested estate, which is necessary for the application of this section, unless they receive a guarantee that the holdings shall not be sold to the tenants at a lower price than they themselves could have obtained. The result is that if the Commissioners were to pay these maximum prices there would be nothing left for them out of which to make the necessary improvements, and, in consequence, this provision of the Act has been a failure.

As regards the evicted tenants, the first condition in the settlement arrived at by the Land Conference, and embodied in the Wyndham Act, was that they--the wounded soldiers in the land war, as they have been called--to whose sacrifices in the common cause is due the ameliorative legislation enacted by Parliament, should be restored to their holdings. In actual practice, by means of restrictive instructions issued by the late Government to the Commissioners, two of whom protested against this action in their report for 1906, the provisions of the Act which promised this reinstatement were made a dead letter--the Executive once again, in a historic phrase, driving a coach and four through the statute.

With the advent to power of the Liberal Government these instructions were withdrawn, but a further serious obstacle was to be found in the refusal of some landlords--and those, too, the worst--to allow their estates to be inspected with a view to find holdings for evicted tenants. This was the condition of affairs to which Mr. Bryce--at that time Chief Secretary--referred, when he said--"If the remedy for this state of things is compulsion, then to compulsion for that remedy we must go."

It is to be observed that the three Estates Commissioners were unanimous in thinking compulsion necessary, and that which was demanded was that the occupants, or planters, who in some cases have been *bona fide* farmers, but whom the Land Commission inspectors reported had in many cases allowed the land to get into a bad and dirty state, should, on dispossession, be generously compensated or given their choice of other lands. It was originally thought that one thousand would be the limit of the number of applications which would be made for reinstatement, but, in the event, out of ten thousand tenants evicted in the last quarter of a century, such applications were made in 6,700 cases, and some notion of the poverty of these peasants who were turned out upon the roadside may be inferred from the fact that nearly one-half paid a rental of less than L10 a year.

At the beginning of the session of 1907, out of the total number of applicants 1,300 had been rejected as not coming within the scope of the provisions relating to them, and 650, or less than 10 per cent. of the whole number who applied, had been reinstated. In the case of more than half the total number of applicants no report had been made, and in more than 450 cases, including, of course, those on the Clanricarde and Lewis estates, inspection of the property had been, as it is still, refused by the landlords. At this juncture Mr. Birrell declared that further legislation was imperatively needed, and to this announcement Mr. Walter Long replied that he accepted the view of his predecessor, Mr. Wyndham, as to the bargain which had been come to in regard to this question, and he went on to say:--[9]

"There can be no doubt whatever that in the interest not merely of these unfortunate people, whatever their past history may have been, but in the interest of the successful working of the Land Purchase Act, their reinstatement is looked upon as an essential element and a thing promised by Parliament."

The voluntary system, to which a tentative agreement was given under the Act of 1903, having broken down, the Evicted Tenants Bill was designed as a tardy act of justice to remove the cause for disaffection on the part of a tenantry to which Mr. T.W. Russell paid a notable tribute the other day as being not naturally lawless, but in point of fact the most God-fearing, purest-minded, and simplest peasantry on the face of the earth. That his diagnosis, that unrest is merely the product of suffering under cruel circumstances, is valid, is illustrated by the complete restoration of peace on the Massereene estate, when, on the death of the late peer, the planters were replaced by the tenants who had been evicted.

The land which it was proposed to affect by the Bill was a mere matter of some 80,000 acres, a bagatelle to the landed interest of Ireland, but involving vital consequences to the poverty-stricken peasants of the West. It was a Bill, as the Lord

Chancellor declared, to deal with the tail of an agrarian revolution, and to effect this with the minimum of suffering, compulsory powers and a simple and expeditious procedure were demanded, but in spite of the lip service which Unionists paid to the principles involved, in spite of their admissions that it proposed only to carry out their part of the agreement, arrived at no less than four years ago; by their amendments in the House of Lords, introducing limitations and appeals involving delays and costs, they succeeded in large measure in destroying the value of the measure. One can understand the attitude of Lord Clanricarde, who roundly denounced the whole proposal as "tainted with the callous levity of despotism," but it is difficult to speak charitably of the members of the Opposition, who, while repeatedly protesting their anxiety to see the evicted tenants restored, took care, through the agency of the House of Lords, to place every possible obstacle in the way of their speedy re-instatement.

Many of the amendments designed by the House of Lords were proposed by two of the Lords of Appeal in Ordinary, who sit in that House primarily as judges, and who are supposed to keep free from political entanglements. They aimed at an enhancement of the prices at which compulsory purchase should take effect, with a view, it was admitted by their organs in the Press, to afford a precedent for further schemes of land purchase at large. Of this nature was the compensation which they demanded--fortunately without success--in accordance with the provisions of the Lands Clauses Consolidation Act, which, if accepted by Government, would have given to the landlords on sale a douceur of 10 per cent. in addition to the 12 per cent. bonus which they already enjoy over and above the market value of the land, and the fixation of such a price would have prevented any reinstatement, for this reason, that the instalments of the tenants in those circumstances would have been too high to have been within the means of the tenants whom it was proposed to reinstate.

There was a curious irony in the spectacle of the House of Lords standing out for the principle of fixity of tenure, and defending tooth and nail the tenant-right of a few hundred planters, when little more than thirty years ago this same body offered the most relentless opposition to any recognition of the right of compensation for disturbance on the part of four millions of Irish tenants. In this matter the Lords gained their point, and compulsory powers are not to be applied under the

Act to the holdings on which the landlords have placed planters, who are held to be *bona fide* farmers. An amendment to this effect was thrown out by the House of Commons, by a majority of more than four to one, on a division in which only 66 voted for the amendment, but although the Bill in its original form offered sitting tenants the fullest compensation ever offered to such persons, and although most of the planters would be only too glad to accept such terms, the Upper House insisted on over-riding the will of the great majority in the Commons.

Lord Lansdowne, on the second reading, gave three reasons why the Bill should not be incontinently rejected by the Peers. In the first place, it came to them, he said, supported by an enormous majority in the other House, "and their Lordships always desired to treat attentively and respectfully Bills which came to them with such a recommendation." Secondly, the late Government, as well as the present, had pledged themselves to a measure of reinstatement of some kind, and if they threw out the Bill on a second reading "it would be said that they had receded from a kind of understanding arrived at in 1903," and lastly, "the summary rejection of the Bill might greatly increase the difficulties of the Executive Government in Ireland." One would have thought that the fact that the Bill was given a second reading did little to exonerate the Upper House from similar consequences as a result of their mutilation of the Bill in Committee.

In its final form the Act allows an appeal on questions of value from the inspector, to two Estates Commissioners, and from them to Mr. Justice Wylie, sitting as Judicial Commissioner with a valuer. On questions of price there is no appeal from him. Other appeals, on questions of law and fact, are, by Section 6, to be heard by a Judge of the King's Bench, with whom rests the final decision whether a particular planter is or is not to be evicted. Demesne lands and other lands, purchase of which would interfere with the value of adjoining property, are omitted from the scope of the statute, and its operation is limited to the case of 2,000 tenants, whose claims must be disposed of within four years. The power vested in the Estates Commissioners compulsorily to acquire untenanted land, not necessarily their former holdings, for the reinstatement of the evicted tenants, is of no practical value in the case of the Clanricarde estate, since all the land on it is occupied, and the fact that on that plague-spot--the nucleus of the whole disturbance--no settlement will be possible under the Act, shows to what an extent was justified Mr. Birrell's declaration that the final form of the statute was a triumph for Lord Clanricarde, and affords a curious commentary on the repeated declarations of the Unionist leaders, that nothing was further from their desire than to effect the wrecking of the Bill.[10]

Rejection of similar measures of relief--notably the Tenants' Compensation Bill of 1880--has led in the past to a recrudescence of strife in Ireland, and Mr. Balfour's unworthy retort to Mr. Redmond's deduction from every precedent in the history of the struggle for the land, that it was an incitement to lawlessness, was a mere partisan retort to an avowal of a danger which every unbiassed observer must see arises from the betrayal by the House of Lords of a confidence in a final settlement which was formerly encouraged by a Conservative Govern merit.

One of the weapons used by the Orangemen in their attack on this Bill was to be found in their repeated insinuations as to the unfitness of the Estates Commissioners to exercise dispassionately the functions which would be demanded of them. In this the Unionists were hoist with their own petard, for the necessity recognised by the Government for placing the Estates Commissioners in a position other than that of mere Executive officers, by giving them a judicial tenure independent of ministerial pressure or party influences, was strongly shown by the incident of the Moore-Bailey correspondence of last session, which should provide food for reflection on the part of those who imagine that intimidation is to be found in Ireland in use only on the National side. Mr. Moore, the most active of the Orangemen, asked in a supplementary question whether it was not a fact that the delay in the Estates Commissioners' Office was due to Mr. Commissioner Bailey's continued presence in London. These visits, it should be noted, were paid to London by Mr. Bailey in the discharge of his official duties for the purpose of consultations with the Government in connection with the Evicted Tenants Bill. On reading in the papers Mr. Moore's question implying negligence to his duties on his part, Mr. Bailey wrote to Mr. Moore the following letter, marked private:--

"UNIVERSITY CLUB,

"DUBLIN, March, 1907.

"DEAR MOORE,--I see that as a supplemental question you asked the other day whether the delay in land purchase was due to the continued absence of Mr. Bailey. I do not know, of course, what was your object, but it may interest you to know that for the last year I attended more days in the office than either of my colleagues, and that, as a matter of fact, I did not take much more than half the vacation to which I was entitled. You will thus see that you have been strangely misinformed, and I can only surmise that another of my colleagues was meant.

"Faithfully yours,

"W.F. BAILEY."

To this Mr. Moore replied:--

"ULSTER CLUB,

"BELFAST, March 19th.

"DEAR BAILEY,--You were appointed by a Unionist Government to see fair play between Wrench and Finucane, and you have sold the pass on every occasion. The first thing my colleagues and I will do when we come back, which will not be very far off, will be to press for an inquiry into the working of your department. You can destroy your evidence now, and show this to whom you please.

"Yours truly,

"W. MOORE."

In reply the Estates Commissioner wrote:--

"Mr. Bailey desires to acknowledge receipt of Mr. Moore's letter of the 19th inst., and inasmuch as it contains grave statements of a threatening and unfounded character he will take an early opportunity of bringing the matter under notice in the proper quarter."

The final letter was Mr. Moore's reply:--

"ULSTER CLUB,

"BELFAST, March 25th.

"Mr. Moore hopes that when Mr. Bailey publishes the correspondence he will make it clear that Mr. Moore's reply was directed to a disloyal attack by Mr. Bailey on one of his colleagues in his letter to Mr. Moore. This is all that was omitted from Mr. Moore's reply."

The next step in this discreditable incident occurred on July 23rd, on which day Mr. Moore denounced Mr. Bailey in the House of Commons for his partisanship towards the Nationalists, and gave a graphic picture of the private letter which Mr. Bailey had written to him to protest against his personal attacks. Mr. Redmond rose and asked that Mr. Russell should read to the House Mr. Moore's reply, and Mr. Russell thereupon read the second of the letters given above, upon which Mr. Balfour, regardless of his own share in the partial suppression of the Wyndham-MacDonnell *dossier* a few years before, demanded the production of the whole correspondence. This was done on July 26th, when Mr. Moore read the letters in the order given above. In his personal explanation he represented it as an extremely suspicious circumstance that Mr. Bailey had been seen in the Lobby in conversation with the Nationalists. "That may be legitimate," he said, "but I think it very undesirable," and in the very next breath he confessed that another of the Commissioners was a particular and personal friend of his own, to whom he would have shown the first letter from Mr. Bailey if it had not been marked private.

The comment of the *Times*--in which Mr. Moore as a rule finds an active admirer of his political methods--is interesting:--

"Mr. Bailey is a public servant entrusted with certain quasi-judicial functions. That a member of Parliament, whatever may be his opinions of the conduct of such an official, should inform him that he had been appointed 'to see fair play' between his colleagues, and that he had not seen it, and should couple this charge with a promise to press for an inquiry into the working of the department whenever there should be a change of Government, is indefensible."

The whole incident is worthy of attention as showing the atmosphere of suspicious hostility with which the Orange faction in Ireland surrounds every act even of Civil Servants and Executive Officers who are not as active supporters of the ascendancy as they would wish.

Of further legislation dealing with the laws of tenure, the Town Tenants Act of 1906, which Mr. Balfour denounced as highway robbery, gives tenants in towns compensation for disturbance so as to prevent a landlord making a vexatious use of his rights. An attempt was made by the House of Lords to limit the compensation so paid to one year's rent, but the rejection of the amendment by the House of Commons was acquiesced in, and no such limitation exists in the Act.

With regard to the question of the agricultural labourers, the fact that the last Census Report discloses that there are in Ireland nearly 10,000 "houses" with one room and one window apiece, wretched cabins inhabited by about 40,000 people, the peat smoke from the fire in which escapes through a hole in the thatch, gives some idea of the miserable conditions existing in parts of the West of Ireland. Of the quarter of a million of cottages in the second class of the Census--those, that is, with from one to four doors and windows--a large number also no doubt are quite unfit for habitation, and do much in the way of leading to the asylum or to emigration. It is to secure the replacement of these by cheap sanitary and comfortable cottages that the Labourers' Acts, ever since the first of the series introduced by the Irish Party in 1883, have been passed. By them Boards of Guardians, and by the Local Government Act, Rural District Councils, may build such cottages. In 1905, 18,000 cottages had been built under existing Acts, and they are let to tenants at rents of from 10d. to 1s. a week, but the difficulty had always been to effect the improvements sufficiently rapidly owing to the costly and elaborate procedure which involved an appeal to the Privy Council and a heavy burden on the rates of a poverty-stricken community. The Act of 1906 has simplified procedure by replacing the appeal to the Privy Council by an appeal to the Local Government Board, and that it was needful is seen from the fact that under Wyndham's Act only 25 cottages were built. It is hoped thereby to circumvent the apathy of District Councils, and their parsimony is to be appeased by the fact that the funds, which are largely derived from economics in the Irish Executive are advanced at a rate of interest, not as heretofore of 4-7/8 per cent., but, as in the case of land purchase advances, of 3-1/4 per cent., repayable in a period of 68-1/2 years. The urgency of the problem is obvious. The bearing of this state of affairs in rural housing on the fact that in 1904 two out of every thirteen deaths were due to tuberculosis shows that it is impossible to overestimate its importance, and I think that this condition of things, put side by side with the other economic facts with which I have dealt, are a sufficient reply to those who declare that conditions in Ireland would appear ***couleur de rose*** were they not seen through the jaundiced eyes of a discontented people.

If the catalogue of Acts of Parliament which have been found necessary to effect the transformation of the system of tenure in Ireland from the state in which it was forty years ago to that in which it is to-day is evidence of the pressing grievance under which the country has suffered; it is also proof that there cannot be legislation other than by shreds and patches on the part of a legislature which lacks sympathy for and knowledge of the country for which it is making laws.

The need for exceptional and separate legislation in Ireland has been admitted, and the system which existed in fact, obtained legal sanction only in 1881, to be in its turn swept away by further legislation which will have a deeper economic bearing on the future of the country than any other change since the relaxation of the Penal Laws. For the rest I cannot do better than quote, in this connection, the opinion of the most dispassionate critic of Ireland of recent years--Herr Moritz Bonn. Speaking of the landlord who has sold his estate he says--"He has no further cause of friction with his former tenants, who now pay him no rent. He no longer regards himself as part of an English garrison. He will again become an Irish patriot. He no longer talks of the unity of the Empire, for Home Rule has few terrors for him now. He talks of 'Devolution,' of the concession of a kind of self-government for Ireland. He will struggle for a while against the designation Home Rule, because not so long ago he was declaring that he would die in the last ditch for the union of the three kingdoms, but he will soon be reconciled to it. It will not be very long till the former landlords, whose chief interests lie in Ireland, have become enthusiastic Nationalists."

CHAPTER V
THE RELIGIOUS QUESTION

"I am convinced that if the void in the lay leadership of the country be filled up by higher education of the better classes among the Catholic laity, the power of the priests, so far as it is abnormal or unnecessary, will pass away."
--DR. O'DEA, now Bishop of Clonfert, speaking in evidence before the Robertson Commission on University Education, as the representative of Maynooth College. Appendix to Third Report, p. 296.

The scruples of George III., who although as King of Ireland he yielded to the claims of Catholics to the suffrage by giving the Royal consent to the enfranchising Act of Grattan's Parliament in 1793, were such that they made him declare that his coronation oath compelled him to maintain the Protestantism of the United Parliament of the three kingdoms and express himself to Dundas of opinion that Pitt's emancipation proposals were "the most Jacobinical thing ever seen."

The continuance for thirty years of these political disabilities, and the obligation incumbent on Catholics to support an alien Church with the full weight of endowments and tithes, did more than anything else to maintain the wall of prejudice between the two creeds which the eighteen years of Grattan's Parliament had done much to destroy.

It was James Anthony Froude who said that the absenteeism of her men of genius was a worse wrong to Ireland than the absenteeism of her landlords. This evil the Union accentuated by reducing Dublin from the seat of Government, which in the middle of the eighteenth century had been the second only to London in size and importance, to the status of a provincial city from which were drawn the leaders of that liberal school of Protestantism the rise of which was the marked feature of Irish politics at the end of the eighteenth century.

The dividing line between parties in England has never been one of caste or of creed, still less of both combined. In the past the Whigs could claim as aristocratic and as exclusive a prestige as could the Tories. In point of wealth there was little to choose, and, most important of all, in respect of religion, though the minor clergy were very largely Tory and the Dissenters were allied to the Whigs, yet the Anglicanism of the great Whig families, and their appointments when in power to the Episcopal bench and to other places of preferment, saved the Church of England from being identified *in toto* with either party in the State.

In Ireland, unfortunately, the case was far different, for there property and the Established Church found themselves ranged side by side in the maintenance of their respective privileges against the democracy, which, as it happened, was Catholic, and which for many years after the Union did not recover from the long and demoralising persecution of the Penal Laws.

The aristocracy resisted emancipation, in spite of the fact that it was advocated by all the greatest statesmen and orators of two generations, and it did so quite as much because it was emancipation of the masses as because it was emancipation of the Catholics. The Church of Ireland at the same time dreaded the reform since it had the foresight to perceive that the outcome would be an attack upon her prerogatives and an assault upon her position. The anticipations of both were well founded. Nine years after the Emancipation Act, tithe, which an English Prime Minister had declared was as sacred as rent, was by Act of Parliament commuted into a rent-charge no longer collected directly from the tenant, but paid by the landlord, who, however, compensated himself for its incidence on his shoulders by raising rents. Forty years later the Church Act was passed, and almost simultaneously was begun the assault on the land system which had given support to, and received it from, the Church Establishment.

I have heard it said by Englishmen who have watched the course of politics for some years that the jingling watchword which Lord Randolph Churchill coined for the Unionists twenty years ago, that Home Rule would spell Rome Rule, if used again to-day would to a very great extent fall flat. They have based this view, not on the assumption that Englishmen love Rome more, but rather upon the opinion that they care for all religions less, and that hence the appeal to bigotry would make less play.

The fact, however, remains that one meets men in England with every sympathy for Irish claims who shrink nevertheless from the advocacy of the principle of self-government through fear lest the Protestant minority should suffer. This fear for the rights of minorities serves always as the last ditch in which a losing cause entrenches itself, and timid souls have always been found who hesitate at the approach of every reform on the ground that the devil you know may turn out to be not so bad as the devil you do not know. The legislative history of the House of Lords during the last century, if examples of this were needed, would provide them in large numbers; and as to the question of whether it is better that the majority or the minority of a nation should be governed against its will, one need scarcely say which is the principle adopted in a normal system of Parliamentary government. The rapidity with which under Grattan's Parliament an emancipated Ireland ceased to be intolerant leads one to suspect that the bigotry of creeds which is attributed to us as a race is not a natural characteristic, but rather the outcome of external causes. This view is borne out by the opinion of Lecky, who declared that the deliberate policy of English statesmen was "to dig a deep chasm between Catholics and Protestants," and if proof of the allegation is needed it is to be found in the fact that in the middle of the eighteenth century the Protestant Primate, Archbishop Boulter, wrote to Government concerning a certain proposal that "it united Protestants and Papists, and if that conciliation takes place, farewell to English influence in Ireland."

Under Grattan's Parliament Trinity College, Dublin, opened its doors, though not its endowments, to Catholics. In 1795 a petition from Maynooth, the lay college in which was not till twenty years later suppressed by Government for political reasons, was presented to the Irish House of Commons by Henry Grattan, protesting against the exclusion of Protestants from its halls. In the ranks of the Volunteers, who secured free trade in 1779 and Parliamentary Independence in 1782, Catholics and Protestants stood shoulder to shoulder, and the independent legislature, which was the outcome of their efforts, granted the franchise to the Catholics.

It was of course natural, when Catholics were excluded from Parliament, that the leaders of the people should have been members of the Protestant Church, but in view of the alleged bigotry at the present day of the mass of the Irish people it is surely significant that Isaac Butt and Parnell were both members of the Church of minority, that to take three of the fiercest opponents of the maintenance of the Union John Mitchell was a Unitarian, Thomas Davis an Episcopalian Protestant, and Joseph Biggar a Presbyterian. At this moment of the Nationalist Members of Parliament nine, or more than ten per cent., are Protestants, and one may well ask if the Orangemen have ever had a like proportion of Catholic members of their party, and *a fortiori* what would be thought of the suggestion that a member of that religion should lead them in the House of Commons. The difficulty experienced in Great Britain by would-be candidates of either party in securing their adoption by local associations if they are Catholics is so common as to make the excessive bigotry alleged against the Irish Catholics, one-tenth of whose representatives are Protestants, appear very much exaggerated.

That bigotry exists among Catholics to some extent I should be the last, albeit regretfully, to deny, but I leave it to the reader to judge how far this is the result and the natural outcome of a policy the direct opposite of that pursued in Scotland, where shortly after the union of her Parliament with that of England, the Church of the majority of the people was for the sake of peace established and has remained in this privileged position ever since. In view of the use to which the "No Popery" cry has been put in its bearings on the Irish question, it is interesting to consider the relations of the English Government with the Catholic Church throughout the last century and to see how far it throws light on the justice and applicability of the taunt that Ireland is priest-ridden.

In 1814 the Catholics of England, in spite of the opposition of the Irish people, secured from Mgr. Quarantotti, the Vice-Prefect of the Propaganda in Rome, who was acting in the absence of Pope Pius VII., at that date still a prisoner in France, a letter declaring that in his judgment the Royal veto should be exercised on ecclesiastical appointments in Ireland. Under O'Connell's leadership, the bishops, clergy, and people of Ireland refused to submit to the decree, and there, in spite of the indignation of the English Catholics as a whole and of the Catholic aristocracy of Ireland, the proposal was allowed to drop, which would have virtually given a right of *conge d'elire* to the English ministry.

In 1782 Edmund Burke had written in his letter to a peer of Ireland on the Penal Laws--"Never were the members of a religious sect fit to appoint the pastors of another. It is a good deal to suppose that even the present Castle would nominate bishops for the Irish Catholic Church with a religious regard for its welfare." If this was the case under Grattan's Parliament, its application thirty years later was very much more cogent. Behind the scenes, however, the wires continued to be pulled, as is seen by what Melbourne told Greville in 1835, after the latter had expressed the opinion that the sound course in Irish affairs was to open a negotiation with Rome.[11] "He then told me ... that an application had been made to the Pope very lately (through Seymour) expressive of the particular wish of the British Government that he would not appoint MacHale to the vacant bishopric--anyone but him. But on this occasion the Pope made a shrewd observation. His Holiness said that he had remarked that no place of preferment of any value ever fell vacant in Ireland that he did not get an application from the British Government asking for the appointment. Lord Melbourne supposed that he was determined to show that he had the power of refusal and of opposing the wishes of the Government, and in reply to my questions he admitted that the Pope had generally conferred the appointment according to the wishes of the Government."

These facts must be borne in mind on the part of those by whom the admitted support given by the Whig Catholic "Castle Bishops" of the early part of the nineteenth century to the Government is urged as evidence of a consistent tendency on the part of the Church in Ireland, the political views of the prelates of which, so soon as in the second half of the nineteenth century Governmental lobbying ceased, were of an entirely different colour.

At a later date Greville returned to the topic and noted that[12] "Palmerston said there was nothing to prevent our sending a minister to Rome; but they had not dared to do it on account of their supposed Popish tendencies. Peel might." Melbourne was not alone among Prime Ministers of the time in his appeals to the Holy See. In 1844 the Government of Sir Robert Peel, when troubled with the manifestations of sympathy which O'Connell was arousing, made an appeal to Gregory XVI. to discourage the agitation, and three years later, when the Whigs under Lord John Russell were in office, Lord Minto, Lord Privy Seal, who was Palmerston's father-in-law, was sent to Rome in the autumn recess to secure the adherence of Pius IX., then in the first months of his Pontificate, to the same line of action, and to bring to the notice of His Holiness the conduct of the Irish priesthood in supporting O'Connell. The fact that neither Gregory XVI. nor Pio Nono made any response to these appeals lends point to the sardonic comment of Disraeli on the Minto mission--that he had gone to teach diplomacy to the countrymen of Machiavelli. The views of Palmerston, on the other hand, are to be seen from a letter addressed to Minto, which is extant, in which, with characteristic bluntness, the Foreign Secretary wrote that public opinion against the Irish priests at home was so exasperated that nothing would give English people more satisfaction than to see a few of them hanged.

"Can anything be more absurd," Greville had written concerning the relations which Melbourne revealed to him as subsisting between Downing Street and the Vatican, and the quotation is as appropriate to these later overtures. "Can anything be more absurd or anomalous than such relations as these? The law prohibits any intercourse with Rome, and the Government, whose business it is to enforce the law, establishes a regular, but underhand, intercourse through the medium of a diplomatic agent, whose character cannot be avowed, and the ministers of this Protestant kingdom are continually soliciting the Pope to confer appointments, the validity, even the existence, of which they do not recognise, while the Pope, who is the chief object of our abhorrence and dread, good humouredly complies with all or nearly all their requests."

Two years after the Minto mission, and a few months before he succeeded to power in place of Peel, Lord John Russell told Charles Greville that the Government was "the greatest curse to Ireland," and he spoke of "their policy of first truckling to the Orangemen, insulting, and then making useless concessions to the Catholics, without firmness and justice."[13] It is only fair to Lord John to say that in the following year he ordered a Bill to be drawn up to legalise intercourse with the Pope and to put an end to these repeated acts of *praemunire* on the part of Ministers of the Crown; for a large number of constitutional authorities believed that their action amounted to this offence, which has been defined as consisting of acts tending to introduce into the realm some foreign power, more particularly that of the Pope, to the diminution of the King's authority.

The Diplomatic Relations with the Court of Rome Bill was introduced and passed into law, with one important amendment which we shall have occasion to notice later, in 1848, less than two years after Peel's ministry had been succeeded by that of Russell. The grounds upon which its acceptance by Parliament was demanded were that the complications resulting from the revolutionary crisis throughout the Continent made it essential that the Foreign Office should be in a position, in dealing with the chancelleries of Europe, to obtain direct recognition, and as a result first-hand information, as to the attitude of the Holy See in any situations which might arise; and the acceptance by Parliament of the change of policy which the Bill was intended to effect, on the understanding that diplomatic negotiations should be confined to foreign affairs, may be seen in the words of Earl Fitzwilliam in the House of Lords. In his speech in support of the Bill he declared that "the very last subject upon which the Government should communicate with the Court of Rome was that which had reference to relations which it should have with its own Roman Catholic subjects."[14]

The Act was an enabling Act, and its proposals, like those as to concurrent endowment which Russell had made three years earlier, were forgotten in 1850, when, in the matter of the Ecclesiastical Titles Bill, the Prime Minister played the part which Leech immortalised as that of "the little boy who chalked up 'No Popery' and then ran away."

Even in the interval before this occurred the provisions of the Act were not put in force. No appointment pursuant to the statute was ever made, but its object was indirectly secured by the fact that a Secretary of Legation, nominally accredited to the Court of the Grand Duke of Tuscany, was kept in residence in Rome, where he served as a *de facto* Minister to the Vatican. This state of affairs was maintained until Lord Derby recalled Jervoise, who was then Secretary, from Rome, and from that date even this measure of diplomatic representation at the Vatican has ceased to exist.

The Bill of 1848, as we have seen, was directed to the establishment of relations with "the Court of Rome." An amendment on the part of the Bishop of Winchester, which was accepted and passed into law, substituted for these words the phrase "Sovereign of the Roman States," and in consequence, after the loss of the Temporal Power, the Act was repealed by the Statute Law Revision Act, 1875, so that the law was restored to that condition, in regard to this subject, in which it had been before Lord John Russell introduced the Act of 1848.

All this, it will be said, is ancient history, but the fact that it is fifty years old does not affect my point, which is this--that the maintenance of an unnatural polity can only be secured by means of a series of subterfuges such as these employed by Unionist Governments, both Whig and Tory, by which, while sympathy was extended to Orangemen in the open, the Ministry endeavoured to twitch the red sleeves of the Roman Curia in the back stairs of the Vatican.

As Macaulay picturesquely put it, at any moment Exeter Hall might raise its war whoop and the Orangemen would begin to bray, and there was no choice, one must suppose, but that you should not let your right hand know what your left hand was doing.

In 1881 Mr. Gladstone appealed to Cardinal Newman to apprise the Pope of the violent speeches which were being delivered by certain priests in Ireland, for whose language he said he held the Pope, if informed of it, morally responsible, and he asked the English Cardinal for his assistance. To this Newman replied that the Pope was not supreme in political matters, his action as to whether a political party is censurable is not direct, and, moreover, it lay with the bishops to censure the clergy for their language if they thought it intemperate, and the interposition of the Holy See was not called for by the circumstances of the case.

The policy, however, which had been applied before was employed once more in another direction in the teeth of British sentiment if not of British law. A mortgage had been foreclosed on Parnell's estate, and the Irish newspapers having obtained knowledge of the fact raised a collection which became known as the Parnell Tribute, and which was headed by a subscription from the Archbishop of Cashel. If precedent were needed for this form of recognition of national services it was to be found in the grant of L50,000--which might, had he been willing, have been double that amount--which was made to Grattan by the emancipated Irish House of Commons, but more exact parallels perhaps are to be found in "O'Connel's Rent," which Greville described as "nobly paid and nobly earned," or in the great collection which marked the popular appreciation in Great Britain of Cobden's services in securing the repeal of the Corn Laws. In the autumn of 1881, when the Parnell Tribute was initiated, the Land League agitation was in full swing in Ireland, and about the same time Mr. George Errington, an English Catholic Whig Member of Parliament, who was about to spend the winter in Rome, called on Lord Granville, the Foreign Secretary, and was given by him an introduction to the Cardinal Secretary of State. In this wise Mr. Errington went, in the phrase of the day, "to keep the Vatican in good humour," and if he was not the accredited representative of Her Brittanic Majesty--for that would have been illegal--at any rate he went with the sanction and under the aegis of the Foreign Office.

The upshot was a Papal rescript, signed by Cardinal Simeoni, the Prefect, and Mgr. Jacobini, the Secretary of the Sacred Congregation De Propagatione Fide, which condemned the Tribute owing to the Land League agitation.

"The collection called 'The Parnell Testimonial Fund,'" so ran the rescript, "cannot be approved, and consequently it cannot be tolerated that any ecclesiastic, much less a bishop, should take any part whatever in recommending or promoting it."

The bishops and clergy withdrew from any further action in connection with the Tribute Fund, but the laity gave the lie to the suggestion that they are under the thumb of their priests in matters which are not within the sphere of faith or morals. The rescript was promulgated in May, and at this time the subscription list amounted to less than L8,000. Within a month it had doubled, and by the end of the year it amounted to L37,000. The amount of the mortgage was L13,000. As Parnell, in a characteristically laconic way, put it in his evidence before the Commission, "The Irish people raised a collection for me to pay off the amount of a mortgage. The amount of the collection considerably exceeded the amount necessary." The retort of the country to the document "***Qualecumque de Parnellio***," had been, in the phrase then current, to "make Peter's pence into Parnell's pounds."

Two years after the Simeoni letter Mr. Errington was again in Rome, attempting this time to secure the exclusion from the successorship to Cardinal M'Cabe, of Dr. Walsh of Maynooth, as Archbishop of Dublin. A letter on the subject fell into the hands of the editor of **United Ireland**, who published it in his paper, and so in this way thwarted the objects of the second Errington mission. "If we want to hold Ireland by force," said Joseph Cowen, the Radical member for Newcastle, "let us do it ourselves; let us not call in the Pope, whom we are always attacking, to help us."

A further instance may be recounted of the manner in which the people of what is, after Spain, the most Catholic country in Europe, while submitting to the Pope implicitly in matters which are *de fide*, refused to take their cue in purely political matters from Rome.

The rejection of the Home Rule Bill and of the Land Bill of 1886, and the return of the Conservatives to power, led to a recrudescence of the land war, to which the hope of ameliorative legislation had temporarily put a truce. The Plan of Campaign, which was then launched--of which it has been said that no agrarian movement was ever so unstained by crime--was of the following nature:--The tenants of a locality were to form themselves into an association, each member of which was to proffer to the landlord or his agent a sum which was estimated by the general body as a fair rent for his holding. These sums, if refused by the landlord, were pooled and divided by the association for the maintenance of those tenants who were evicted.

The wheels were set in motion in Rome to obtain a ruling from the Holy Office as to whether such action was justifiable or not. Mgr. Persico, the head of the Oriental rite in the Propaganda, who had had much experience of English speaking people in the East, was sent to Ireland in July, 1887, to investigate the question on the spot. In April, 1888, a rescript was issued by the Holy Office to the bishops of Ireland condemning the Plan of Campaign and boycotting on the ground that they were contrary to both natural justice and Christian charity. With the Decree was sent to the bishops a circular letter, signed by Cardinal Monaco, the Secretary of the Holy Office, which contained the following statement:--"The justice of the decision will be readily seen by anyone who applies his mind to consider that a rent agreed upon by mutual consent cannot, without violation of a contract, be diminished at the mere will of a tenant, especially when there are tribunals appointed for settling such controversies and reducing unjust rents within the bounds of equity after taking into account the causes which diminish the value of the land.... Finally, it is contrary to justice and to charity to persecute by a social interdict those who are satisfied to pay rents agreed upon, or those who, in the exercise of their right, take vacant lands."

The *Tablet*, the organ of English Catholicism, speaking of the decision, said that happily there was no suspicion of politics about it, and as to the letter of Cardinal Monaco la Valetta, it wrote--"It adds certain reasons which perhaps may have led the Congregation to answer as they have done, but these constitute no part of the official reply." The next step in this episode should be well pondered by those who accuse the Irish of a blind Ultramontanism. The bishops, with one exception, omitted to publish the rescript to their flocks, and the Archbishop of Cashel went so far as to send L50 to the funds of the Plan of Campaign. Parnell, referring publicly to the rescript as "a document from a distant country," declared that his Catholic colleagues must decide for themselves what action to take. Mr. Dillon contradicted the statements in Cardinal Monaco's letter to the effect that the contracts were voluntary or that the campaign fund of the Land League had been collected by extortion. A meeting of forty Catholic members of Parliament assembled in Dublin, and in the Mansion House in that city signed a document denying the allegations about free contracts, fair rent, the Land Commission, and the rest, declared that the conclusions had been drawn from erroneous premises, and while asserting their complete obedience to the Holy See in spiritual matters, no less strongly repudiated the suggestion that Rome had any right to interfere in matters of a political nature. Mass meetings were held in the Phoenix Park in Dublin, and in Cork, which indorsed this position by popular vote. The Orangemen were delighted at the imminence of a schism, and the discomfiture of the Catholics under a decree, the result of internal division, was hailed with pleasure only by the enemies of the Church. In the event they were doomed to disappointment, for in the closing days of the year the Holy Father wrote a letter to the Archbishop of Dublin concerning his action, which had been "so sadly misunderstood," in which he wrote that "as to the counsels that we have given to the people of Ireland from time to time and our recent decree, we were moved in these things, not only by the consideration of what is conformable to truth and justice, but also by the desire of advancing your interests. For such is our affection for you that it does not suffer us to allow the cause in which Ireland is struggling to be weakened by the introduction of anything that could justly be brought in reproach against it."

In this manner was closed an incident which was expected by its foes to threaten the allegiance of Ireland, and with it that of more than half the Catholics in England, to the Holy See.

The Nationalist members at the Mansion House had flatly declared that the decree was an instrument of the unscrupulous enemies both of Ireland and of the Holy See. The *Tablet*, which declared that it had been promulgated with full and intimate knowledge of all the circumstances, retorted--"As a matter of fact we believe that the English Government has taken no steps, direct or indirect, to obtain the pronouncement, which is based solely on the reports of Mgr. Persico and the documents and evidence which accompanied them." And it went on to add that Persico was expected to return to Ireland to watch the application of the decree.

Beyond this, until recently, nothing more was known except that it was remarked that negotiations between the Duke of Norfolk and the Vatican were broken off, and that the former left Rome suddenly for England without having an audience with the Pope, for which arrangements had been made. The forecast of the *Tablet* as to Mgr. Persico's return to Ireland to see that the terms of the decree were enforced and applied, was not correct. The responsibility for the decree was everywhere laid on his shoulders, and the *Tablet* for April 27th, 1889, records that an Address was presented to Mgr. Persico after his return to Rome "as an expression of respect, and in the fervent hope that his Excellency's mission might largely conduce to the glory of God, the increase of charity, and the restoration of peace and goodwill among men."

It is only in the last couple of years, with the publications of Persico's correspondence with Cardinal Manning,[15] that the real facts of the case have been known. After spending six months in Ireland, the envoy was obliged, for reasons of health, to move to Devonshire in January, 1888. He had orders from Rome to remain in the British Islands, but further, so he told the Cardinal in his letter, "I must not reside in London so as to give not the least suspicion that I have anything to do with the British Government." As to the promulgation of the decree, it was done without his knowledge and, what is more, against his judgment. Having arrived in Ireland in July, 1887, he had concluded his investigations by the middle of the month of December of that year. His requests that the mission might be terminated were met by the reply that it was to continue indefinitely, and he was told that if he wished, for reasons of health, to leave Ireland during the winter months he might do so, but that he must remain in the British Isles.

After the issue of the rescript he wrote to the English Cardinal in these words:--"It is known to your Eminence that I did not expect at all the said decree, that I was never so much surprised in my life as when I received the bare circular from Propaganda on the morning of the 28th ulto. And fancy, I received the bare circular, as I suppose every Irish bishop did, without a letter or a word of instruction or explanation. And what is more unaccountable to me, only the day before I had received a letter from the Secretary for the Extraordinary Ecclesiastical Affairs, telling me that nothing had been done about Irish affairs, and that my report and other letters were still ***nell casetta del Emo. Rampolla!*** And yet the whole world thinks and says that the Holy Office has acted on my report, and that the decree is based upon the same! Not only all the Roman correspondents but all the newspapers ***avec le Tablet en tete*** proclaim and report the same thing! I wish that my report and all my letters had been studied and seriously considered, and that action had been taken from the same! Above all, I had proposed and insisted upon it, that whatever was necessary to be done ought to be done with, and through, the bishops." Of this there is ample proof in the earlier letters, and the proposal which he made was that the four archbishops and one bishop for every province should be summoned to Rome to "prepare and settle things." Writing on the Feast of the Epiphany in 1888, he said to Manning:--"I agree fully with your Eminence that the true Nunciatura for England and Ireland is the Episcopate. If the bishops do not know the state of the country they are not fit to be bishops. If they do, what more can ***una persona ufficiosa o ufficiale*** do for the Holy See?" And again--"I fully understand what your Eminence adds, the English people tolerate the Catholic Church as a spiritual body. The first sign of a political action on the Government would rekindle all the old fears, suspicions, and hostility. It is a great pity they do not realise this in Rome. And it is also a great pity that English Catholics do not understand all this. I am sure that His Holiness understands it well, but I share your fears that those about him may harass him with the fickle and vain glory that would accrue to the Holy See by having an accredited representative from England also."

It is impossible not to infer from this that the English Catholics were engaged in an attempt to secure diplomatic recognition by Great Britain of the Holy See, and that their anxiety to secure this was in some measure connected with their desire to override the feelings and opinions of the Irish Episcopate, but the overtures of Lord Salisbury were as fruitless as those of Russell forty years before.

The last letter from Mgr. Persico to the English Cardinal, which has been reprinted, reiterates the disclaimer of responsibility for the action of the Vatican, in these words:--

"I had no idea that anything had been done about Irish affairs much less thought that some questions had been referred to the Holy Office, and the first knowledge I had of the decree was on the morning of the 28th April, when I received the bare circular sent me by Propaganda. I must add that had I known of such a thing I would have felt it my duty to make proper representations to the Holy See."

In view of this it is interesting to read the naive record in the *Tablet* of those who signed the address to Persico on the totally wrong assumption that he and his report were the *causa causans* of the decree. "The signatures," says the *Tablet*, "comprise those of all the Catholic peers in Ireland (14 in number), four Privy Councillors, ten honourables, two Lords Lieutenants of counties, nineteen baronets, fifty-four deputy-lieutenants, two hundred and ninety-seven magistrates, and a large number of the learned and military professions." The remarkable thing about this memorial was the absence of the names of any clerics, regular or secular, parish priests or prelates.

There are in Ireland a great many more Protestant Nationalists than the English Press allows its readers to suspect, and it is one of these who, in a recent novel, declares in a wild hyperbole that if the bishops can secure the continuance of English Government for the next half century Ireland will have become the Church's property. No one, of course, with any sense of proportion takes seriously such a statement as this, but I allude to it as showing, in its extreme anti-clericalism, the same tendency, very much magnified, as I have observed to a great extent in the Protestant Nationalist as a class, who has not, as I believe, had time to eliminate the last taint of No Popery feeling in which for generations he and his forbears have been steeped. The existence of this anti-clerical spirit, and, what is more to the point, its expression with the proverbial tactlessness of the political convert, for such a one the Protestant Nationalist usually is, make it very essential that the Catholic clergy should walk warily and avoid giving any handle to their detractors, for in Ireland, and perhaps most of all in the Church in Ireland, there is need to use the prayer of the faithful Commons--"that the best possible construction be put on one's motives." How small is the basis for the allegation that the clergy are playing only for the Church's hand and are prepared to sacrifice for this end the welfare of the country is shown, I think, by the evidence which I have adduced. But in spite of their ill success in the past there is a persistent notion on the part of both English parties that they can drag in ecclesiastical influence to redress the political balance in their favour. The exposure in the Life of Lord Randolph Churchill of the manner in which he proposed to Lord Salisbury to win over the Church to Unionism is an example of what I mean:--[16]

"I have no objection to Sexton and Healy knowing the deliberate intention of the Government on the subject of Irish education, but it would not do for the letter or communication to be made public, for the effect of publicity on Lancashire would be unfortunate.... It is the bishops entirely to whom I look in future to mitigate or postpone the Home Rule onslaught. Let us only be enabled to occupy a year with the education question. By that time I am certain Parnell's party will have become seriously disintegrated. Personal jealousies, Government influences, Davitt and Fenian intrigues, will be at work upon the devoted band of eighty. The bishops, who in their hearts hate Parnell, and don't care a scrap for Home Rule, having safely acquired control of Irish education, will, according to my calculation, complete the rout. That is my policy, and I know it is sound and good, and the only possible Tory policy." And again he wrote--"My opinion is that if you approach the archbishops through proper channels, if you deal in friendly remonstrances and active assurances ... the tremendous force of the Catholic Church will gradually and insensibly come over to the side of the Tory Party."

All this, of course, is perfectly consistent with the views which in 1884 the leader of the Fourth Party had expressed when, speaking on the Franchise Bill, he declared his opinion that "the agricultural peasant is much more under the proper and legitimate influence of the Roman Catholic priesthood than the lower classes in the towns."[17] But how is one to reconcile either of these declarations with his action in 1886, when, the tremendous force of the Catholic Church not having come over to the Tory side, he "decided to play the Orange card, which, please God, will prove a trump," and went, with his hands red from making overtures to what they considered the scarlet woman, to rally the Orangemen with the haunting jingle that Home Rule would be Rome Rule.

This was before the general election of 1886. Seven years later, when another election was approaching, he returned to the charge, this time in a letter to Lord Justice FitzGibbon:--"What is the great feature," he wrote, "of the political situation in Ireland now? The resurrection in great force of priestly domination in political matters. Now I would cool the ardour of these potentates for Mr. G. by at once offering them the largest concessions on education--primary, intermediate, and university--which justice and generosity could admit of. I would not give them everything before the general election, but I would give a good lot, and keep a good lot for the new Parliament. I do not think they could resist the bribe, and the soothing effect of such a policy on the Irish vote and attitude would be marked. Of course the concessions would have to be very large--almost as large as what the bishops have ever asked for, but preserving intact Trinity College. It would assume the material shape of a money subsidy."[18]

I have set down without omissions and with nothing extenuate the data on which is based the indictment that the clergy have been, and are, anti-national, and I ask the reader to say whether the charge is unsupported or not. That overtures have again and again been made *sub rosa* to the clergy to wean them from the popular side is proved up to the hilt, but that in any single instance they have closed with the offers or been forced by the rigours of ecclesiastical discipline into compliance, appears to me not proven, as is also the imputation that the people have in any degree departed from the lines of O'Connell's dictum--that we take our theology from Rome, but our politics we prefer of home manufacture. If the action of Cardinal Cullen with regard to the Tenant League in 1855 be adduced as an argument in favour of the proposition, it must be remembered that though as Primate his voice was preponderant and his policy was affected, in Dr. MacHale, the Archbishop of Tuam, an exponent of opposite views was to be found, and that it is on the lines laid down by MacHale, and not those advocated by Cullen, that the policy of the Catholic Church in Ireland has as a rule been based.

The clergy in the early part of the nineteenth century were brought up in foreign seminaries, where passive obedience to the established order was inculcated, and where, as was natural in such places, a horror of the Jacobinical principles of the French revolution created among them an antagonism to any violent agitation, which admittedly or not drew its inspiration from that source, but the names of Dr. Doyle of Kildare, of Dr. Duggan of Clonfert, of Dr. Croke of Cashel, of Dr. M'Cormick, to name only four, show how much support was given to the popular cause in Ireland by a considerable section of the higher clergy.

To Protestant Nationalists I would commend that expression of opinion of the greatest of their number--Edmund Burke--who, speaking of the religion of the mass of his countrymen, declared that in his opinion "it ought to be cherished as a good, though not the most preferable good if a choice was now to be made, and not tolerated as an inevitable evil. It is extraordinary that there should still be need to emphasise the fact that the Catholicism of Ireland is inevitable and that there is no hope of making the country abjure it--but this is the case."

Half a century ago, when proselytism was in full swing in a country weakened by famine, Protestants were sanguine on this point. Sir Francis Head, in a volume which bears the very naive title of "A Fortnight in Ireland," declared that within a couple of years there can exist no doubt whatever that the Protestant population of Ireland will form the majority, and Rev. A.R. Dallas, one of the leading proselytisers in the country, borrowing a Biblical metaphor, announced that "the walls of Irish Romanism had been circumvented again and again, and at the trumpet blast that sounded in the wailings of the famine they may be said to have fallen flat. This is the point of hope in Ireland's present crisis."

With the maintenance by the Church of her hold over the people governments have recognised the influence of the priests, and have tried to turn it to their own use by methods into which they have been afraid to let the light of day; and for the rest, with every trouble and every discontent, has arisen the parrot cry of ***cherchez le pretre***. Conscientious objections to certain forms of education are respected in England when they are emphasised by passive resistance. How many times have the same objections in Ireland been put down to clerical obscurantism? The priest in politics we have been told ***ad nauseam*** is the curse of Ireland, but clerical interference is not unknown in English villages, and one has heard of dissenting ministers whose hands are not quite unstained by the defilement of political partisanship. It is not the habit that makes the monk, and it is possible for sacerdotalism to be as rampant among the most rigid of dissenters as in Church itself. An example of the falsehoods which have at intervals to be nailed to the counter was the one which declared that under the compulsion of their priests a considerable part of the Irish electorate falsely declared themselves to be illiterate, so that the secrecy of the ballot might be avoided and their votes might be regulated by the clergy. On a comparison of the statistics of illiterate voters and the Census of illiteracy a similar proportion was found to exist as that between the total number of voters and the whole population, in this way completely disproving the allegation.

A great deal of capital has of late been made of the alleged excessive church building in Ireland during the last few years. In the light of the fact that less than forty years have passed since the money of these same peasants for the expenditure of which so much concern is now expressed, was devoted to the maintenance of what Disraeli admitted to be an alien Church, it is a little surprising to hear this taunt from Englishmen and Protestants. Relieved, as the people have been only in the last generation, from this obligation it is not strange that the work of providing churches for their own worship should have been undertaken. The Catholic churches have in large measure been built by the contributions of successful emigrants, subscribed in many instances with the secondary object of providing work in building during times of distress. There are 2,400 Catholic and 1,500 Protestant churches in Ireland at the present moment, and there is one Episcopalian Protestant church for every 320 members of that creed and one Catholic church for every 1,368 Catholics.

Sir Horace Plunkett, who started this new fashion of attack by giving it the cachet of respectability in the first edition of "Ireland in the New Century," after declaring that he has "come to the conclusion that the immense power of the Irish Roman Catholic clergy has been singularly little abused," goes on to add in connection with the topic on which we are touching that "without a doubt a good many motives are unfortunately at work in the church-building movement which have but remote connection with religion." What is meant by this I cannot pretend to say. It seems to me unworthy of a gentleman in Sir Horace's position, and with his acknowledged good intentions to adopt an attitude which can only be compared to that which Pope satirised in the lines:--

"Damn with faint praise, assent with civil leer,   And without sneering teach the rest to sneer,   Willing to wound, and yet afraid to strike,   Just hint a fault, and hesitate dislike."

But the remarkable part of the facts about this unframed charge is that in the popular edition of Sir Horace's book, published in 1905, the passage which I have quoted is omitted, and in spite of the fact that nearly forty pages are devoted to an Epilogue containing answers to his critics, the author makes no mention of its omission, and gives no reason for the implied retractation of what may be interpreted as being a very grave charge.

The books of one or two writers on the abuses of clericalism in Ireland, written in violent, unmeasured invective, and innocent--which is more important--of all notion of the value of evidence, are, I understand, eagerly snapped up and readily believed by pious Protestants in England, and it is from these books that many Englishmen have learnt all that they know to-day about the Church in Ireland.

The picture which is presented of the Irish priest as a money-grabbing martinet, whom his flock regard with mingled sentiments of detestation and fear, is a caricature as libellous as it is grotesque. Even the high standard of sexual morality which prevails in the country is attacked as being merely the result of early marriages, inculcated by a priesthood thirsting for marriage fees, and virtue itself is in this way depicted as being nothing but the bye-product of grasping avarice. I would not have thought it necessary to have touched on this subject if I were not assured of the vast circulation of the type of books to which I refer, which are not worth powder and shot, more particularly in dissenting and evangelical circles in England. The reiterated assertion by their author that he is a Catholic produces the entirely false impression that he is the spokesman of a considerable body of Catholics in Ireland whose mouths are closed by the fear of consequences.

One fact which shows how bitter is the hatred towards the religion of Ireland on the part of a section of the population of England is this--that there is no more certain method by which a book on that country can be assured of advertisement and quotation in the English party Press of the baser kind, which for partisan reasons plays on the bigotry of English people by the booming of such books, no matter how scurrilous or how vile are their innuendoes. The comment of M. Paul-Dubois on these attempts to foist on the Catholic Church responsibility for the evil case in which Ireland finds herself, deserves quotation:--"Cette these grossiere et fanatique ne vaut l'honneur d'un devellopment ni d'une discussion: contentons nous de remarquer comme il est habile et simple de rejeter sur Rome la responsabilite des malheurs d'Erin en disculpant ainsi et l'Angleterre et la colonie anglaise en Irlande!"

The energy of the Irish priesthood in the advocacy of temperance--an energy which in a climate like that of Ireland can never be excessive; their social work in the encouragement of the industrial revival by the starting of agricultural and co-operative societies, and, most of all at this time, of the Industrial Development

Association; their whole-hearted assistance in the work of the Gaelic League, and their aid in the discouragement of emigration--all these, apart from their spiritual labours, are factors which have increased their claims to the affection of the people to whom they minister and the respect of their non-Catholic fellow-countrymen. They have discouraged violence, and the weight of their Church has always been directed against secret societies, and if their power has been great it is only because they have been in full sympathy with their flocks. In 1848 the clergy made such efforts to check the excesses of the abortive insurrection of that year that Lord Clarendon, the Viceroy, wrote to Lord John Russell to tell him that something must be done for the clergy, but the bigotry of the English and Scottish people stood in the way. The No Rent Manifesto of 1881 fell flat owing to the ecclesiastical condemnation which it incurred on the ground that it involved repudiation of debts. Every article in the Press of Europe and America on the problem of "race suicide" contained a well-deserved tribute to the moral influence of the Irish clergy on their flocks in this direction, and the figures of illegitimacy show the same results of their inculcation of sexual morality. In 1904 there were 3.9 per cent. of such births in England and Wales, in Scotland 6.46, and in Ireland 2.5. The highest rate in Ireland--3.4 in Ulster--is almost the same as the lowest in Scotland--in Dumbartonshire--and the contrast between the Scottish maximum of 14.3 in Kincardine and the Irish minimum of .7 in Connacht needs no comment.

With regard to ecclesiasticism in the lower branches of education, while convinced that popular control over the secular branches, leaving the religious branches of such education completely in the hands of the clergy, is the ideal arrangement, one must admit that there is a striking testimony contained in the Report on Primary Education drawn up in 1904 by Mr. F.H. Dale, as to the efficiency and good management of the Convent Schools in Ireland, which, it should be noted, are at the same time those of least expense to the State. The cleanliness and neatness of the premises, the supervision and management on the part of the Community, the order and tone of the children, are all highly praised; and in a further Report on Intermediate Education, prepared by the same Inspector of Schools jointly with a colleague, will be found equally strong insistence on the well-known success and efficiency of the three hundred schools of the Christian Brothers, in which, without a penny of State aid, are educated some 30,000 pupils; and it was no doubt to the education given by the Christian Brothers that the Protestant Bishop of Killaloe referred when, in an address to his diocesan synod five years ago, he generously recognised the superiority of the Catholic over the Protestant schools in Ireland.

It was Lord Lytton, I think, who described the Established Church in Ireland as the greatest bull in the language, since it was so called because it was a church not for the Irish. All who are acquainted with those masterpieces of Swift's satire--the Drapier Letters--and who appreciate the fact that Berkeley--the most distinguished of Irish Protestant bishops--was refused the Primacy of Ireland because he was an Irishman, and that to appoint any but an Englishman or a Scotsman would be to depart from the policy followed throughout the whole of the eighteenth century, will see that at that time, at any rate, it deserved the censure which it has received as a foreign body maintained for denationalising purposes.

The maintenance until thirty-eight years ago of the Established Church, which raised its mitred head in a country where its adherents formed one-eighth of the population, but where its funds were extorted from those who regarded its doctrines as heresy, was, I verily believe, the ***fons et origo*** of the sectarian bitterness which still persists among Catholics, "Lui demander," wrote a French observer of the position of the Catholic Church in the days before 1870, "de s'associer a une telle entreprise lui parait une injure; lui forcer est une violence; la continuance de cette violence est une persecution." You would find it hard to make me believe that had England been the scene of a similar anomaly, with the ***roles***, of course, exchanged, the feelings towards the Catholic Church, even forty years after its disestablishment, would be the most cordial. The proposals of Pitt for the State payment of the Catholic priesthood were constantly revived and advocated throughout the century. Lord Clarendon's views, which have just been quoted, were a mere echo of the opinion expressed by Lord John Russell in favour of concurrent endowment in 1844, and there is a significant allusion on the part of Charles Greville fourteen years earlier to the feeling of that time, in which, after speaking about Irish disaffection, he shows the results which were expected from concurrent endowment by commenting unfavourably on the policy which the Government pursued "instead of depriving him (O'Connell) of half his influence by paying the priests and so getting them under the influence of the Government."[19]

The whole question was considered merely in the abstract until the Fenian outburst of the sixties--as Mr. Gladstone freely admitted--opened men's eyes to this among the other serious problems of Irish government. It required all the violence of desperate men to call, attention to a condition of things in which the Church which was established numbered less than one-eighth of the inhabitants of the country among its adherents.

The part of the country in which the greatest proportion of Episcopalian Protestants was to be found was Ulster, and there they were only 20 per cent. of the people, while in Munster and Connacht they were only 5 and 4 per cent. respectively. In 199 out of 2,428 parishes in Ireland there was not a single member of the Established Church. The net revenue of the Church was L600,000, and of this two archbishops and ten bishops received one-tenth. The mode of solving the inequitable state of affairs which produced least resistance lay in the direction of concurrent endowment. Earl Russell suggested the endowment of Catholics and Presbyterians and the reduction of Episcopalian revenues to one-eighth of their existing amount. To the Presbyterians his plan would have entailed a gain, in so far as the Regium Donum would have been increased, but the opposition to it of the Catholics, in spite of the fact that levelling up rather than planing down appealed not only to Russell but to Grey and Disraeli, resulted in its abandonment, and the question of disestablishment became the recognised solution of the difficulty.

With the introduction of the Bill in 1869 began those dire prophecies and grim forebodings which have formed a running accompaniment to every Irish reform, and Mr. Gladstone and the Liberals were denounced for having sanctioned sacrilege. In the end the Church saved from the burning more than in any equitable sense she was entitled to claim. The Representative Body, which was incorporated in 1870, received about nine millions for commuted salaries, half a million in lieu of private endowments, and another three-quarters of a million was handed over to lay patrons.

The commutation paid to the Non-Conformists for the Regium Donum and other payments was nearly L800,000, and in lieu of the Maynooth grant the Catholic Church received less than L400,000, the income from which fund only covers about one-third of the annual cost of maintenance of Maynooth. The history of this grant dates from the L9,000 given to the College by the Irish Parliament, which was increased by Peel in 1844 to L26,000 a year. When in the following year he brought in a Bill to make it a vote of £30,000 for building purposes, the *Times*, according to Greville, "kept pegging away at Peel in a series of articles as mischievous as malignity could make them, and by far the most disgraceful that have ever appeared on a political subject in any public journal."

That on the purely financial side the Catholic Church in Ireland would have gained by concurrent endowment these figures, which represent the whole of her receipts from public funds, amply bear witness, but that she gained in a moral sense far more than in a material sense she might have secured, no one will for one moment deny. The glaring discrepancy between the amount of public funds at her disposal and the amount held by the other religious bodies from public sources did not abate the virulence with which the Church Act was assailed, but at this day what is of interest is that the jeremiads of the Protestants as to the consequences either to the country at large or to their Church in particular were in every respect uncalled for, as was acknowledged by no less a person than Lord Plunket, at a later time Archbishop of Dublin, who, when in that position, admitted that the Church Act had proved not a curse, as was expected, but a blessing to the Episcopalian Protestant Church. This body has at the present moment in Ireland 1,500 churches, to which 1,600 clergy minister, and as the population of that sect amounts to very little more than half a million it appears that there is one parson for every 363 parishioners, 800 Presbyterian ministers serve nearly a half million of people in the proportion of one for every 554 of that communion. 250 Methodist ministers are sufficient for 62,000 people in the ratio of one for every 248, and the 3,711 Catholic priests, who serve nearly four million of souls, are in the proportion of one for every 891, while in England the priests of the same communion amount to one for every 542. These figures show the measure of truth in the alleged swamping of Ireland with priests. In proportion to the number of their flocks all the other denominations have a much larger relative number of clergy in the country, and until the very much more flagrant drainage due to emigration has ceased, it is to be hoped that we shall hear a good deal less about the danger in an increase of celibates in Ireland, a danger--if it be one--which after all she shares with every other Catholic country in the world. The alleged extortion of money by the clergy from a poverty-stricken peasantry is scarcely borne out by the evidence before the Royal Commission on the Financial Relations, in which Dr. O'Donnell, Bishop of Raphoe, calculated that the average contribution to the clergy in the West of Ireland, including subscriptions for the building and maintenance of churches, is 6s. or 7s. a year per family.

That strange accusation of Sir Horace Plunkett, that "the clergy are taking the joy--the innocent joy--from the social side of the home life," was, I think, sufficiently answered by the apposite reply of M. Paul-Dubois, that this is a strange reproach in the mouth of a Protestant who has undergone the experience of spending a Sunday in Belfast. The truth is that attacks on the Irish priesthood came ill from Englishmen or Anglo-Irishmen who have found in the Catholic Church the most powerful agent of social peace in the country. That Irishmen have on this ground any reason to blame the priesthood for lack of patriotism I as strongly deny, for though one may not think necessarily that God is on the side of the big battalions, armed resistance, which from the nature of things must be borne down by sheer force of weight, is as insensate as it is destructive.

The figure of Father O'Flynn, drawn by the son of a bishop of the Protestant Church, professes to be as much a picture of a type as the French *cure* whom Mr. Austin Dobson has so gracefully depicted, and it is difficult to see how such a figure of genial kindliness could have been portrayed in such a quarter or have received such general acceptance if there were to be found in any number worth considering the hard and worldly beggars on horseback whom their enemies allege constitute the characteristic type of the Irish clergy.

If in the religious nature of the Irish people is to be found one reason for the influence of the clergy in secular matters, a far more potent factor is to be seen in the historical fact that the priest has for centuries been the only guide, counsellor, and friend of the Irish peasant. The absence of a well-educated middle class, which, failing a sympathetic aristocracy, would, in a normal condition of things, provide popular leaders, is the only thing which has maintained any such undue predominance on the part of the clergy in secular affairs as exists. With the development of an educated Catholic laity, among some members of which one may expect to see evolved that critical acumen and balanced judgment which are what the fine flower of a university culture is supposed to produce, this preponderance will disappear, but in the meanwhile, be it noted, it is the refusal of Englishmen to found an acceptable university which is maintaining the very state of affairs in this direction against which they protest.

CHAPTER VI
THE EDUCATIONAL PROBLEM

"When I consider how munificently the Colleges of Oxford and Cambridge are endowed ... when I remember from whom all this splendour and plenty is derived; when I remember what was the faith of Edward the Third, and of Henry the Sixth, of Margaret of Anjou, and Margaret of Richmond, of William of Wykeham, and of William of Waynefleet, of Archbishop Chicheley, and Cardinal Wolsey; when I remember what we have taken from the Roman Catholics, King's College, New College, Christ Church, my own Trinity; and when I look at the miserable Dotheboys Hall which we have given them in exchange, I feel, I must own, less proud than I could wish of being a Protestant and a Cambridge man."--T.B. MACAULAY, Speech on the Maynooth Grant, 1845.

"What the Irish are proposing is nothing so enormous or chimerical. They propose merely to put an end to one very cruel result of the Protestant ascendancy, the result that they--the immense majority of the Irish people--have no University, while the Protestants in Ireland, the small minority, have one. For this plain hardship they propose a plain remedy, and to their proposal they want a plain, straightforward answer."
--MATTHEW ARNOLD, **Mixed Essays**, 1880.

The fact that the recurrent educational problem in England is that of the Elementary Schools, while as to Ireland the only question which is ever to any extent ventilated is that of University Education, has led to the totally wrong impression that everything in this sphere in Ireland, with the exception of Higher Education, is in a satisfactory condition. Nothing, in point of fact, could be further from the truth, and perhaps the strongest indictment against the present Executive system in the country is to be found in the chaos which exists in educational matters.

The National system of Education in Ireland was started by Lord Stanley in 1833. Up to that date there had been no organised education in the country, and in fact there were still many living who could recall the time when for a Catholic to receive education from his co-religionists was a penal offence, involving legal and equitable disabilities.

The main vehicles of elementary education up to this date were the Charter Schools and the Kildare Street Schools. The former, which were founded about 1730 by Primate Boulter, and lasted a hundred years, were frankly proselytising agencies--the address for the charter to the Crown specifically setting out that it was a society for teaching the Protestant religion to Papist children. John Howard, the philanthropist, condemned them as a disgrace to Protestantism and a disgrace to all society, but for all that, in the course of their career, they cost the public nearly two millions of money. The Kildare Street Schools, which were founded in 1811, and which secured a Government grant for the first time in 1814, professed to be non-sectarian, and so long as they kept to their professions were successful, but their subsequent association with proselytising agencies, such as the Hibernian Society, was their ruin, and in 1831 the public grant was withdrawn from them by the Chief Secretary, who two years later introduced the National System.

On the establishment of the National Board all creeds and parties in Ireland were anxious that the basis of the system should be denominational, but in the teeth of this unanimity the principle adopted was that of united secular and separate religious instruction.

One would have thought that on the establishment of the National System the danger of its capture by the Protestant ascendancy, which was very obviously anxious to secure its control, would have ensured the insistence on safeguards for the rights of the weaker section of the community at a time when no longer held good that *obiter dictum* pronounced from the Bench in 1758, which was equally true for many years after, that "the law does not suppose a Papist to exist in the kingdom, nor can they breathe without the connivance of the Government." On its formation the National Board included among its members Dr. Murray, the Catholic Archbishop of Dublin; Dr. Whately, the Protestant Archbishop of that city; and Dr. Carlisle, a Presbyterian Minister. No attempt was made to effect anything approaching a proportional representation of the creeds concerned, and the two Catholic members were outvoted by their five Protestant colleagues on the Board for the control of the education of the children of a population in which Catholics were to Protestants in the ratio of about 4 to 1.

The English Archbishop and the Scottish Presbyterian, in whom power was in this way placed, set themselves by their regulations to effect the Anglicising of the Irish children in the schools of the country. The use of the English language was enforced for the education of children, thousands of whom spoke Gaelic, and though this may possibly be justified on grounds of its greater use in the transactions of everyday life, the same cannot be said of the manner in which the history books employed were of a kind in which the subjection of Ireland by Elizabeth, James I., and William of Orange were extolled, as was also the defection from Rome of England in the sixteenth century.

Whately's policy was avowedly to Anglicise the children in the schools, to effect the "consolidation," as he called it, of Great Britain and Ireland, and in a reading book produced under his auspices occur the following lines, written with that aim in view:--"On the east of Ireland is England, where the Queen lives. Many people who live in Ireland were born in England, and we speak the same language, and are called one nation."

From the reading-books as first published were expunged such verses as Campbell's "Downfall of Roland" and Scott's "Breathes There a Man with a Soul so Dead," owing to their tendency, one must suppose, to suggest emotions other than those which it was deemed fitting to inculcate, and in their place was inserted a verse from the Archbishop's own pen which is familiar to most Irishmen, but which is, I find, unknown to most Englishmen:--

"I thank the goodness and the grace which on my birth have smiled,   And made me in these Christian days a happy English child."

To appreciate fully the irony of the divergence between the sentiments expressed and the real facts, one must remember that these lines were written at a time when land reform and church disestablishment were regarded by those in authority as the proposals of unspeakable demagogues.

The views of Whately on the value of the educational machine which he controlled, as an instrument of proselytism are very frankly set out in a conversation which he had with Nassau Senior, which is quoted from the diary of the latter in the Archbishop's biography:--

"I believe," he said, "that mixed education is gradually enlightening the mass of the people, and that if we give it up we give up the only hope of weaning the Irish from the abuses of Popery. But I cannot venture openly to profess this opinion. I cannot openly support the Education Board as an instrument of conversion. I have to fight its battles with one hand, and that my best, tied behind me."[20]

This extract more than justifies the policy by which, when Dr. MacHale succeeded Dr. Murray in Dublin, a bland acquiescence in Governmental action began to be no longer the line of action of Catholic prelates.

The system of National Education was, as I have said, founded at its inception on the principles of undenominationalism, but, as a matter of fact, the determined views of all creeds in Ireland prevailed to a very great extent, so that at the end of the nineteenth century out of a total of 8,700 schools in the country more than 5,000 were attended by children of one religion only; of these 4,000 were Catholic schools, the remaining 1,000 belonging to one or other of the Protestant denominations. Of the 3,700 schools which are not purely denominational, there are many in which the great majority of the pupils belong to one religion, but in these, of course, the minority is safeguarded by a conscience clause.

The members of the National Board are appointed to-day--as they were in 1833--by Dublin Castle. They are nominees in no sense responsible to anyone, amateurs in educational matters, whose debates are carried on *in camera*, and when they have arrived at decisions their fiat goes forth without reason being given for changes of system or of policy, and without opportunity being afforded for revision or appeal.

In these circumstances it is not surprising that the system of elementary education in Ireland does not meet with the popular attention that it should. There is no consultation on the part of the Board with those responsible for carrying on changes which it orders, and when innovations are introduced without reasons being offered, those who have to apply them are not likely to do so with good grace, still less with enthusiasm. When the arguments and reasons in favour of alterations are unknown to the public such changes almost invariably meet with opposition at the hands of those who have to effect them.

The multiplication of schools arising partly from the denominationalism which so largely holds the field is accentuated by the financial system which is adopted by the National Board. In all the schools under its control, with the exception of the 300 convent and monastery schools, where the State-aid takes the form of a capitation grant, the grant is ear-marked for the payment of teachers' salaries, the largest charge incurred by the school; and in this way the responsibility on that account and the occasion for economy on that score of the managers is removed, leaving to them only the control of the school buildings. Moreover, the non-application of the capitation system of grants fails to bring into play what would be a direct financial inducement to the locality to improve the school attendance of the children, as would also any system of local control. The small size of existing school areas results in inevitable mischief, for under it the poorest districts are those in which the school accommodation is worst, and since more money has to be raised than in richer localities the poorer districts have to pay most and the richest least for elementary education.

A primary effect of the larger number of schools is that the average attendance is much smaller than in Scotland, where conditions are in many respects similar, and side by side with the small size of the schools goes the very low standard of salaries paid to the teachers, which begin at L56 a year for men and L44 each for women, and advance by triennial increments to L172 for men and L140 for women. Two-thirds of the primary school teachers of Ireland have a salary of less than 30s. a week. The average payment to head teachers is in Scotland 75 per cent. and in England 48 per cent. higher than in Ireland. The general state of inefficiency of education in Ireland may be gathered from the fact that the Census of 1901 showed that of persons over five years of age no less than 13.7 per cent. could neither read nor write, the percentage of illiteracy being in the four provinces, 11.3 in Leinster, 12.5 in Ulster, 14 in Munster, and 20.7 in Connaught. The children in Scottish schools attend on 85 per cent. of the days on which the schools are open, in English on 84 per cent., and in Irish schools only on 65 per cent.; but in considering these figures allowance must be made for the fact that school attendance in Great Britain has been compulsory for just over thirty years, while in Ireland it was only in 1892 that an Act was passed sanctioning the formation of School Attendance Committees with power to enforce the attendance of children at school.

In addition to the Board of National Education there are in Dublin the Intermediate Board, the Commissioners of Education, who deal with the few Educational endowments in the country, the Department of Agriculture and Technical Instruction, the Senate of the Royal University, the Local Government Board attending to the education of children in work-houses, industrial, and reformatory schools, all concerned with primary and secondary education in its administrative aspect, while the Board of Works is occupied with the erection of school buildings. The extravagance and inefficiency which results from this diffusion and consequent overlapping of power and duties on the part of officials scattered about in Tyrone House, in Hume Street, in Merrion Place, and three or four other parts of Dublin, is well illustrated by the fact that out of every 20s. given as Exchequer aid to education--

In England and Wales
17/- goes to Education and 3/- to Administration and Inspection.

In Scotland
16/2 goes to Education and 3/10 to Administration and Inspection.

In Ireland
13/6 goes to Education and 6/6 to Administration and Inspection.

Administrative extravagance, it will be seen, is in inverse ratio to the quality of the educational service. If we take the three Irish Boards of National, Intermediate, and Technical Education, the total cost of administration and inspection is L120,000 per annum; the similar charge on Scotland is exactly half that sum, and yet Scotland prides herself on her education, and Ireland is taunted with her illiteracy.

The state of secondary education in Ireland differs fundamentally from that of England in this--that the number of educational endowments in the country are extremely few. Practically the whole of the money spent on this branch of education comes from taxation and school fees. It is controlled by the Intermediate Board, which was established some thirty years ago, and is in its management entirely dissociated from the National Board, so that all arrangements with a view to the transfer of clever pupils from the schools of the one type to those of the other are made as difficult as possible.

The Intermediate schools are, on the other hand, subject to the Department of Technical Instruction as well as to the Intermediate Board. Each of these awards grants, in some instances, for the same subjects, but dependent in many cases on different standards and conditions, so that it sometimes happens that schools earn grants twice over for the same subjects; and in other cases they enjoy aid from one Department of State which is refused for the same subject by another, owing to failure to comply with its conditions or to attain to its standard. Just as the connection of the Elementary schools with the Intermediate schools is very imperfect, so at the other end is the connection with the universities. The system of payment by results, under which the Intermediate schools are subsidised, is notoriously unsound from the point of view of education, since it leads to "cramming," and, moreover, under it the amount of grant earned by a school is subject to extreme variations. Lastly, if the pupils suffer from existing arrangements, the case of the teachers is no better, for from a recent report it will be seen that the average salary of lay teachers in Intermediate schools in Ireland is at least half what it is in corresponding schools in England.

In a country where elementary and intermediate education are in so unsatisfactory condition as we have seen them to be, one would expect university education to be seriously crippled, but in Ireland there arise in this connection further complications from religious differences which serve to perpetuate a state of affairs which twenty years ago Mr. Balfour declared was an intolerable grievance, and which still remains one of the chief disabilities of Ireland. There are at the present moment two universities in the country, but since one of these is only an examining board let us begin by considering the status of the other. Trinity College, Dublin, was founded by Queen Elizabeth with the proceeds of confiscated Catholic lands, both monastic and lay, with the avowed intention of propagating the principles of the Protestant religion. During Grattan's Parliament, at the end of the eighteenth century, it threw open its gates to others than members of the Established Church--an example which was not followed by Oxford and Cambridge for three-quarters of a century. There could be no greater mistake than to imply from this that it thereby lost its strong sectarian character. After Mr. Gladstone's attempt in 1873 to solve the University question had failed, Fawcett's Act removed the religious tests which barred not only Catholics but also Presbyterians from its offices and scholarships, and thereby made the College, in theory, undenominational. In point of fact it is little less Episcopalian than it has ever been. Its chapel services are Protestant, as are also its Divinity schools. Its governing body, comprising the Provost and seven Senior Fellows, is entirely Protestant, while of the 4,200 names on its electoral roll 2,600 are those of Protestant clergymen.

Of other institutions affording opportunities for higher education in Ireland, the three Queen's Colleges in Cork, Galway, and Belfast were destined by their founder, Sir Robert Peel, who established them in 1838, to supply the higher education which was lacking among the Catholics of the country. The Protestant "atmosphere" of Trinity being the great obstacle in the way of Catholics who wished for higher education for their sons, it was thought that by removing this and setting up undenominational colleges all would be well and the religious difficulty would be solved. It was as great a mistake as it was possible to commit. They were stigmatised by a leading Protestant of the time as godless colleges; they ran counter to all Catholic principles of education, which demand at least some connection between secular and religious teaching, and the taboo to which they have in large measure been subjected has to a great extent resulted in making a failure of Cork College, and still more of Galway College. The undenominationalism of Queen's College, Belfast, not being in opposition to the consciences of the Presbyterians of that city, has resulted in the fact that the College there has succeeded to a far greater extent than have the other two.

The Royal University, founded in 1882, is, as I have said, nothing more than an examining body, established on the lines of the London University as it existed at that date, with power to award scholarships and fellowships. About fifty years ago John Henry Newman founded the Catholic University in St. Stephen's Green.

Unendowed and depending on the voluntary contributions of the poorest people in Western Europe, it is not surprising that the venture failed. From it, however, rose the University College, controlled by the Jesuit Fathers, which occupies the same buildings, and the pupils of which compete for the degrees of the Royal University as those of the Queen's Colleges have done ever since, on the foundation of the Royal University, the Queen's University--of which the three colleges were components--was destroyed. The indirect mode in which the Catholic University College is endowed is worthy of attention. The Royal University, out of its income from the Irish Church Fund, maintains twenty-nine fellows, each with an income of L400 a year on condition that they should act as examiners in the Royal University, and in addition give their services as teachers in colleges appointed by the Senate (namely, the three Queen's Colleges, University College, Dublin, and the Magee College in Derry). Of these Fellows fifteen are allotted to University College. On the assumption that of their salary one-quarter represents the payment as examiners to the University--and the estimate is generous in view of the payment of only L30 to each examiner in the Cambridge Triposes--if this be assumed to be the case, the remaining L300 stands for the salary given as teacher in University College, which thus, albeit indirectly, is endowed to the extent of L4,500 a year--a fact which, though contrasting unfavourably with the L12,000 or L13,000 enjoyed by each of the Queen's Colleges, nevertheless would have seemed to cut the ground from under the feet of those who argued that the University question was insoluble since they would not countenance the application of public funds to a sectarian college.

It is often alleged that the anxiety of the Irish for other facilities for higher education than are at present afforded arises from their priest-ridden condition, and that the clergy urge the demand only in order that they may obtain more power than they already possess. The conditions in University College are some answer to this charge. It is, as I have said, under the control of the Jesuits, and a very able member of that Society is its President. Founded though it was for Catholics, the proportion--namely, about 10 per cent.--of non-Catholic students has for the last twenty years been greater than that of Catholics attending Queen's College, Belfast. Of its professorial staff only five out of twenty-one are priests. There have always been some Protestants among them, and on the governing council only one member is a priest, and of the five laymen one is a Protestant.

The history of the University question in recent years is instructive. In 1868 Lord Mayo, the Chief Secretary, endeavoured without success to formulate a scheme. In 1873 Mr. Gladstone brought in a Bill which risked the life of his Government, and failed to pass. Three years later a Bill of Isaac Butt's was introduced, but was unsuccessful, and after another three years, in 1879, was established the federal Royal University. In 1885 the Conservative Chief Secretary, Sir Michael Hicks Beach, expressed a hope on the part of the Government that in the following session they would be able to bring in a Bill in settlement of the question. The letter of Lord Randolph Churchill to Lord Justice FitzGibbon, which has been quoted elsewhere, shows that at the end of the same year the Conservative Government was anxious to make an end of the matter by legislation. In 1889 Mr. Balfour, as Chief Secretary, on two occasions expressed in the House of Commons the intention of the Government to proceed to a solution, for the conditions in Ireland, he went on to say, were "such as to leave them no alternative but to devise a scheme by which the wants of the Roman Catholics would be met." We have seen in another connection the quotation from the Life of Lord Randolph Churchill urging legislation in 1892, and in 1896 Lord Cadogan, as Viceroy, explicitly spoke of it as "a question with which the present Government will have to deal."

Eight years ago, in 1899, Mr. Balfour launched a manifesto on this question which proposed the maintenance of Dublin University with its Episcopalian atmosphere, while a St. Patrick's University was to be founded in Dublin with a Catholic atmosphere, and a University of Belfast with a Presbyterian atmosphere was to be founded on the basis of the existing Queen's College in that city. The reasons which Mr. Balfour gave for desiring a settlement of the question deserve quotation:--

"For myself I hope a University will be granted, and I hope it will be granted soon. I hope so, as a Unionist, because otherwise I do not know how to claim for a British Parliament that it can do for Ireland all, and more than all, that Ireland could do for herself. I hope so as a lover of education, because otherwise the educational interests both of Irish Protestants and of Irish Roman Catholics must grievously suffer, and suffer in that department of education, the national importance of which is from day to day more fully recognised. I hope so as a Protestant, because otherwise too easy an occasion is given for the taunt that in the judgment of Protestants themselves Protestantism has something to fear from the spread of knowledge."

Two years after this declaration a Royal Commission on the whole question was mooted, and immediately the cry of "Hands off Trinity" was raised, in spite of the fact that no Royal Commission had sat on that College since 1853, an interval of time in which there had been four Commissions on Oxford and Cambridge, and three on the Scottish Universities. The terms of reference of the Commission of 1901 on its appointment under the chairmanship of Lord Robertson were vague. A Judge of the High Court in Ireland threatened to resign if Trinity College--the main centre of University education in the island--were included in the scope of the inquiry of a Commission on the means for obtaining such education in the country. The Commission sat in private, and it was not till the first volume of evidence was published that it was discovered that the terms of reference had been so interpreted as to exclude Trinity from the inquiry, and to retain the services of the learned Judge.

After discussing the alternatives of a new Catholic University, or a reconstitution of the Royal University with the addition of a new Catholic College, the Commissioners decided in favour of the latter. Their plan comprised a federal teaching University with four constituent Colleges, the three Queen's Colleges and a new Catholic College to be situated in Dublin. Changes in the constitution of the Queen's Colleges, to remove the religious objections at present entertained towards them were proposed, and in reference to the endowment of the new Catholic College it was claimed that it was not truly open to the objection that it introduced denominational endowment into the University system of Ireland since the Jesuit University College receives, and has received for nearly a quarter of a century, a large annual sum out of moneys provided by Acts of Parliament for University purposes. The reason which the Commissioners gave fer not making this institution the basis of a new College was declared to be its meagre scale which makes it unsuitable for expansion.

In January, 1904, Lord Dunraven propounded a scheme in a letter to the Press by which the question was to be solved by enlarging the University of Dublin so as to include the present Queen's College, Belfast, and a new College which should satisfy Catholic needs in Dublin, each of the Colleges being autonomous and residential, and on August 3rd, 1904, Mr. Clancy, in the House of Commons, read a telegram from the Archbishop of Dublin saying that the bishops would accept either the Dunraven scheme or that of the Robertson Commission.

So matters were allowed to rest until, with the advent to power of the present Government, the lacuna, which owing to the recalcitrancy of Mr. Justice Madden, had been left in the public information on the problem by the omission of Trinity from the Robertson report, was filled up by the appointment of a new Royal Commission.

Early this year their report was published. Five of the Commissioners are in favour of a modified Dunraven scheme, three follow the Robertson scheme, and one--the only Catholic Fellow of Trinity, one of the very few of that faith who had ever been elected to that office--is in favour of no change, an opinion which he expounds in three lines.

It must be remembered in connection with the minority recommendation that the importance of its coincidence with that of the Robertson report may easily be exaggerated if sufficiently strong insistence be not laid upon the exclusion of the University of Dublin from the purview of the latter.

The chief respect in which the majority recommendations differ from those of Lord Dunraven is in the inclusion in the new federal Dublin University of the present Queen's College in Cork, and possibly of that of Galway. It is important to study this proposal, because it is, according to Mr. Bryce's last words on resigning office, to be the means by which the Government hope to effect a solution.

The fact that both the Robertson and the Fry Commissions reported against Mr. Balfour's plan, to the promotion of the success of which in the eight years which have elapsed he has done nothing, on the grounds of the difficulty of bringing it into play, show that for the moment opinion is set against the multiplication of Universities, and the choice for the present lies between the two methods of dealing with the two existing Universities, one of which does not teach, while to the other the students of the country cannot in conscience go to be taught.

After Mr. Bryce's speech we can no longer ask British statesmen, "How long halt ye between two opinions?" That the plan adopted by the Government is the better of the two at present mooted I shall endeavour to show. In the first place, it is a mere accident that Trinity College has continued so long the sole College in the University of Dublin, Chief Baron Palles, in a very able note appended to the report, disentangles from a number of legal decisions and statutory declarations the distinctions between Trinity College and the University of Dublin which it is endeavoured to confound. The Charter of James I., conferring on Dublin the privilege of a University, foreshadowed the establishment of other Colleges. Both the Act of Settlement, 14 & 15 Car. II. (1660), and the Roman Catholic Relief Act, 1793, expressly authorise the erection of another College in the University--a fact which makes the proposed change which partisans are anxious to paint as revolutionary vandalism appear in truth merely the belated performance of a long-expressed intention. The advantages to Trinity in making it a part of a great National University are hard to exaggerate. She has long been described as the only successful British institution in Ireland, and in that may perhaps be found the comparatively evil days on which she has fallen, as her admission lists every year testify, and as was explained to me recently by a member of the very class from which she used to draw her undergraduates, when he said--"The respectable Protestant country gentry don't send their sons to Trinity now in the numbers in which they used to. They send them to Oxford and Cambridge." The last part of his remark I was able to indorse from my own personal observation.

On two occasions advances have been made by the Board of Trinity College to the heads of the Catholic hierarchy, asking them what would be their attitude if Trinity were to allow Catholic students in the College the same facilities for religious teaching by the members of their own Church as are at present provided for undergraduate members of the Episcopalian Protestant Church. On the first occasion Cardinal Cullen, shortly after the passing of the University Tests Act, replied that he could be no party to such a proposal. When the process of sounding the Catholic bishops was repeated in November, 1903, the Provost and Senior Fellows expressed their willingness to consent to the erection of a Catholic chapel in the College grounds provided a sufficient sum of money was forthcoming for its erection. A similar advance was made to the Moderator of the General Assembly of the Presbyterian Church, and the reply in each case was the same--that the parties concerned could not accept the offers made by the College Board. The failure on the part of Presbyterians to make use of the College has been attributed by the Commissioners to the ancient alienation of the Presbyterians from Trinity, as well as to the existence of the useful work done for that body by the Queen's College, Belfast.

That this ancient alienation exists in the case of Catholics far more than in that of the Presbyterians is but natural, seeing that the College was founded by Elizabeth to undermine the Catholicism of the people. For all that, however, the taunt is raised with some superficial measure of plausibility that in refusing the offer the Catholics and their bishops lay themselves open to a charge of narrowmindedness, seeing that they have not a College suitable to their needs as have the Presbyterians in Belfast. That the ***genius loci*** is Episcopalian Protestant no one will deny. At an inaugural meeting of the College Historical Society a few years ago Judge Webb declared--"Their University was founded by Protestants, for Protestants, and in the Protestant interest. A Protestant spirit had from the first animated every member of its body corporate. At the present moment, with all its toleration, all its liberality, all its comprehensiveness, and all its scrupulous honour, the ***genius loci***, the guardian spirit of the place, was Protestant. And as a Protestant he said, and said it boldly, Protestant might it evermore remain." To this exposition of the spirit of the College two of its most distinguished members--Lord Justice FitzGibbon and Professor Mahaffy--gave their assent.

In the light of this frank admission the attitude of the Catholics takes a new complexion. No suggestion, it will be noted, is made in the overtures to the bishops to give Catholics any--not to speak of a proportionate--representation on the Councils of the College. As at present constituted, the Board, owing to the abolition of celibacy as a condition of Fellowship and the extinction of the advowsons belonging to the College by the Irish Church Act of 1869, has become a body of men, the average age of whom is over seventy and the average time since the graduation of whom is a little more than half a century. There is at present one Catholic Junior Fellow in the College, and from the above facts it will be seen that he may get on the governing board, if he survives, in about forty years from now.

The government in a college by men whose undergraduate days were fifty years ago is not calculated to inspire hope for a liberality of treatment with which a more modern generation might be imbued. The suggestion that Catholics show narrowmindedness in refusing to throng the halls of a College admittedly envious of its Protestantism and maintaining automatically its purely Protestant government for three-quarters of a century more is very disingenuous.

That if they were to comply, Protestantism would have by some special means to maintain its supremacy is obvious, for the Episcopalian Protestants are only thirteen per cent. of the population of Ireland, and if Catholics were to swamp Trinity and to succeed in obtaining a share in its councils proportionate to their numbers in the country, the body for which Trinity was founded would find themselves unable to obtain any dominant voice in its government.

"Trinity College is quite free from clerical control," said the Vice-Provost in his statement to the Commissioners, regardless apparently of the fact that of the seven Senior Fellows who, together with the Provost, form the College Board, no less than four are clergymen. In this connection I cannot do better than quote from the statement submitted by the Committee on Higher Education of the General Assembly of the Presbyterian Church in Ireland for the information of the last Royal Commission:--

"So long as Trinity College remains practically as it is there is a real grievance for all denominations except the Protestant Episcopalian, and the members of those denominations will still be able to say that the best education in the country--and whether it is the best academically or simply possesses a greater social acceptance and prestige it is needless here to discuss--is withheld from them, except on conditions that tempt their sons to abandon the faith of their fathers or to become weakened in their attachment to it."

No one--least of all an Irishman--can deny the greatness of a College on the boards of which are such names as Berkeley, Swift, Grattan, Flood, and Burke, but it will be admitted by all that as far as the fame of her *alumni* is concerned--and there is no other test for a collegiate foundation--Trinity reached the zenith of her greatness during the years in which a free Parliament served to break down the barriers of religion in the island. With the passing of that phase of political history she relapsed into her place as the "silent sister" in the country, but not of it, taking no part in national life other than to offer opposition to the legislative changes, which even she is now constrained to admit were reforms.

As owner of some 200,000 acres, Trinity College has proved herself one of the worst landlords in Ireland. An estate belonging to the College in County Kerry gave rise to one of the bitterest struggles of the land war. In view of the cry which is being raised in England to-day as to the broad tolerance which is alleged to hold the field in the College to-day, the bitterly anti-Catholic spirit of the present Provost and of his predecessors deserves mention; but I must further call the reader's notice to a recent event which attracted much attention in Ireland, but was passed unnoticed in Great Britain. In a sonnet, written by a leading Fellow of the College in "T.C.D.," the College magazine, the writer spoke of the Catholic churches in Ireland as "grim monuments of cold observance, the incestuous mate of superstition," of which "to seeing eyes each tall steeple lifts its tall head and lies." Sentiments of this kind, expressed in such taste, are not calculated to encourage Catholic parents to send their sons to a college where they may come under influences of which the writer is an example.

The idea of putting into practice the proposed expedient of swamping Trinity by the encouragement of all Catholics to send their sons to that College is to a member of an old university as attractive as on paper it appears easy, but there are drawbacks to its practical application other than the presence in the College of such a spirit as I have exemplified.

In England, where there are public schools, and Oxford and Cambridge colleges, many of which have behind them a career of three or four hundred years, one is inclined to overestimate the value of tradition in a country where educational endowments are rare and ancient endowments are the exception. The traditions, moreover, of the origin and of the mission of Trinity are not such as to foster for her the same feelings as Oxford and Cambridge have the power of provoking in England. The part which Trinity has played in Irish history is in no sense analogous to that played by the English Universities in the history of that country. English Catholics make use of Oxford and Cambridge for the education of their sons because in view of their numbers the notion of a separate university or even a separate college would be ridiculous. In England Catholics are a small sect. In Ireland they form the great bulk of the nation. In Montreal, where Catholics form only forty per cent. of the population, a Catholic University was established by Royal Charter, and the same principle has been applied in the establishment of Catholic Universities in Nova Scotia, in Malta, in New South Wales, and in the founding of the Mahommedan Gordon College at Khartoum.

As long as Trinity maintained tests, so long did the Catholics demand as of right a purely Catholic University on the grounds of civic equity, but in these days of open doors they have again and again expressed their demand for a college or university open to men of all creeds--Catholic in the sense that Oxford and Cambridge are Protestant, and are in consequence thronged with young Englishmen; Catholic in the way that the Scottish Universities are Presbyterian and that Trinity, Dublin, is Episcopalian. Not a rich man's college, but one to which all may go as they do to those in Scotland and like those racy of the soil, and for the rest, in Cardinal Newman's words--"Not a seminary, not a convent, but a place where men of the world may be fitted for the world."

Everyone recognises to-day the grievance of the Dissenters in England and Wales in single school areas under the Education Act of 1902. Ireland may not unjustly be said to be a single university area, for to call an examining Board a university is a misnomer. It is surely not too much to assert that the conscientious scruples of the Irish Catholics to forms of education of which they do not approve are as strong as the feelings of the Non-conformist conscience. The attempt to force undenominationalism on the country has been an expensive failure. Recognising this, the denominational--nay, more, the Jesuit--University College has in a niggardly fashion and by a back door been subsidised by the State. The demand is for no more than a university which shall be Catholic in the sense that it shall be national, and this in a preponderatingly Catholic country implies Catholicism. The Irish Catholic bishops in 1897 declared they are prepared to accept a university without tests in which the majority of the governing body are laymen, with a provision that no State funds should be employed for the promotion of religious education. It is idle, in view of this, to protest that the demand is urged only on behalf of rampant clericalism, and that the only form of university which Catholics will accept is of such a kind as would serve to strengthen the hand of the priests, whose sole aim in this demand is to secure that increase of power. The shifts of intolerance are many, but I cannot believe that it will long continue to masquerade in this manner as the statesmanlike buffer between a priest-ridden country and an aggressive clergy. Granting, for the sake of argument, that this was the case, one would have thought that a well-educated laity was better able than one without education to withstand the encroaches of clericalism. We do not ask for a denominational college, but remember that the only colleges, Keble and Selwyn, founded in Oxford and Cambridge in the last eighty years are purely denominational. In the last forty years six new universities have been founded in England, and the number of university students has risen from 2,300 to 13,000. In Ireland, on the other hand, for three-fourths of the population knowledge must still remain a fountain sealed; it is as though one were applying literally to that country the text--"He that increaseth knowledge increaseth sorrow."

In connection with what one may call the Bryce scheme it may be well to point out that as long ago as 1871 the hierarchy proposed a solution on the same lines. In a Pastoral letter of that year, after insisting on the principle of equality, the following passage occurred--"All this can, we believe, be attained by modifying the constitution of the University of Dublin, so as to admit the establishment of a second College within it, in every respect equal to Trinity College, and conducted on purely Catholic principles."

On the motion to go into Committee on the Bill for the abolition of tests in 1873 an Irish member moved a motion to the effect that a Catholic College should be founded in the University of Dublin, in addition to Trinity College. Two years later Mr. Isaac Butt, the Protestant leader of the Irish Nationalists (himself a Trinity man), and The O'Conor Don, a Catholic Unionist, brought in a Bill on the same lines, but both motion and Bill were defeated. The advantages of this mode of dealing with the question are seen from its acceptance by the hierarchy and the general mass of the Catholic laity. The Senate of the Royal University have since its promulgation readily recognised its soundness and have given it their support, as have the Professors of University College, Dublin. It will serve to make an end of the underhand manner by which, as we have seen, that College, though not merely a denominational, but, moreover, a Jesuit institution, is subsidised by public money, though we are always told that State endowment of religious education is alien to all modern principles of government.

One would have thought that the authorities of Trinity would have felt themselves estopped from refusing to accept this solution. The offer of facilities inside Trinity itself--if it is the generous concession it professes to be--must be made with a full recognition that, if accepted, the process of "capturing" the College would be effected before long, thus modifying the Protestantism which is its proudest boast. If, on the other hand, the expense of life in Trinity College would prove prohibitive to any but a small section of the four thousand matriculated students in the Royal University, the much-vaunted liberality of Trinity is seen to be very greatly restricted, since the results of acceptance of the offer would only touch the mere fringe of the educational demand.

Last year, of the 1,114 students on the books of the College only 261 were resident within the College--there being accommodation for only 275. Of the 853 returned as residing outside the College, more than a hundred do not attend lectures or classes, and are entitled to call themselves members of the College though their only connection with it is in the examination hall--an evil system which the Commission has condemned, and which one must suppose was borrowed from the Royal University.

Everyone is agreed that a university to be worth the name should, if possible, be residential. The absence of disciplinary control in Trinity on those residing out of College, the omission on the part of the authorities to enact rules which would allow terms to be kept only in licensed lodging-houses, subject to inspection and to a rigid "lock-up rule" at twelve o'clock, are absent in Dublin not only at Trinity, but at the University College, where one can only suppose its absence to be due to the unorganised condition of a small and temporary makeshift. Not only, however, for the exercise of disciplinary control, but also because of the close association of men with each other which residence ensures, is this to be regarded as the best means of getting the heart out of a university education.

This being the case, if Trinity were to receive a new accession of numbers its accommodation would have to be largely increased, so that the line of least resistance, which leaves the very largely autonomous constitution of Trinity unimpaired, will be seen to lie in the direction of the establishment of a new college, in which, moreover, it will be possible to make expenses more economical than they are in Trinity.

"It is not for us," said Mr. Balfour at Partick in December, 1889, "to consider how far the undoubtedly conscientious objections of the Roman Catholic population to use the means at their disposal are wise or unwise. That is not our business. What we have to do is to consider what we can do consistently with our conscience to meet their wants."

The proposals of the Government, as outlined by Mr. Bryce and recommended by the Royal Commission, offend against no one's conscience. They assail no vested interest unless one so calls that of which Matthew Arnold spoke as one very cruel result of the Protestant ascendancy; they tend to establish something approaching equality between creeds; they make an end of the mischievous system by which the Royal University has encouraged a false ideal of success by making examination the end-all and the be-all of a so-called university education, and which, moreover, according to the final report of the Robertson Commission, "fails to exhibit the one virtue which is associated with a university of this kind--that of inspiring public confidence in its examination results." The advantages of the present proposal over a reorganised Royal University are that the size and poverty of the country are strong reasons against the creation of two universities when one would be equally efficient. The scheme will be readily accepted by the Presbyterians as well as by the Catholics, which would not be the case with a reconstituted Royal University, and it is the only solution of the question which will bring the young men of different creeds in the country together at an impressionable age when friendships are formed which may serve to break down the barrier between creeds.

The objection of Trinity College to the inclusion on the roll of the University under the new conditions of the present M.A.s of the Royal University is scarcely consistent with its recent action in admitting to ***ad eundem*** degrees women who have passed the final degree examinations at Oxford and Cambridge, and if the objection to the proposal is based on the change in political complexion which the electoral roll of the University would undergo, the answer is that University representation is an anomaly which in any circumstances is not likely to continue for many years more in the case, not merely of Dublin, but of the other universities of the three kingdoms.

* * * * *

Since the foregoing chapter was written the Provost of Trinity has announced to a meeting of Graduates of the College that he has received assurances from the Chief Secretary that in the forthcoming Bill the University of Dublin will be left untouched. I have said enough to show that Irish Nationalist opinion has not been committed to the Bryce scheme to the exclusion of every other solution, but it is to be regretted, in the interests of education, that the proposal which the majority of

Irishmen regarded as the solution nearest approaching the ideal should have been launched by the Government merely as a ***ballon d'essai***, to be withdrawn at the first breath of opposition, and to be replaced by what, at the best, can only prove to be a less hopeful compromise. One guarantee of a speedy solution the country at any rate holds--namely, that the Government is pledged to introduce legislation next session, and that the Chief Secretary has bound himself to stand or fall by the fate of the Bill.

CHAPTER VII
UNIONISM IN IRELAND

"When I hear any man talk of an unalterable law, the only effect it produces upon me is to convince me that he is an unalterable fool. There are always a set of worthy and moderately gifted men who bawl out death and ruin upon every valuable change which the varying aspect of human affairs absolutely and imperiously requires ... I admit that to a certain extent the Government will lose the affections of the Orangemen ... but you must perceive that it is better to have four friends and one enemy than four enemies and one friend."
--SYDNEY SMITH, *Letters of Peter Plymley*, 1807.

From the outcry which arose in the last years of the late Government at the revelations which came to be known as the MacDonnell mystery one would have thought that Conservatives could look back to a record unstained by any traffic with the unclean thing for which they express such horror. I will try to show how small is the measure of truth in this belief, and in what manner it has proved impossible to maintain the *status quo* in the teeth of democratic feeling without *pourparlers* behind the scenes, even when in the open such dealings have had perforce to be denounced as impossible.

Twenty-five years ago the rigid application of the Crimes Act by Lord Spencer, the Viceroy, after the Phoenix Park murders had put an end to the "Kilmainham Treaty," and the failure on the part of the Government to amend the Land Act of 1881, together with the sympathetic attitude of Lord Randolph Churchill, then conducting his guerilla tactics as leader of the Fourth Party, all served to make opposition on the part of the Irish members to the Liberal Government increase, and it was by their aid that in June, 1885, it was thrown out of office on a defeat by twelve votes on the Budget. Lord Salisbury then took office with his "ministry of caretakers," with a minority in the House of Commons, for a general election could not take place until the provisions of the new Franchise Act had come into force.

Colour was lent to the general impression which was abroad that the Conservatives were flirting with Home Rule by the appointment to the Lord Lieutenancy with a seat in the Cabinet of Lord Carnarvon, the statesman who had established federation in Canada and had attempted to bring it about in South Africa, who was familiar with the machinery of subordinate legislatures and Colonial parliaments, and whose sympathies with the Irish people were to be inferred from the fact that he had voted for Disestablishment in 1869, and for the Land Bill of the following year, in a speech on which measure he had urged the House of Lords not to delay concession till it could no longer have the charm of free consent, nor be regulated by the counsels of prudent statesmanship.

The defeat of the Liberals had been primarily due to the revolt on the part of the radical section over the question of whether a new Coercion Bill should be introduced. In the light of this fact special importance was attached to the declaration, made in the House of Lords, as to the Irish policy of the Government, the more so because in an unprecedented manner not the Premier but the Viceroy was the spokesman. He began by a repudiation of coercion, with which he declared the recent enfranchisement of the Irish people would not be consistent. "My Lords," he went on to say, speaking of the general question, "I do not believe that with honesty and singlemindedness of purpose on the one side, and with the willingness of the Irish people on the other, it is hopeless to look for some satisfactory solution of this terrible question. My Lords, these I believe to be the opinions and views of my colleagues."

A further step in securing Irish support occurred at the end of July, and perhaps of all the strange events which have occurred in the government of Ireland it is the strangest. Lord Carnarvon solicited through one of his colleagues, and obtained, an interview with Mr. Parnell, and the circumstances under which this occurred between the Queen's Lord Lieutenant and the leader to whom men attributed treason and condoning assassinations is perhaps the most curious part of the whole story.

The meeting took place at the very end of the London season, not in the Houses of Parliament nor in a club of which one or other of the parties was a member, but in an empty house in Grosvenor Square, from which all the servants had gone away. It is a piquant feature of the event, shrouded as it was with all these circumstances of mystery, that the gentleman who was in the secret and offered his house for the meeting was no other than that rigid Imperialist, Col. Sir Howard Vincent, who had only the year before retired from the Criminal Investigation Department at Scotland Yard. When the occurrence of this interview became known, nearly a year later, Mr. Parnell declared--and the fact was never denied by Lord Carnarvon--that the latter had pronounced himself in favour of an Irish Parliament with the power of protecting Irish industries. The insistence by the Viceroy that he spoke only for himself appeared to the Irish leader to be mere formality, but in truth the Cabinet knew nothing of the interview. Lord Salisbury was informed that it was going to take place, raised no objection to its occurrence, and on receiving afterwards, both *verbatim* and in writing, accounts of what had occurred, praised the discretion of his Viceroy.

In view of what had happened it was not surprising that in the month of August Mr. Parnell made an explicit demand for the restoration of Grattan's Parliament, with the right of taxing foreign and even English imports for the benefit of the Irish home trade--a proposal not so revolutionary as it would now appear, seeing that less than forty years had elapsed since the Irish Custom House had for the first time begun to admit all English goods duty free.

Mr. Parnell's manifesto was followed by Lord Salisbury's speech at Newport, from which quotation has already been made, in which he expressed himself of opinion that Home Rule would be safer than popular local government, and further enhanced the impression that he was moving in the direction of the safer policy, by proceeding to frame what has been described as the nearest approach to an apologia for boycotting which has ever been made by an English statesman. The election address of Lord Randolph Churchill--the most popular and influential minister in the country--contained no allusion to the threatened "dismemberment of the Empire," and in his campaign his only allusion to Ireland was comprised in boasts of the success of the anti-coercion policy of Carnarvon; while Sir John Gorst, who had been

Solicitor-General, referred in his election address in disparaging terms to "the reactionary Ulster members." All the symptoms pointed in the one direction of an alliance between Salisbury and Parnell on the basis of a scheme for self-government, and an additional point was given to the indications in that direction by the fact that Mr. Chamberlain and Lord Hartington, at variance on most points of policy, were united in opposition to Mr. Parnell's demand.

The statesmanlike manner in which at this juncture Mr. Gladstone endeavoured, as he himself put it, to keep the strife of nations from forming the dividing line between parties, has become very apparent with the recent publication of documents of the period. Two years before, he had told the Queen that the Irish question could only be settled by a conjunction of parties, and on December 20th, 1885, he wrote to the Conservative leader on the urgency of the Irish question, and declared that it would be a public calamity if this great subject should fall into lines of party conflict. If Salisbury would bring forward a proposal for settling the whole question of future government in Ireland he would treat it in the same spirit as that which he had shown in the matters of Afghanistan and the Balkans, and he illustrated the advantages which such a spirit of concession could produce by the conferences on the Reform Bill, and the fact that the existing Conservative ministry had been maintained in office by Liberal forbearance. "His hypocrisy," wrote a minister to whom this letter had been shown, "makes me sick." In this connection a letter from Lord Randolph Churchill to Lord Salisbury, written on the following day, is of interest:--

"Labouchere came to see me this morning.... He proceeded to tell me that, on Sunday week last, Lord Carnarvon had met Justin MacCarthy and had confided to him that he was in favour of Home Rule in some shape, but that his colleagues and his party were not ready, and asked whether Justin MacCarthy's party would agree to an inquiry which he thought there was a chance of the Government agreeing to, and which would educate his colleagues and his party if granted and carried through. I was consternated, but replied that such a statement was an obvious lie, but, between ourselves, I fear it is not, perhaps not even an exaggeration or a misrepresentation. Justin MacCarthy is on the staff of the ***Daily News***, Labouchere is one of the proprietors, and I cannot imagine any motive for his inventing such a statement. If it is true Lord Carnarvon has played the devil."[21]

With regard to the overtures which Mr. Gladstone had made, for which precedents in plenty were supplied by the repeal of the Test Act in 1828, Catholic Emancipation in 1829, the Repeal of the Corn Laws in 1848, and the extension of the franchise in 1867, Lord Salisbury saw in it only anxiety to take office on the part of his great opponent, and prophesied that if his hunger were not prematurely gratified he would be forced into some line of conduct which would be discreditable to him and disastrous, and when the Liberal leader on the 23rd again pressed for a definite answer to his approaches he was refused a communication of views.

"Thus idly," says Mr. Winston Churchill, "drifted away what was perhaps the best hope of the settlement of Ireland which that generation was to see."

The view which Mr. Gladstone took of the events of the winter of 1885-6 is illustrated by a memorandum which he wrote in 1897, in which he says:--

"I attached value to the acts and language of Lord Carnarvon and the other favourable manifestations. Subsequently we had but too much evidence of a deliberate intention to deceive the Irish with a view to their support at the election."[22]

The attitude of the Tories and the rankling memory of the bitter debates on the Liberal Coercion Bill of 1882, coupled with the attitude of the Tories and the deception which they practised, resulted, not unnaturally, in the fact that Parnell threw his weight in favour of the Conservatives at the general election which ensued, and by this means, it is estimated, lost at least twenty seats to the Liberals. Immediately after the election the Viceroy and the Chief Secretary retired, but though their successors were appointed in the third week in December, it was not till the middle of January that the resignations were made public. The first act of the new Chief Secretary was to announce that, in spite of the emphatic disclaimers of the previous June, a Coercion Bill was to be introduced, and as a result of the Irish voting with the Liberals the Tories were defeated, and Mr. Gladstone took office. The Home Rule Bill which was introduced was thrown out in the month of June, the Government being in a minority of thirty. Had it not been for Parnell's manifesto, urging Irishmen in Great Britain to vote for Conservatives, the Government would have had a majority of between ten and twenty, and, moreover, if a general election had followed, the morale of the Liberals would have been much greater if they had been fighting for the second time within a few months shoulder to shoulder with the Irishmen, and not been in the position in which in fact they were--of enjoying the support in June of those who had opposed them in November.

Let us now turn to the MacDonnell incident. One of the first acts of Mr. Balfour, on becoming Prime Minister in July, 1902, on the retirement of Lord Salisbury was to give Mr. Wyndham, the Chief Secretary, a seat in the Cabinet. In September Mr. Wyndham appointed as Under Secretary Sir Antony MacDonnell, a distinguished Indian Civil Servant and Member of the Indian Council, who had been in turn head of the Government of Burma, the Central Provinces, and the North-West Provinces, and who had with conspicuous ability carried on financial and agrarian reforms in the East. Lord Lansdowne, during his tenure of the Viceroyalty, formed a high estimate of his knowledge and ability, and it was on his recommendation that Mr. Wyndham appointed this official to the post. The correspondence between the two, which Mr. Redmond elicited from the Government two and a half years later, shows that it was with some reluctance that the Under Secretary yielded to the pressure brought to bear on him to accept the office.

"I am an Irishman, a Roman Catholic, and a Liberal in politics," he wrote. "I have strong Irish sympathies. I do not see eye to eye with you in all matters of Irish administration, and I think that there is no likelihood of good coming from such a *regime* of coercion as the *Times* has recently outlined." For all that, being anxious to do some service to Ireland, he declared his willingness to take office provided there was some chance of his succeeding, which he thought there would be, "on this condition, that I should have adequate opportunities of influencing the policy and acts of the Irish administration, and subject, of course, to your control, freedom of action in Executive matters. For many years in India I directed administration on the largest scale, and I know that if you send me to Ireland the opportunity of mere secretarial criticism would fall short of the requirements of my position. If I were installed in office in Ireland my aims, broadly stated, would be:--(1) The maintenance of order; (2) the solution of the land question on the basis of voluntary sale; (3) where sale does not operate the fixation of rent on some self-acting principle whereby local inquiries would be obviated; (4) the co-ordination, control, and direction of boards and other administrative bodies; (5) the settlement of the education question in the general spirit of Mr. Balfour's views, and generally the promotion of general administrative improvement and conciliation."

Mr. Wyndham's acceptance of these terms was explicit, and it was understood, as the Chief Secretary put it in the House of Commons when the whole subject came up for review, that Sir Antony was appointed rather as a colleague than as a mere Under Secretary to register Mr. Wyndham's will, and although in the House of Commons Mr. Balfour said that Sir Antony was bound by the rules applying to all Civil Servants, in the House of Lords Lord Lansdowne declared that, "it had been recognised that the Under Secretary would have greater freedom of action, greater opportunities of initiative, than if he had been a candidate in the ordinary way."

One of the first results of the new departure was the withdrawal of the application of the Coercion Act, which had been in force since April, 1902, an action which roused angry protests from the Orangemen, as did also the words used, in what was almost his first speech, by Lord Dudley, the new Viceroy, who had succeeded Lord Cadogan, and who announced that, "the opinion of the Government was, and it was his own opinion, that the only way to govern Ireland properly was to govern it according to Irish ideas instead of according to British ideas."

During 1903 interest was largely engrossed in the fate of the Land Act, and it was not till the autumn of 1904 that it became known that before drafting in its final form the programme of the Irish Reform Association Lord Dunraven had secured the assistance of the Under Secretary with the knowledge of the Chief Secretary and the Viceroy, the latter of whom, according to Lord Lansdowne's declaration in the House of Lords, "did not think that Sir Antony was exceeding his functions"--a fact to which colour was given by the circumstance that on several occasions the Under Secretary discussed the reforms with the Lord Lieutenant.

Mr. Wyndham, on behalf of the Government, had taken the unusual course of repudiating the Dunraven scheme in a letter to the *Times*, but in spite of this, Irish Unionists wrote to the *Times* to express their suspicions "whether in short the devolution scheme is not the price secretly arranged to be paid for the Nationalist acquiescence in a settlement of the land question on generous terms."

Then it was that the *Times* expressed its opinion that when a Unionist Lord Lieutenant and a Unionist Under Secretary are discussing reforms which the Cabinet condemn as Home Rule in a thin disguise, it is obviously time that they quitted their posts. Three weeks later Mr. Wyndham resigned, but Sir Antony, who had had the refusal of the Governorship of Bombay--the third greatest Governorship in the British Empire--retained his position, though his presence at Dublin Castle had been described by some fervent Orangemen as a menace to the loyal and law-abiding inhabitants of Ireland, and by the Irish Attorney-General as a gross betrayal of the Unionist position and an injury to the Unionist cause. Mr. Long, however, very rapidly won the hearts of those who had succeeded in securing the resignation of Mr. Wyndham by his description of devolution as "a cowardly surrender to the forces of disorder," and in the same strain the Earl of Westmeath spoke of "truckling to disloyalty and trying to conciliate those who will not be conciliated."

At the opening of the session of 1905 the whole question was ventilated. The official explanations proving unsatisfactory, the Orangemen decided to withdraw their support from the Government on all questions affecting Ireland, and the leader of the party went so far as to utter the threat that "Ulster might have to draw upon her reserves," which was taken to mean that the Orangemen who were members of the Government would resign *en masse* --an action which, in the moribund condition of the Ministry, would have meant an instant dissolution. At the very beginning of the session Mr. Wyndham had announced that the matter of Sir Antony's dealings with Lord Dunraven had been considered by the Cabinet, and "the Government expressed through me their view that the action of Sir Antony MacDonnell was indefensible. But they authorised me to add that they were thoroughly satisfied that his conduct was not open to the imputation of disloyalty."

The equivocal and ambiguous position in which the Unionists placed themselves in the course of this episode is a striking commentary on the impossibility of governing a country against its will. The Tories tried once again, in the historic phrase, to catch the Whigs bathing and steal their clothes, but this time they failed. When the Orangemen held a pistol at the Government's head and bade its members stand and deliver, Mr. Wyndham had perforce to resign, but the mystery, which has not yet been cleared up, is the reason why the Viceroy and the Under Secretary, who were tarred with the same brush, retained their posts.

It should in frankness be stated, however, that when during the session of 1907 the Prime Minister remarked on a certain occasion that he always thought Mr. Wyndham resigned the Chief Secretaryship in consequence of criticisms from the Orangemen below the gangway on his own side, Mr. Balfour interrupted with the remark--"That is a complete mis-statement, and I think the right honourable gentleman must know it."

One may well ask, in view of this, what was meant by Mr. Wyndham when, speaking on the reasons for his retirement, on May 9th, 1905, he accounted for it by the fact that "the situation in Ireland was complicated by personal misunderstandings," producing "an atmosphere of suspicion," which was an obvious reference, as most people supposed, to such denunciations as that of Mr. William Moore of the Chief Secretary's "wretched, rotten, sickening policy of conciliation." The disingenuousness marking the whole proceeding is well shown by the fact that although on announcing Mr. Wyndham's resignation Mr. Balfour said:--"The ground of his resignation is not ill-health,"[23] less than a year later, when asked during the election at Manchester by a heckler to state the reason why Mr. Wyndham retired, the reply of Mr. Balfour was--"He retired chiefly on account of health."[24]

From the correspondence which passed in March, 1906, between Lord Dudley and Sir Edward Carson, and which was published in the Press, we have the express statement from the ex-Lord Lieutenant that Mr. Balfour "never conveyed to me any intimation that he or the Government disapproved strongly or otherwise of my conduct."

The correspondence arose over a remark made by Sir Edward Carson, to the effect that Lord Dudley had made statements both ways as to the desirability of governing Ireland according to Irish ideas. Challenged to make good the assertion, which he declared was based on a private conversation, Sir Edward Carson went on to assert that the Viceroy had on another occasion expressed the opinion to him that Ireland should be governed through the agency of the Catholic priesthood. This Lord Dudley denied as vehemently as he did the imputation of facing both ways, and in reply went on to write:--

"That you should have formed an impression of that kind from any conversation with me confirms my belief that the violence of your opinions on Irish political questions make it quite impossible for you to estimate justly the standpoint of anyone whose views on such questions may be more moderate and tolerant than your own. It is not, however, by violence and intolerance that the cause of union is best served, and my experience in Ireland has shown me very clearly that the present system of government constantly receives from its most clamorous advocates blows as heavy and as effective as any that could be dealt to it by its avowed enemies."

The Government tried to ride two horses abreast--to rule Ireland otherwise than by force, and to maintain itself in power with the help of Orange votes--two courses, each irreconcilable with the other. Their position reminds me of Alphonse Daudet's immortal creation, Tartarin de Tarascon, with a double nature, partly that of Don Quixote and partly of Sancho Panza, at one moment urged on by the glory, and at the next held back by the prospect of the hardships, of lion-hunting in Africa--"Couvre toi de gloire," dit Tartarin Quichotte, "Couvre toi de flanelle dit Tartarin Sancho."

It is easier for a camel to pass through the eye of a needle than for a government which does not recognise democratic principles to make any headway in the work of amelioration in Ireland. The moral is that those responsible for the administration of the country have found themselves by the force of circumstances, even against their will, driven to apply popular principles of government in order that they may secure fairness and efficiency, and my contention that this is so is borne out by the two incidents to which I have referred, in which the Conservatives escaped only by the skin of their teeth from committing themselves to a policy which would have won them the hostility of their Orange allies.

The latter have in truth secured their own way to a remarkable extent. The promise has not been fulfilled which Mr. Chamberlain made after the Unionist victory of 1886, to the effect that Lord Salisbury and the Conservative leaders were prepared to consider and review the "irritating centralising system of administration which is known as Dublin Castle." At the time of the ill-fated Round Table Conference, which Sir William Harcourt convened, Mr. Chamberlain committed himself to the expediency of establishing some form of legislative authority in Dublin, and admitted that such a body should be allowed to organise the form of Executive Government on whatever lines it thought fit, and Sir West Ridgeway, as Under Secretary, subsequently carried out the behests of the same Government by outlining a scheme of self-government by means of Provincial Councils with a partly elected board to control finance. All these facts serve to show the injustice--in view of acknowledged facts--of the description by the late Attorney-General for Ireland of the Wyndham proposals as "mean and cruel desertion."

There is no part of the Irish question in respect of which more has been said which is misleading than what is known as the problem of Ulster. I have already explained what a misnomer this is. In the Counties of Donegal, Tyrone, Monaghan,

Fermanagh, and Cavan there are more Catholics than Protestants, while in the Counties of Armagh and Down the numbers of the two creeds are almost equally divided. What is known as the question of Ulster should in truth be known as that of Belfast, for it is only in that city and in the adjacent Counties of Antrim and Down that the religious question is most acute.

The social conditions of the country, which have always been to some extent, though not to that existing in recent years, agricultural, lead one to seek a cause in the conditions of Land Tenure for the different degrees of prosperity pervading the North-East corner of Ulster and the rest of Ireland. It is impossible to doubt that the Ulster Custom of Tenant Right had an immense effect on the economic status of the province. Under it the system of tenure which held the field in the other three provinces was replaced by one in which the tenants had security against arbitrary eviction so long as they paid their rents, and, in addition, were entitled to sell their interest in the property to the incoming tenant, and this Tenant Right sold often for as much as half, and sometimes for as much as the full, fee-simple of the holding. The sum could be obtained on the tenant voluntarily vacating the holding or on his being unable to pay the rent, the landlord being entitled to be consulted with a view to approval by him of the incoming tenant.

The importance of the custom can be recognised in the light of the fact that in England, where improvements are effected in nearly every case not by the tenant but by the landlord, it has been found necessary, nevertheless, to give legislative sanction to Tenant Right.

This has been effected by the Agricultural Holdings Acts, 1875, 1883, and 1900, under which tenants are entitled to statutory compensation for improvements, whether permanent, as, for example, buildings; for drainage purposes; or, as in the case of manure, for the improvement of the soil.

The result of the Ulster Custom on the industry of the Northern tenant-farmer, who enjoyed a freedom of sale and a fixity of tenure, and, further, a compensation for improvements long before the tenants of the South and West secured these advantages, are impossible to over-estimate. Again, in considering the relative economic positions of the members of the two religions, it is impossible to blink the fact that little more than a century has passed since the Irish Catholics were treated as helots under a penal code, and that, if they have been behind hand in the industrial race, account must be taken of the lead in the saddle to which in that way they were subjected. The resulting preponderance of Protestants among the landed gentry led to a further factor in the ostracism which in the past they exercised as employers of labour, whether agricultural or industrial, which, besides its direct effect of breeding and perpetuating sectarian hate, served in an economic sense to unfit Catholics for employment, and to persuade those who in fact were least unfitted and retained their perceptive faculties, that the scope for their energies was to be found only abroad, and so tended to leave behind a residue of labourers rendered unfit for employment as against the time when the prejudice of the richer classes was removed. The non-application in the more purely Protestant parts of Ulster of the principles which held the field in other parts of Ireland made for prosperity in that province by tending towards an economic condition of the labour market, unimpeded by artificial restrictions, arising from religious differences and imposed at the hands of employers of labour. Another factor in the contentment of the Ulster Presbyterians under the varying vicissitudes of Irish government is to be found in the history of the Regium Donum. The Scottish settlers in 1610 having brought with them their ministers, the latter were put in possession of the tithes of the parishes in which they were planted. These they enjoyed till the death of Charles I., but payments were stopped on their refusal to recognise the Commonwealth. Henry Cromwell, however, allowed the body L100, which Charles II. increased to L600, per annum, but towards the end of his reign, and during that of James II., it was discontinued. William III. renewed the grant, increasing it to L1,200, and it was still further augmented in 1785 and 1792. After the Union Castlereagh largely increased the amount of the Regium Donum, and completely altered its mode of distribution, making it in fact contingent on the loyalty of the parson to the Union. The spirit in which it was granted is well shown in a letter in Castlereagh's memoirs, in which the writer, addressing the Chief Secretary just after the votes had been passed by Parliament, declared--"Never before was Ulster under the dominion of the British Crown. It had a distinct moral existence before, and now the Presbyterian ministry will be a subordinate ecclesiastical aristocracy, whose feeling will be that of zealous loyalty, and whose influence on those people will be as purely sedative when it should be, and exciting when it should be, as it was the reverse before." Those who blame Pitt for not having carried through his schemes of concurrent endowment, and who see in his failure to do so, one reason for the ill success of his policy of Union, must admit the importance of the fact that the Presbyterian clergy were pensioners of the State. A notion of the extent to which they were subsidised may be inferred from the fact that by the Commutation Clauses of the Church Disestablishment Act of 1869, the Dissenters secured as compensation for the loss of the Regium Donum and other payments a sum of L770,000, while the equivalent amount paid in lieu of the Maynooth grant to the Catholics--numbering at least eight times as many--amounted to only L372,000.

It was Froude who declared that if the woollen and linen industries had not been hampered there would now be four Ulsters instead of one. Even in the days before restrictions were placed on the production of Irish linen for the better encouragement of the English trade, the North of Ireland was far ahead of the rest of the country in the matter of flax-spinning, and this pre-eminence was mainly due to the fact that the climate there is more suited to that plant than in other parts of Ireland.

Starting with this advantage, linen was able in that province to survive the impositions placed on its production, while in places less favoured by a suitable climate the industry went to the wall. To assume off-hand, without going into the innumerable causes which effect such movements of commerce, that innate thrift was responsible, apart from all other causes, for the progress of Belfast is an attitude similar to that of one who should hold that nothing but the stupidity of the East Anglian yokel has prevented that country from becoming as much a centre of industry as is Lancashire, for such a sweeping generalisation would take no account of other forces at work in the development of the great commercial centres of the North as, for example, the fact that the peculiar conditions of the Lancashire climate are such that the processes of cotton-spinning can be best effected in an atmosphere containing the amount of moisture which there prevails.

In Belfast the interdependence of the linen and the ship-building trades--in one of which the men, while in the other the women, of many families are employed--is one of the most powerful instruments of social progress. The narrow sea which separates it from Scotland and the geographical conformation of Belfast Lough have, moreover, a great bearing on its prosperity. Independence of Irish railways with their excessive freights, crippling by their incidence all export trade, in a town like Belfast, nine-tenths of the industrial output of which goes across the sea, and the advantage which it has over all other Irish towns in its proximity, again independently of Irish railways, to the Lanarkshire, Ayrshire, and Cumberland coalfields, are very important considerations in view of the obstacle which the scarcity of coal is to all commercial enterprises in the island.

Finally, it must not be forgotten, in reference to the greatest of the industries of the North of Ireland, that a very exceptional impetus was given to the development of the commercial enterprise of Belfast at a time which might otherwise have proved a critical period in her industrial career, by the fact that the American Civil War caused a slump in cotton which resulted in the failure of a very large number of Lancashire cotton mills, the place of which was taken by the linen mills of Belfast, which have profited ever since from the advantage gained in that crisis and the growth of their trade which it effected.

I have said enough, I think, to show that the attempt to foist the blame for the backwardness--in an industrial sense--of the rest of the country as compared with the North-East corner, on the difference of religion, is to close one's eyes to half a dozen other factors which must in truth also be appreciated in order that one may arrive at a proper estimate of the real reason for the disparity which undoubtedly exists. The facts which I have mentioned serve to show the unwarrantable nature of the assumption which accounts for the prosperity of North-East Ulster by considerations of race and religion alone. That several generations of progress in the industrial field have had a great effect on the character of the people of Belfast in respect of thrift, energy, and industry I am not concerned to deny, but on what ground in this light is to be explained the decrease in population of Antrim and Down which has gone on concurrently with the enormous increase in that of Belfast? That extrinsic factors such as those of geographical situation have much to do with increase of prosperity is well illustrated by the industrial growth of Wexford, with its manufactories of agricultural implements and dairy machinery, which is largely attributable to the close proximity of that town to the coalfields and iron of South Wales.

As to the argument that political preoccupation is responsible for national backwardness, in the case of Finland the convulsions of a bitter political agitation have not been found incompatible with an increase of wealth and of population.

In this connection it is germane to ask what the Protestant people of Ulster have done for the rest of the country, and to inquire if, with all their commercial success, they have been in the van of progress. That they have never produced a great leader of men or framer of policy is a remarkable fact, and to every demand of their fellow-countrymen they have answered with a reiterated ***non possumus***, backed by threats of their intentions in case they are ignored, which, in point of fact, they have never carried into effect.

The Orangemen in turn opposed Emancipation, Tithe Reform, Land Reform, Church Disestablishment, the Ballot, Local Government, and the settlement of the University question. Their attitude to the Land Conference we have seen elsewhere, and in view of this record one may ask whether or not they deserve Mr. Morley's condemnation as "an irreconcilable junto, always unteachable, always wrong."

That their loyalty is contingent on the maintenance of their ascendancy and the enforcement of their views, their reception of the Church Act of 1869 well shows, as does also the manner in which in 1886 they threatened armed resistance if the Bill to which they were opposed was carried. That they submitted to the Church Act without carrying out their threats is a matter of history, and there is at least a strong probability that in the latter event a similar effect would have been witnessed.

The removal of religious tests in the public life of Great Britain has been accomplished so completely that it is difficult for Englishmen to realise the extent to which the spirit, if not the letter, of tests at this day persists in Ireland.

We have recently seen the adjournment of the House of Commons moved by the Orangemen because a rate collector in Ballinasloe did not receive the appointment to a post for which he applied, and the demands of Catholics for a due share of position and of influence is denounced as a claim for monopoly.

To show how much evidence there is to sustain the charge I will quote a Protestant writer on this question of preferment--"Three-quarters of the Irish people," she writes, "are Catholics. Of 23 Lords Lieutenant since 1832 not one has been a Catholic, nor ever by law can be a Catholic, and only 3 have been Irishmen, tame Irish, as the word goes in Ireland of the denationalised Irishman who has shaken off allegiance to his own people. Of 30 Chief Secretaries, almost all English, not one has been a Catholic. It is not necessary that the Chief Secretary or the Commander of the Forces should be Protestant, but no Catholic has ever yet been allowed to fill either of these exalted offices. Of the 173 Irish peers only 14 (including Viscount Taafe of Austria) are Catholics, and the 28 representative peers in the House of Lords are all free from the taint of the religion of the Irish people, and powerful to drive opinion against it. Out of 60 Privy Councillors in Ireland 4 only are Catholics, and 3 out of 17 judges. Eleven out of the 60 Sub-Commissioners are Catholics; 7 out of the 21 County Court Judges. The head of the police is a Protestant. One only of the 36 County Inspectors is a Catholic. Of 170 District Inspectors only 10 are of that faith, and of 65 Resident Magistrates only 15 are Catholics. If we take the Valuation Offices, the Registration Offices, the Inspectorship of Factories, the Board of Works, the Woods and Forests, the Ordnance Survey, and any and every public department, Protestants hold three places out of four, though they are but one-quarter of the whole population. The extreme party, as we have seen, have secured no less than seven offices in the Government, and their followers and friends hold about 90 per cent. of the higher salaried posts under the Crown in Ireland."[25]

The same writer attributes the glaring discrepancy between the figures which have just been quoted and the ratio of Catholics and Protestants in the population of Ireland to "a union of Protestant fanaticism and place-hunting greed." That it is due to any lack of ability among Irish Catholics I scarcely think anyone will urge, and in this connection an amazing article, which I remember reading in an English paper, is of interest. The writer, a Unionist from Ulster, strove to show the manner in which the influence of the Vatican was making itself felt in English politics by pointing to the number of Catholics--mostly Irishmen--who held high posts in the British Diplomatic, Civil, Military, and Naval Services, the presence of whom, which he tried to indicate as a menace, but which most Englishmen view with equanimity, shows by contrast the extent to which a taboo is placed in Ireland on officials who adhere to the creed of the majority of their countrymen.

Enough has been said as to the preference shown to one caste, religious and political, to explain the reason for the fact that in Ireland the *soi-disant* loyalist has become synonymous with place-hunter. If Unionism in Ireland pervades the richer classes, it does so also in Great Britain, but in Ireland the inherent weakness of an established Church, by which its prestige and the cachet which it gives, make it a harbour of refuge for those who wish for advancement, and who think that if they creep and intrude and climb into the fold they will secure it, all these are factors, which are present in Dublin, where the Establishment is Unionism with Dublin Castle as its cathedral. Social ambition, anxiety for preferment or for an *entree* into society, are all at work to bring it to pass that a large amount of wealth and influence are ranged on the side of the Union. It is a damaging indictment which has been drawn up against the Irish landlords by Mr. T.W. Russell in his recent book, where he declares of this class, with which he fought side by side against the two Home Rule Bills, that he has come to the conclusion, slowly but surely, "that in pretending to fight for the Union these men were simply fighting for their own interests, that Rent and not Patriotism was their guiding motive,"[26] and the same charge was formulated a few years ago by Lord Rossmore, a former Grand Master of the Orange Society, when he made a public declaration that the so-called Loyalist minority in Ireland were blindly following the lead of a few professional politicians, who felt that their salaries and positions depended on the divisions and antipathies of those who should be working together for the good of their common country.

There is no aspect of the Irish question in regard to which more dust is thrown in Englishmen's eyes than that which is summed up in the one word disloyalty. The prestige of the Crown in Great Britain, where its functions are atrophied to a greater extent than in any other country in Europe, is one of the most striking features in contemporary English life. The loyalty of a nation is chiefly due to associations formed by events in its history. The extreme unpopularity of Queen Victoria in Great Britain in the earlier years of her reign, which arose from her retirement as far as possible from public life on the death of the Prince Consort, completely disappeared with the passage of years, when her age, her sex, and her private virtues overcame the antipathy which a very natural reticence on the part of a grief-stricken widow had aroused throughout Great Britain. The associations connected with the Crown in Ireland are not many. From the day on which Dutch William beat English James at the Boyne in circumstances not calculated to arouse the enthusiasm of Irish Catholics for either the lawful king or the usurper, no Sovereign set foot in Ireland till George IV. visited the country in 1824. The main function of Ireland as regards the monarchs of that time was that its pension list served to provide for the maintenance of Royal favourites as to whose income they wished no questions to be asked. Curran thundered against the Irish pension list as "containing every variety of person, from the excellence of a Hawke or a Rodney to the base situation of a lady who humbleth herself that she may be exalted." In saying this he was understating rather than overstating the case, since a very cursory inspection of the State papers will reveal the fact that the mistresses and bastards of every English King, from Charles II. to George II., drew their incomes from the Irish establishment free from the inquisitive prying of the English House of Commons. Although George III. had no need to conceal any palace scandals in this way, we have seen how the bigotry of "an old, mad, blind, despised, and dying king" postponed Emancipation for more than a generation, and one of the "princes, the dregs of their dull race," of whom Shelley went on to speak, the Duke of York, declared in the House of Lords in 1825--"I will oppose the Catholic claims whatever may be my situation in life. So help me God."

The respectful reception accorded to Queen Victoria--whose dislike of Ireland was notorious--on the very rare occasions on which she visited the country serves to show the absence of hostility to the Crown on the part of the great mass of the people, but the small number of these visits during the course of the longest reign in English history lends point to a question asked by Mr. James Bryce in a book published more than twenty years ago--Why has the most obvious service a monarch can render been so strangely neglected? When the present King visited the South of Ireland as Prince of Wales in 1885, at a time when Mr. Charles Parnell's prestige was at its zenith, he was greeted with the half humorous sally--"We will have no Prince but Charley," which at any rate contrasts favourably with the shouts of "Popish Ned," which his alleged sympathy with the popular side evoked on his visit a few years later to Londonderry.

The trivial fact that the English National Anthem was drowned at the degree day of the Royal University a few years ago by the fact that the students insisted on singing "God Save Ireland" at the end of a ceremony which even in the decorous surroundings of the Sheldonian and the Senate House is marked by a large amount of disrespectful licence, nevertheless provided the *Times* and the Unionist Press in general, for several days with a text upon which they hung their leading articles in the exploitation of their favourite theme, but no attention has been drawn in these quarters to the periodical threat of Orange exponents of a contingent loyalty to "throw the Crown into the Boyne" as a protest against the various assaults which have been made upon their prerogative by Parliament, and no mention was made in the English Press of the fact that on the day of the postponement of the coronation, owing to the illness of the King, the organ of the "disloyalists"--the *Freeman's Journal*--ended its leading article with the words "God Save the King," which were a mere expression of the feelings of the bulk of its readers.

Loyalty, said Swift, is the foible of the Irish people, and it is a remarkable fact, in spite of the detestable insult to their religious views which the law exacts from the Sovereign at his accession, that the popular welcome accorded to his Majesty, on the part of individuals, should remove any ground for the suggestion that the Crown, which Grattan always declared was an Imperial Crown, is viewed with any animus in Ireland.

That public bodies as such refuse to offer addresses of welcome is due to a conviction that to do so would be interpreted as an abdication of the popular position, an acquiescence in the *status quo*, a recognition of the system of government of which the Sovereign is head; and it must not be forgotten in this connection that, if the Sovereign is neutral, his representative in Ireland is a strong party man, and that the tendency which his Majesty has so strongly deprecated in England on more than one occasion, of employing emblems of royalty as symbols of party, has been ineradicably established by the ascendancy faction in Ireland, where the Union Jack is a party badge and God Save the King has been monopolised as a party song.

CHAPTER VIII
IRELAND AND DEMOCRACY

"A majority of Irish members turned the balance in favour of the great Reform Bill of 1832, and from that day there has been scarcely a democratic measure which they have not powerfully assisted. When, indeed, we consider the votes which they have given, the principles they have been the means of introducing into English legislation, and the influence they have exercised upon the tone and character of the House of Commons, it is probably not too much to say that their presence in the British Parliament has proved the most powerful of all agents in accelerating the democratic transformation of English politics."
--W.E.H. LECKY, ***History of England in the Eighteenth Century***, Vol. VIII., p. 483.

In Ireland perhaps more than in most countries history repeats itself. The lament of Lord Anglesea, the Lord Lieutenant, in 1831, who, finding himself a ***roi faineant***, declared that "Things are now come to that pass that the question is whether O'Connell or I shall govern Ireland," found its echo just fifty years later when Parnell enjoyed so powerful a position that writers were fain to draw a contrast between the coroneted impotence of the head of the Executive and the uncrowned power of the Irish leader.

The history of Irish representation at Westminster is one of the most curious chapters in Parliamentary annals. It is only in the last thirty years that it has reached the importance which it now possesses, although of all Liberal Governments since the great Reform Bill, that of 1880 and that which is in power to-day are the only two which have had a majority independently of the Irish vote, and it is worth remembering that the Ministry of 1880 ended its career amid the pitfalls of an Irish Coercion Bill. The maxim to beware when all men speak well of you, there has been no need to impress on Irish members since the days of Parnell, as there was at the time when under Butt's leadership a punctilious observance of Parliamentary procedure earned for the Irish representatives a contumelious respect which laughed their demands out of court.

If Parnell had not set out with the deliberate intention of making Ireland stink in the nostrils of the respectable English gentlemen who thronged the benches of the finest club in London, the protest against misgovernment would have taken the form of violence in Ireland and not of obstruction in the House of Commons. The orderly debates of Butt's time were as unproductive in showing the Irish representatives to be in earnest as were the wholesale suspensions of the later *regime* profitable, and if proof of this be needed it is to be found in the fact that in 1877 there were but eight English Home Rulers in the House of Commons, and that to attempt to secure reforms was to knock one's head against a stone wall. Speaking of the Irish representation in 1880 Mr. Gladstone made this solemn declaration:--"I believe a greater calumny, a more gross and injurious statement, could not possibly be made against the Irish nation. We believe we are at issue with an organised attempt to override the free will and judgment of the Irish nation." That bubble was pricked after the Franchise Act of 1885, when Parnell returned to the House of Commons with nearly twenty more followers than he had had before.

There is a quotation of Blackstone's from Lord Burghley to the effect that England could never be ruined but by a Parliament, and Englishmen must admit that they have paid a price, though by no means as we think too dearly, for insisting on the maintenance in their chamber, under existing conditions of a foreign body against its will and admittedly hostile to the traditions of which they are so proud. The closure, which Lord Randolph Churchill used to pronounce with elaborate emphasis as *cloture*, the curtailment of the rights of private members, the growth in the power of the Cabinet, and *pari passu* the loss in power on the part of the House, all these are instances of the way in which the sand in the bearings has been able to thwart the Parliamentary machine. "If we cannot rule ourselves," said Parnell in 1884, "we can, at least, cause them to be ruled as we choose."

In spite of the odium which it entailed, Parnell, once he had "taken his coat off," maintained this attitude regardless of the feelings it evoked, which are perhaps as well expressed as anywhere in a letter of Lord Salisbury to Lord Randolph Churchill when he declared "the instinctive feeling of an Englishman is to wish to get rid of an Irishman," to which one may reply--"What! did the hand then of the Potter shake?"

Though abuse of the plaintiff's attorney has been indulged in so often, neither English party has scorned, as from its expressions one would have expected, to make use of the Irish vote when its own career has been in danger. The appeals which in spite of this one sees addressed at intervals to the Irish leaders to abandon their attitude of **Nolo episcopari** and take Ministerial office, for which some, at any rate, of their number have by their ability been conspicuously fitted, is to ignore the fundamental protest on which this self-denying ordnance depends. The protest against the **status quo** has been traditionally made in this manner; to waive it would be tantamount to an abdication of the claims which have been so consistently made. To accept office might be to curry favour with one party or the other, but its refusal--especially as compared with its acceptance by the Irish Unionists--does much to deprive the enemy of the occasion to suggest sordid motives as reasons for the continuance of the Parliamentary agitation.

In urging his great reform, Lord Durham was wont to lay great stress on the evil effect of the English party system on Canadian politics. The party system in Great Britain acts as a corrective and an adjusting mechanism to a degree which is never known in Ireland, where the principle of government with consent of the governed has only been applied to one corner of the island.

The supreme example of so many, in which concessions have been made to Ireland in times of public danger, which had been obstinately refused in times of public security is that of Emancipation, concerning which Peel in June, 1828, reaffirmed his determination never to surrender, but in January, 1829, on the ground that five-sixths of the infantry force of the three kingdoms was engaged in police work in Ireland, introduced the Bill which obtained the Royal consent in circumstances such as to rob it of its grace and to make gratitude impossible. I am not, however, here concerned with emancipation as such, but with the set-off for its concession, under which on the principle of taking away with one hand, while giving with the other, the forty shilling freeholders, who had returned O'Connell at the Clare election, were disfranchised to the number of 200,000, and in this way was gilded the pill for the purpose of placating the English governing classes. The same principle was followed in 1841, when the Corporations of Ireland were thrown open to Catholics, for out of some sixty-five all except ten or eleven were abolished. The results of the disfranchising clauses of the Act of 1829 are to be seen in the fact that in 1850, while in England the electors were twenty-eight per cent. of the adult male population, in Ireland they were only two per cent. A Bill introduced in that year would, if it had passed into law, have raised the percentage in Ireland to fifteen. The Lords amendments altered the percentage to eight, and in its final form it was left at about ten. Instead of imposing an L8 rental qualification one of L12 was imposed, and by this means were excluded 900,000 voters who would have secured the suffrage under the lower qualification. Speaking of the Franchise, Mr. Lecky, in "Democracy and Liberty," declared that--"The elements of good government must be sought for in Ireland, on a higher electoral plane than in England." This is a matter of opinion, and I find it interesting to reflect that the ablest Conservative of my acquaintance--a Tory of the school of Lord Eldon--has on several occasions expressed to me a deliberate opinion in exact contradiction of this, to the effect that owing to the relative mental calibres of the races there is need of a higher franchise qualification in England than in either Ireland or Scotland. Speculations of this kind, however, are unprofitable, seeing that the competency of the Irish peasants as citizens has been acknowledged by the grant of a wide household suffrage safeguarded by a careful system of ballot.

When the last great extension of the franchise to householders in the country was made in 1884 there were those who asserted that its application to Ireland would be folly. Mr. W.H. Smith, the leader of the Conservatives in the House of Commons, declared that any extension of the suffrage in Ireland would lead to "confiscation of property, ruin of industry, withdrawal of capital, misery, wretchedness, and war"; the leading Whig statesman said the concession to Ireland of equal electoral privileges with those of England would be folly, but in spite of these gloomy prognostications the omission of Ireland from the scope of the Act was not proposed by Conservative statesmen, and Lord Hartington himself undertook the duty of moving the second reading of a Bill containing provisions which a few weeks before he had described as most unwise. By this Act the enfranchised inhabitants of Ireland were multiplied more than threefold, and the share of Ireland of the "two million intelligent voters" who were added to the electorate was 200,000. In the redistribution of seats which accompanied the Franchise Act of 1884 the representation of Ireland was, by an arrangement between parties, left unimpaired, and this leads me to a matter which serves, I think, to show with what speed events move and how true was that remark of Disraeli's to Lord Lytton that "in politics two years are an eternity." It is little more than two years since the burning political question was the redistribution of seats on the lines proposed by Mr. Gerald Balfour. The Unionist Press has for some years been endeavouring to rouse public opinion on this question of the alleged over-representation of Ireland in the House of Commons, and in view of the share of attention which the matter received in the closing days of the last Parliament it is as well to devote some attention to the topic.

By the Act of Union, which our opponents hold so sacred, Ireland was given 100 members in the House of Commons, and in the House of Lords 28 representative Peers, together with Bishops of the then Established Church, and it was further enacted that this should be her representation "for ever." On the population basis, which to-day is urged by Unionists as the only fair mode of apportioning representatives, Ireland was entitled at the date of the Union to many more members than in fact she obtained. Her population at that time was nearly five and a half millions, that of Great Britain was less than ten and a half millions, and so, though she could claim more than a third of the inhabitants of the three kingdoms, her representation was less than one-sixth.

By the Reform Bill of 1832 the Irish members were increased to 105. Two seats have since been disfranchised, and we thus arrive at 103--the figure at which the representation of the country stands to-day. The disproportion from which Ireland suffered at the time of the Union had become still more acute by the time of the great Reform Bill, and no one can seriously suggest that the addition of five seats redressed the inequality. According to the Census of 1831 the population of Great Britain was little over sixteen millions, and that of Ireland was seven and three-quarter millions. If these figures had formed the basis of a proportionate representation, Ireland would have had a little more than 200 members--just about double the number which she actually returned.

By an agreement between parties, as I have said, in the last Redistribution of Seats Bill--that of 1885--the number of representatives of Ireland was left unchanged, and it is only since the Conservative Party has definitely thrown in its lot as an opponent of Irish demands as formulated to-day that this method of reducing the force of their political opponents has begun to find favour amongst its members: Under the Bill of Mr. Gerald Balfour, by an ingenious arrangement of raising the limits of population under which boroughs and counties should no longer have separate representation, the scheme secured the transfer of twenty-two seats from Ireland to Great Britain.

The limit of population above which boroughs would have had to reach to maintain their separate existence was fixed at 18,500, and under this arrangement three boroughs in Ireland and six in Great Britain would have lost their seats. If the limit had been fixed at 25,000 a total of 19 seats in Great Britain and still only 3 in Ireland would have lost their member, while a minimum population of 35,000 would have disfranchised 25 boroughs in Great Britain and only 4 in Ireland.

The actual proposal was elaborately calculated so as to produce the least possible disturbance to the small boroughs in Great Britain, while securing the maximum of disfranchisement in Ireland.

At the same time the standard of population per member, which in the case of counties was fixed at 65,000, secured the disfranchisement of one Scottish county, the net disfranchisement of two English counties, and the deprivation of no less than 20 Irish counties of their member.

The grant of a new member to Belfast would have made the net loss to Ireland 22 seats, and these were to be redistributed as between England, Scotland and Wales in the proportion of 17:4:1.

These, then, are the data upon which we have to reckon. The Conservative Government, it should be added, greeted by a howl of disapproval even from its own supporters at the anomalies which it proposed to leave unredressed, appointed a Special Committee, the report of which was a posthumous child of the ministry which created it.

It is true that according to the terms of this report the borough limit of population was raised to 25,000, and the rotten boroughs which for "historical reasons"

Mr. Balfour had been loth to disfranchise, were to be swept away, but so far as we are concerned the results would have been much the same, for under its provisions Ireland would have suffered a net loss of 23 seats.

O'Connell pointed out to the Corporation of Dublin in 1843 far greater inconsistencies than can be indicated to-day. The population of Wales at that day was 800,000, that of County of Cork was more than 700,000, but the former was represented by 28 members and the latter by two; and further, he was able to point to five English counties with a total population of less than a million having 20 members to represent them, while five Irish counties with a population of over two millions returned only ten members.

If it is the mere passion for a representation proportionate to population which is evinced, it is remarkable that it has only arisen since the time at which it began to tell against Ireland, that when the boot was on the other leg there was no suggestion of redistribution on the part of Conservatives. The truth is that for Unionists the idea of paring the claws of the Irish Party offers a tempting prospect. Our position in the matter is quite plain: so long as Great Britain insists on maintaining the Act of Union she must do so consistently in the sense that it is a contract, albeit secured by chicanery, to the breach of any term of which the consent of the party which it trammelled at least is necessary. It will be answered that the Disestablishment of the Irish Church made a breach in a clause of as binding a solemnity as that which guaranteed 100 members in the Imperial Parliament "for ever." The difference is that in that case the consent of the two parties was given by their representatives in the House of Commons, and the consent and the sanction which it entails will never be secured--even possibly from Ulster Orangemen--to a proposal for the curtailment of representation in the Imperial Parliament under the present system of government.

We do not pretend for one moment that according to the rule of three we are not represented in the House of Commons by a number of members greater than that to which our population at the present moment would, taking the three kingdoms as whole, entitle us, but one must point out that the system of electing representative peers robs us of even that modicum of democratic peers of Parliament which Great Britain is able to secure, and we repeat the argument of Mr. Gladstone that the distance of Dublin from Westminster and the consequent deafness of the House of Commons to Irish opinion is to a slight extent redressed by the small excess--calculated on lines of proportion--which Irish representation secures at Westminster.

At any rate one has the satisfaction of knowing where one stands in the matter, and one is aware that one part of the Conservative programme to be applied whenever that party returns to power is that of which someone has spoken as the detestable principle that to keep Ireland weak is the most convenient way of governing her. And here let me in parenthesis remark on one fact in the conditions of Irish representation--namely, its solidarity. It is one of the commonplaces of politics that office is the best adhesive which a party can enjoy, and the cold shades of opposition are apt too often to dissolve a unity which in office appeared secure. We have seen it of late years in the demoralisation of the Liberals, who, after the retirement of Mr. Gladstone, fell to pieces as a party only on their resignation of office in 1895; we are seeing it now in the disintegration of the Unionists ever since the debacle of the general election.

There is a term which the Unionist Press is never tired of using in connection with the Irish Party, the "fissiparous tendency" of which it is passionately fond of dinning into English ears, regardless of the many cleavages which have occurred in English parties in the last fifty or even twenty years.

Those divisions which there have been in the Nationalist ranks have been for the most part concerned, not with measures, but with men, and even so it cannot be urged that they have been more than temporary in duration. The strength of wrist which has been displayed during the last eight years by Mr. John Redmond in leading the United Irish Party has been a source of admiration to all. "You need greater qualities," said Cardinal de Retz, "to be a party leader than to be Emperor of the Universe." Much wisdom is demanded of an Irish leader in deciding the tactical questions arising from the vicissitudes of British parties. That Irish Nationalists and British Liberals do not see eye to eye on several points of policy is well known. It may well be urged that no better proof of the unnatural form of the polity which holds the field can be adduced than is to be found in the political allies of the two parties in Ireland; for the Catholics, democratic though they may be, are not associated with the party to which the traditions of a Church, the most Conservative force in Europe, one might think would ally them, and the Orange Presbyterians, who are at heart Radicals, are divorced from their dissenting kinsmen in Great Britain and form the tail of the Conservative Party. Hence it is that we have fallen between two stools, and University reform, to the principle of which Lord Salisbury, Lord Randolph Churchill, Sir Michael Hicks Beach, Mr. Balfour, and Mr. Wyndham have been pledged, was shelved over and over again at the bidding of the Ulster Unionists, while the Conservative House of Lords thwarted the application of the principles of self-government to which a Liberal majority in the House of Commons gave its consent. Can anyone, in view of these facts, feel surprised that "a plague on both your Houses" expresses the feelings of the Irish people.

Those nice people, to whom political barter is abhorrent, who at the time of the general election deprecated the "sale for a price" of the Nationalist vote, for so they were pleased to call what occurred, closed their eyes to the very obvious price of the Orange vote in the last Parliament, which took the form of the retirement from office of Mr. Wyndham, on failure to secure which, as the Orange leader declared--"Ulster would have to call upon her reserves," meaning, one must suppose, that the Irish Unionist office holders who were members of the Ministry in numbers altogether disproportionate to their strength would be called upon by the Orange Lodges to hand in their seals.

English Catholics are apt to say that if the Irish people in England had been directed by the Nationalist Party to vote for Conservative candidates the safety of Catholic schools would thereby have been safeguarded, but they forget that to put a Conservative Party in power would be to give a blank cheque to a party pledged to cut down the Irish, and *pari passu* the Catholic, representation in the House of Commons. That the fate of the Catholic voluntary schools in England is a direct concern of the Irish members is admitted by all who are aware how vast a majority of the Catholic poor in Great Britain are Irish, if not by birth, at any rate by origin.

That the efforts in this connection of the Irish Party were appreciated by the head of the Catholic Church in England is seen by the very gracious letter which Archbishop Bourne addressed to Mr. Redmond at the end of the session of 1906, and it is significant that the letter of protest against the Archbishop's action in regard to the moderate counsels to secure a compromise on the part of the Irish, which was sent by certain English Catholic Peers to the Catholic bishops of Great

Britain, was treated by the latter, with only two exceptions, with the contumelious neglect which its disloyalty, the outcome of Tory *intransigeance*, deserved.

English Catholics, among whom knights harbingers and banneret bearers of the Primrose League are numerous, who have leant all their weight in the scale to maintain the Protestant ascendancy in Ireland, have been ever ready when occasion arose to appeal to the religious loyalty of the Irish members to support their interests. Their position has not been very dignified, and its fruits will perhaps be seen if the reduction of the Irish representation enters the sphere of practical politics. Party loyalty will claim their support, but at the same time they will realise that if they give it they will be taking a step to reduce the only body in the House of Commons which can ever hope to represent Catholic principles and uphold Catholic interests.

I do not know whether it struck many people in the course of the general election that the country in which the elections made the least difference was the one of the three kingdoms in which politics claim most public attention. There was a monotony in the unopposed returns, and, in the result, in the place of 80 Nationalists, 1 Liberal, and 22 Unionists, there appeared 83 Nationalists, 3 Liberals, and 18 Unionists, To appreciate the full force of these numbers one must realise, moreover, that of the Unionists in both cases, two out of the total represent University seats, the Conservative nature of which, whether in England, Ireland, or Scotland, is one of the features of political life which is, it appears, immutable. A study of the results shows that Unionism is in a minority in Ulster. There are in the present Parliament 15 Unionists as against 15 Nationalists, who, with 3 Liberals, go to make up the 33 members sitting at Westminster for that province.

These figures relieve me from the necessity of entering a caveat against the use of the word Ulster as though the whole province were Unionist. Virtually, all that is Unionist in Ireland is in Ulster, but it is very far from the truth to say that all Ulster is Unionist. Not one of the Counties of Donegal, Tyrone, Monaghan, or Cavan, out of the whole nine of which the province consists, returns a Unionist. In the three Counties of Down, Armagh, and Fermanagh, the representation is divided, and as for the two Counties of Londonderry and Antrim, which are ordinarily the sole strongholds of the Orangemen, even in them a breach was effected in West Belfast, where the Labour vote returned a Nationalist for the first time since Mr. Sexton sat for it from 1886-1892.

The obviousness and permanence of the Irish representation in Parliament is apt to cause its significance to be forgotten. "It doesn't matter what we say, but for God's sake *let* us be consistent," Lord Palmerston is reported to have said concerning some question of policy at a Cabinet Council. The Irish people, its worst enemies must admit, have been consistent for the last thirty years in the demands which their representatives have made ever since Isaac Butt crystallised the Irish antagonism to the ***status quo*** in the "Home Government Association," which he formed and on the programme of which he returned, after the general election of 1874, with 59 followers in the House of Commons, pledged to support the demand for Irish self-government. If we exclude the fact that the extension of the franchise in 1884 increased the number of the popular representatives to more than 80, it is true to say that since then there has been no change in the position of Irish representation, just as there has been none in Irish demands. The Liberalism of Non-conformist Wales, and to a lesser degree of Presbyterian Scotland, are traditional, but their adherence to one side or the other in politics appears vacillating if one studies the election figures, compared with the unwavering permanence of the Irish returns. When Lord Dudley declared that his aim as Viceroy would be to govern Ireland according to Irish ideas a shout of protest arose from the ***Times*** and the Irish Unionists, whose organ the ***Times*** has constituted itself. Let us clear our minds of cant on the matter, and ask in view of this open disclaimer of the democratic principles which are so much vaunted in England, for what reason is maintained the travesty of representative government, the decrees of which it is frankly avowed are to be ignored? Every English Liberal must be impressed by the fact that the party which has tried to arrogate to itself the sole claim to be thought Imperialist has scouted Home Rule resolutions passed again and again by the legislatures of every one of the self-governing colonies. It was at Montreal that Parnell was first hailed as the uncrowned king of Ireland, and what is more, that great apostle of Imperialism, Cecil Rhodes, so far from seeing in Home Rule the first step towards the dismemberment of the Empire, signified his sympathy with the movement in that direction by giving Mr. Parnell a cheque for L10,000 for the Irish Party funds on the one condition that he would support the retention of some of the Irish members in the Imperial Parliament, as tending in the direction of Imperial federation.

Twenty years ago, when the present good feelings of England towards the United States were not in existence, it was easy, as it has been since on the occasions on which relations have been strained over the Venezuelan and Alaskan questions, to denounce the aid granted to the National movement by the Irish in America. To-day things are different; these denunciations are not heard, and, moreover, as much aid and encouragement has been forthcoming in a proportional degree from the colonies of the British Empire as from the Republic of North America. As a matter of fact there are twice as many people of Irish blood in the United States as there are in Ireland, and thus, when in 1880 Congress threw open its doors and invited Parnell to address it on the Irish question, it was acting in accordance with the sentiments of a vast number of the citizens of the United States.

The Government of Lord North roused the American Colonies by attempts to rule them against their own wishes, and the result was that they secured their independence. Austria refused self-government to Italy, and in consequence lost its Italian territory, while Hungary, to which it granted the boon, was retained in the dual monarchy. Spain, by refusing autonomy to her colonies, suffered the loss of South. America, Cuba, Puerto Rica, and the Philippines, and the action of Holland in the same way led to the separation from it of the kingdom of the Belgians.

All these are cases in point, but the most interesting parallel is that of Lower Canada, which, like Ireland, is Celtic and Catholic, and is, moreover, a French-speaking province. There, too, there was a struggle between races, and it was only by "merging"--as Lord Durham expressed it--"the odious animosities of origin in the feelings of a nobler and more comprehensive nationality" that peace was restored. The Tory Cabinet of Peel gave Canada Parliamentary Government, and proclaimed rebels became Ministers of the Crown, and who is there who will contend that the application of the maxim "trust in the people" of that great Imperial statesman, Lord Durham, was not justified by the results of the grant of self-government not to a peaceful and loyal colony, but to one which was boiling with discontent and rebellion. Twelve years after Lord Durham's experiment, the Government of Lord Derby gave Australia similar institutions, and that fact alone shows how successful the policy had proved. Great Britain has just given representative government to the Transvaal and the Orange River Colony. Within five years of the peace of Vereeniging the pledges of that compact were honourably fulfilled in spite of the forebodings of one of the political parties, and Louis Botha, the Premier of one of the new colonies, is the most distinguished of the generals who less than six years ago were leading their armies against those of Great Britain.

England has realised that it is only by government with the consent of the governed that she can maintain her colonies, and the contrast between her treatment of Ireland and that of her colonies is to be seen in the fact that to them is extended the protection of the British fleet, while they are at the same time left free to legislate in the matter of trade, to deal with their own defence, and all the while contribute nothing to Imperial charges.

The failure of the policy of North and the success of that of Durham are apparent. The former has been applied in Ireland, although the country has consistently cried out for the latter. How long do those with whom the last word in government is the policy applied to-day, imagine that they can govern a country at the bayonet's edge in such a way that she has neither the weight of an equal nor the freedom of a dependency? Lord Rosebery, whose liberalism may be described in the same terms as those in which Disraeli denounced the Conservatism of Peel--"the mule of politics which engenders nothing"--has more than once in the last few years declared his hostility to the principle of Irish self-government, and the explanation of his position which he offers is that the absence of loyalty on the part of Ireland is the obstacle which stands in the way of his advocacy of such a policy. One may well ask in reply whether Lord Rosebery is aware of the complete absence of loyalty at the time when Canada was granted self-government, and the state of feeling towards England in the new South African colonies two years ago is a further case in point; but the most pertinent question which can be asked of Lord Rosebery is on what ground he makes this his condition precedent, in view of the fact that the loyalty or disloyalty of Irishmen stands exactly as it did in 1886 and 1893, in both of which years Lord Rosebery was a member of the Ministries which introduced Home Rule Bills into Parliament.

That hostility is evinced by large sections of Irishmen to England, as well as by Englishmen to Ireland, and that much sympathy was felt, as it was by the most distinguished of the members of the present Cabinet, for the South African Republics, which Irishmen regarded as struggling nationalities like their own, I am not concerned to deny. The same feeling of hostility, as I have already said, was rampant at the time of the Crimean war, and may be expected to continue till the end of the present system of government arrives; but to those who, for party purposes, declare that they see a risk that possible European complications would be accentuated for Great Britain to the point of danger by the proximity of an Ireland with a Parliament in Dublin, the answer is, that it is difficult to conceive a state of affairs more fraught with danger to England than would be found in the existence during a great war of an adjacent island which has been haughtily denied that mode of government which she claims, and which in the troubles of the other country will see an opportunity of extracting by threats and from fear in an hour of peril that which she was unable to secure by other means in the day of prosperity. One may well ask whether this prospect is one to which Great Britain can look forward with calmness, that she should have to legislate at fever heat to cope with the contingencies of the moment with no well-ordered scheme of things; not that way lies an end by which she will secure peace conceived in the spirit of peace.

CHAPTER IX
IRELAND AND GREAT BRITAIN

> "In reason all government without the consent of the governed is the very definition of slavery; but in fact eleven men well armed will certainly subdue one single man in his shirt.... Those who have used to cramp liberty have gone so far as to resent even the liberty of complaining, although a man upon the rack was never known to be refused the liberty of roaring as loud as he thought fit."--JONATHAN SWIFT.

The loss of her language by Ireland was, politically, the worst calamity which could have befallen her, for it lent colour to the otherwise unsupported assertion that she was a mere geographical expression in no way differing from the adjoining island. The manner in which the revival of the Irish tongue has been taken up by the whole country with, literally, the support of peasant and peer is one of the most remarkable phenomena of modern Irish life. That it has any direct political significance is untrue, for the aim of its pioneers in the Gaelic League has been fulfilled, and it remains strictly non-sectarian and non-political. From the purely utilitarian point of view, no doubt a polytechnic could provide a dozen subjects in which a more profitable return could be made for the money and time invested than does the study of Gaelic, but book-keeping or shorthand would not have roused the enthusiasm which this revival of a half dead language has evoked and which is incidentally an educative movement in that the learning of a new language is of a direct value as a mental training, while as a social organisation it has done more in inculcating a public spirit and a proper pride than could otherwise possibly have been achieved. The revival of the Czech language when almost dead, at the beginning of the nineteenth century, and the eminent success of bi-lingualism in Flanders, are hopeful signs for the preservation of a National characteristic, the disappearance of which would have been welcomed only by those who hold that Ireland as a nationality has no existence apart from Great Britain, and the preservation of which will produce the mental alertness characteristic of a bi-lingual people.

The temperance work done by the Gaelic League in providing occupation of a pleasant nature and social intercourse of a harmless kind is one of its chief titles to distinction, for in this aspect it has encouraged the preservation of Irish songs, music, dances, and games. One other thing it, and it alone, can do. One-half of the emigrants from Ireland go on tickets or money sent from friends in the United States, and in my opinion one of the most powerful influences in staying the present lamentable tide in that direction will be to foster in the branches in America the notion that the time has come when every Irishman and woman who can by any possible means do so should be persuaded to remain in Ireland, and not to emigrate.

The ridiculous situation which was allowed by successive Governments to persist in the Gaelic-speaking districts of the West until a few years ago, in which teachers were appointed to the schools without any knowledge of the only language spoken by the children whom they purported to educate, is well illustrated by the statement on the part of one of their number to the effect that it took two years to extirpate, to "wring" the Irish speech out of the children and replace it, one must suppose, by English, and this process, it must be remembered, was gone through with the children of a peasantry whom a distinguished French publicist-- M.L. Paul-Dubois--has described as perhaps the most intellectual in Europe.

It is characteristic of English government that, whereas from 1878 onwards Irish figured in the programme of the National Board, and Government grants were made for proficiency therein as in other subjects, one of the last acts of the late Government was to withdraw these grants for the teaching of Irish. So long as there was no large number of people anxious to learn Gaelic in Ireland, Government gave help towards its study, but the very moment in which, with the rise of the Gaelic League, the number learning the language began to increase, Government put its foot down and proceeded to discourage it by a withdrawal of grants. The order effecting this was withdrawn by Mr. Bryce. The signal failure of the attempts made to kill the Gaelic movement with ridicule, on the part of those who saw in it an evil-disposed attempt to stop the Anglicising of the country, was as conspicuous as has been the ill success of the petty tyranny of the Inland Revenue authorities, who took out summonses against those who had their names engraved on their dogs' collars in Gaelic. Trinity College has had for half a century two scholarships and a prize in Gaelic attached to its Divinity School, and the fact that the ultimate trust of the fund of its Gaelic Professorship on cesser of appointment is to a Protestant proselytising society shows the interest which has actuated the study of Gaelic in that foundation, and its attitude towards the Gaelic League found expression in Dr. Mahaffy, one of its most distinguished scholars, who, having failed to kill the movement with ridicule, changed his line and declared that the revival of Gaelic would be unreasonable and dishonest if it were not impossible.

In spite of this, the success of the League, which was only established in 1893, is astonishing. In 1900 it consisted of 120 branches; to-day there are more than 1,000. The circulation of Gaelic books published under its auspices is over 200,000 a year. In the year 1899 it was taught in 100 Primary Schools, it is now taught in 3,000.

The number of people, including adults, learning Irish in evening continuation classes was in 1899 little over 1,000, and is to-day over 100,000.

The circumstance that in London on the Sunday nearest St. Patrick's Day a service with Gaelic hymns and a Gaelic sermon is conducted every year, and has been conducted for the last three years, at the Cathedral at Westminster, and is attended by 6,000 or 7,000 Irish people, and that last year Dr. Alexander held a Gaelic service in a Protestant Cathedral in Dublin, should do much to show the manner in which the movement is spreading among all classes, and to indicate that it will in time demolish that false situation by which, for the greater part of the Continent, Ireland has been looked upon as merely an island on the other side of England to be seen through English glasses.

That strange recuperative power which the country has evinced at intervals in her history is, without a doubt, once again asserting itself, and a new spirit of restlessness and of effort, which in no sense can be supposed to supplant, or to do more than to supplement, political aspirations, is making itself felt.

It is doing so in a number of different directions, but the ultimate aim of all the forces which are at work may be said to be, in a cant phrase, to make it as much an object to desire to live in the country as hitherto it has been to die for it.

The inculcation of a spirit of self-reliance, the discouragement among the poorer classes of the notion that emigration is an object at which one should aim, the destruction among the richer of that spirit which is known at "West British," and which implies an apologetic air on the part of its owner for being Irish at all, these are among the effects of the new movement.

The desire to see Ireland Irish, and not a burlesque of what is English, is its *raison d'etre*, and that it has made progress along the lines mapped out, the Gaelic League, from which it gains its driving force, the literary revival, and the movement for industrial development bear ample witness.

From the impression made by a few wits, English people have jumped to the conclusion that as a people we are specially blessed with a sense of humour, a curious *non sequitur* which the restraint, consciously or unconsciously inculcated by the Gaelic League, is likely to make more apparent, for it is killing that conception of the Irishman as typically a boisterous buffoon with intervals of maudlin sentimentality which the stage and the popular song have so long been content to depict without protest from us, and which left Englishmen with feelings not more exalted than those of their sixteenth and seventeenth century ancestors, to whom "mere Irish" was a term of opprobrium.

In their appeals to sentiment, Englishmen have not been more successful. The appointment of Mr. Wyndham to the Irish Office was hailed by them as a certain success on the ground of his descent from Lord Edward Fitzgerald, a traitor, on their own showing, descent from whom one would have thought should have been rather concealed than advertised. They waxed sentimental over the bravery of the Irish soldiers in the South African war, among which the achievements of the Inniskillings at Pieter's Hill and the Connaught Rangers at Colenso were only surpassed by the Dublin Fusiliers at Talana Hill, out of a thousand of whom only three hundred survived. But the strange thing was that while English people in honour of these men wore shamrock on St. Patrick's Day, just as in the case of the Crimea, the sympathy of their own country was not on the side upon which they fought, and the people of their country looked upon the Irish soldiers as *condottieri* fighting in an alien cause. One cannot draw up an indictment against a whole nation, and if this be treason in the opinion of Englishmen, one can only reply that to commit the unpardonable sin against the body politic there must be something more on the part of a people than a continuance of feelings towards a state of affairs against which they have always protested, and in which they have never acquiesced.

Historically we have been the home of lost causes, and the fact that so many of the national heroes of Ireland have ended their lives in failure has had no small effect in bringing it to pass that there, at any rate, it is not true to say that nothing succeeds like success. Hugh O'Neill, Red Hugh O'Donnell, Owen Roe O'Neill, Sarsfield, Wolfe Tone, Grattan, the Young Irelanders, O'Connell, Butt, Parnell, not one of these ended his career amid the glamour of achieved success, and the result of this, I think, is an irresponsibility which looks not so much to the probability of the fruition of movements as to their inception; and, after all, a flash in the pan is apt to do more harm than good.

To this fact I attribute the circumstance that there has always been a small section of the population to which the ordinary methods of constitutional agitation have appeared feeble and unavailing, but to understand to the full the reason for it one must realise that if there have been three insurrections in the history of the United Parliament, there has twelve times in the same course of time been famine, that parent of despairing violence, throughout the country.

The ordinary Englishman seeing in the state a polity maintained by a long tradition, which has undergone change gradually and in measured progress, in which agitation, when it has been rife as it was before the first Reform Bill, has died down on redress of grievances, almost as soon as it has arisen has no conception of the relative, and indeed absolute, unstable state of equilibrium in the affairs of Ireland.

The fact that one has to go back to the battle of Sedgemoor for the last occasion when in anything dignified by a higher name than riot, blood has been shed in England; the fact that when a retiring English Attorney-General appointed his son to a third-rate position in the legal profession an outcry arose in which the salient feature was surprise that so flagrant a job should have been perpetrated, are indications of what I mean when I say that English people are in every circumstance of their outlook precluded from eliminating in their view of Irish affairs that deep-seated conviction, which in the case of their own country is founded on indisputable fact, that radical change in the well-ordered evolution of the State is out of keeping with the sequence which has hitherto held sway, and in so far as it is so is a thing to be guarded against and avoided.

In Ireland no one can claim to see a similar gradual metamorphosis in the light-of the history of the last one hundred, or even fifty, years, Radicalism, experimentalism, empiricism have been let loose on every institution of the country, and it is only when we take the greatest common measure of the results that we can see that the upshot has been on the whole rather good than bad. When Parnell declared that while accepting Mr. Gladstone's Home Rule proposals he must nevertheless state definitely that no one could set a limit to the march of a nation, he was stating an axiom which is every day illustrated by English statesmen of either party when they say, on the one hand, that the refusal, and on the other hand the concession, of certain fiscal proposals will lead to the dismemberment of the Empire. What can be stated in cold blood as a possible contingency in the case of, say, Canada or New Zealand has only to be adumbrated in that of Ireland to be denounced, not as a justifiable retort to the flouting of local demands, but as a treasonable aspiration to be put down with a strong hand.

The new aspect of Imperial responsibility as entailing on the mother country a position not of contempt of, but rather of deference to, the wishes of the colonies cannot but have a direct bearing on Anglo-Irish relations.

It is the greatest feature in Parnell's achievement that he succeeded in persuading ardent spirits to lay aside other weapons, while he strove what he could do by stretching the British Constitution to the utmost, linking up as he did all the forces of discontent to a methodical use of the Parliamentary machine. In the very depth of the winter of our discontent, in 1881, when he was in Kilmainham Gaol, crime became most rampant; in truth--as he had grimly said would be the case--Captain Moonlight had taken his place, and in the following year when he was let out of gaol it was expressly to slow down the agitation. More than one Prime Minister has had to echo those words of the Duke of Wellington of seventy years ago--"If we don't preserve peace in Ireland we shall not be a Government," and the periodic recrudescence of lawlessness which the island has seen has, it is freely admitted, forced the hands of Governments which were inflexible in the face of mere constitutional opposition.

The latest aspect which this anti-constitutional movement has taken in Ireland is what is known as Sinn Fein, which adopts a rigid attitude of protest against the existing condition of things, and which declares that the recognition of the *status quo* involved in any acquiescence in the present mode of government is a betrayal of the whole position. The existence of this spirit, which is entirely negligible outside two or three large towns, is not surprising; although it advocates a passive resistance it is the direct descendant of the party which advocated physical force in the past, and in so far as it proposes to use morally defensible weapons it is likely to have the more driving power. The consistent opposition which the Catholic Church offered to revolutionary violence and her sympathy with constitutionally-expressed Parliamentary agitation have resulted in an anti-clerical colour which this new movement has acquired, and to this, force is added by the measure of strength which it has gained among a certain number of young Protestants in Belfast, whose fathers must turn in their graves at this reversal of opinion on a question which was to them a *chose jugee*, a veritable article of faith. The proposals of Sinn Fein include a boycott of all English institutions in Ireland, educational and of other kinds, the abandonment of the attendance of Irish members in the Imperial Parliament at Westminster, elections to which Sinn Fein candidates are, if necessary, to contest on the undertaking that if elected they will not take the oath at Westminster, but will attend a self-constituted National Council in Dublin, under the control of which a system of National education and of National arbitration courts, in addition to a National Stock Exchange, will be established. To develop Irish industries this body, it is suggested, will appoint in foreign ports Irish Consuls, completely independent of the British Consular service, who will attend to the interests and the development of Irish trade. Lastly, the most practical of their proposals lies in the discouragement of recruiting, a movement which, if applied on a large scale, would have a remarkable effect on the resources of the three kingdoms under a voluntary system of military service.

These proposals, which, until a Gaelic name was thought necessary for their acceptance in Ireland, were known as the Hungarian policy, are admittedly based on the success of the struggle for Hungarian autonomy which culminated in 1867, but the fact which the advocates of the application of this policy to Ireland omit to mention, is that Hungary was face to face with a divided and distracted Austria, defeated by the Prussians at Sadowa, while in the case of Ireland we are concerned with a united Great Britain, which has shown no great signs of diminution in her power. A closer parallel than that of Hungary is to be found in the case of Bohemia, which, in respect of general social conditions and the proportion of national to hostile forces, bore a much stronger resemblance to Ireland, and which adopted in 1867 a policy of withdrawal of its representatives from a hostile legislature with results so disastrous that after a few years she returned to the methods which the Sinn Fein party are anxious to make an end of in Ireland.

All foreign parallels, however, are apt to be misleading, but Irishmen have only to remember the fact that the secession of Grattan and his followers from the Irish Parliament in 1797 paved the way for the passing of the Act of Union to find in it a warning against what is the main plank in the platform of Sinn Fein--"the policy of withdrawal"--which, moreover, would leave the control of Irish legislation to the tender mercies of such Irish members as Mr. Walter Long and Mr. William Moore, which would further involve the condemnation of the policy pursued by every Irish leader since the Union, and would mean the abandonment of the weapon by which every Irish reform has been wrested from English prejudice--namely, an independent party in the House of Commons, backed up by a vigorous organisation in Ireland.

For the rest, those who have read the high-flown manifestoes of the Sinn Fein party will be concerned to look around for the result of the proposal which they have been preaching for the last three years, and if they find nothing but a ridiculous mouse in the matter of achievement will be inclined to declare that not a mountain but a molehill has been in labour. It is a singular fact that although since the general election there have been no less than ten by-elections in Ireland, of which only two were in "safe" Unionist seats, in no single instance have the advocates of the policy of abstention from attendance from Westminster had the courage to go to the polls with a candidate of their own. We are told by the exponents of the new policy that they are sweeping the country before them, but the only certain data which Irishmen have as to its popularity is that in ten per cent. of the constituencies in the country, the only ones to which any test has been applied, in no instance has Sinn Fein dared to show its face at the hustings.

Two Irish members, it is true, resigned uncompromisingly from the Irish Party and joined the new organisation in disgust at the scope of the Irish Council Bill. Sir Thomas Esmonde, who expressed his intention of resigning, was, with what it must have come to regret as indecent haste, elected a member of the Sinn Fein organisation, but within a few weeks declared his willingness "to act with the Parliamentary Party, or any other set of men who put the National question in the forefront," and went on to express his opinion that the chances of a Sinn Fein candidate in his constituency of North Wexford would be nil.

So far at any rate Sinn Feiners must admit that "***beacoup de bruit, pen de fruit***" sums up their action in regard to Irish affairs. Any success in propagandism which they may have achieved is to be traced to a natural impatience, especially among ***dilletante*** politicians, whose experience is purely academic, at the slowness of the Parliamentary machine in effecting reforms, but any force which it possesses is discounted by the fact that men whose views are extreme in youth tend to become the most moderate with advancing years--a fact of which a classic example is to be found in the career of Sir Charles Gavan Duffy, one of the most distinguished of the Young Irelanders, who, after a brilliant career in Australia, returned to European his old age and spent several years in the attempt to persuade Conservatives to adopt the policy of Home Rule--a propaganda on his part to which the episode of Lord Carnarvon bears witness, and which was advocated by him in the ***National*** and ***Contemporary Reviews*** in 1884 and 1885. It may well be that the political groundlings who are at present the backbone of the Sinn Fein movement will, when they gain political experience, alter their views in as complete a manner. One can draw an English parallel to this movement in Ireland. There are in the former, as in the latter, country a certain limited number of people who hold extreme political views, which in the case of the English are pure socialism. The English extremists have been so far successful as to secure the return of one Member of Parliament in full sympathy with their aspirations. The Irish extremists have not so far dared to put to the test their chance of obtaining even one Parliamentary ewe lamb. Without the advantage which the English ***intransigeants*** possess, of a few weeks' knowledge on the part of one person of the inside working of Parliamentary government, in exactly the same manner as do the Englishmen of the same type, these Irishmen spend their time reviling popular representatives as ignorant, venal, and beneath contempt. A prophet who, on the basis of the election of Mr. Grayson, foretold an imminent dissolution of the democratic forces in Great Britain, would in truth have more ground on which to base his forecast than has one who from the nebulous movements of the Sinn Fein party, arrives at an analogous conclusion in the case of Ireland. That the political landmarks in Ireland have in the last few years shifted is obvious to the most superficial observer. The devolutionist secession from orthodox Unionism, the Independent Orange Lodge represented by Mr. Sloan, the "Russellite" Ulster tenant-farmers, and the rise of a democratic vote in Belfast regardless of the strife of sects, all serve as indications of this fact; but let it be noted that while we have evidences in these directions of the forces at work in the disintegration of the old Orange strongholds, we have no such obvious indications of the upheaval going on in the traditional Nationalist Party, save only the mere *ipse dixit* of the very people who assure us that they themselves are making it felt. There is every reason to suppose that the Sinn Fein movement, in so far as it consists of passive resistance, will be regarded by the Irish people as merely doing nothing. They could understand a non-Parliamentary action were it replaced by physical force, and the weakness of passive resistance lies precisely in this, that the logical result of its failure is an appeal to armed revolt which no man in his senses can in modern conditions in Ireland think possible, or, if possible, calculated to be other than disastrous. The attempt which the Sinn Fein organisation has consistently, if unsuccessfully, made to arrogate to itself all credit for the progress of the Gaelic League and of the Industrial Revival, is singularly disingenuous in view of the assistance which both those movements have received and are receiving from the Parliamentary Party and its allies. The provisions of the Merchandise Marks Act, and the fact that through the agency of members of the Irish Party the Foreign Office has directed British Consuls abroad to publish separately the returns of Irish imports, which have hitherto been lost by their inclusion in the returns under the one head "British," will do far more for the development of the Irish export trade than the well-meaning but academic resolutions of their critics; and in the matter of social reform I have yet to learn that any body of men have done such good work for their country as have the Irish members by the passing into law, on their initiative, of the Labourers Act, by which nearly half a million of the Irish population will be rescued from conditions of life which, with a population lacking the religious sense of the Irish poor, would have resulted in absolute moral degradation.

I have spoken throughout of the exponents of Sinn Fein as of a party, but it is difficult to find the common measure of agreement which such a term connotes in the heterogeneous elements which for the moment call themselves by the same name. We read of old Fenians, who have ever hankered after physical force, presiding over meetings to expound passive resistance in which young Republicans from Belfast rub shoulders with men whose ideal is vaguely expressed as repeal--a return one must suppose to that anomalous constitution of Grattan's Parliament in which, while the legislature was independent the Executive was not responsible thereto, but went out of office with the Ministry in the Parliament at Westminster.

Irish Parliamentary candidates are selected under a system in which the party caucus has far less share than in any part of the three kingdoms. They have behind them the credentials of popular election which are not possessed by a single one of the self-constituted group of critics who assail them; and one need only say that vague, unfounded charges as to political probity, in no instance substantiated by a single shred of proof, do not redound to the credit of those who frame them.

When the advocates of Sinn Fein can point to a record of services as disinterested and as consistent as those of the Irish Parliamentary Party, when they can produce evidence of work in the immediate past as fruitful for the good of their country as the Labourers Act, the Town Tenants Act, and the Merchandise Marks Act, they will have some ground upon which to claim a hearing from their countrymen. Till then they have no cause to throw stones at those who are honestly working for the good of their country, although they do not proclaim themselves on the housetops the only patriotic section of the Irish people.

Not one of the advocates of this bloodless war which they propose has, so far as I am aware, in spite of three years spent in preaching on the subject, refused to pay income tax, the only tax resistance to which is possible in Ireland. Those who hold Civil Service appointments under the British Crown have not in a single instance, unless I am mistaken, handed in their resignations. These are the criticisms which they inevitably draw down on their heads by stooping to make imputations as to men whose services to the country should put them above reach of anything of the kind. Within the last few months two of the leaders of Sinn Fein appeared, in the course of a few weeks--the one as plaintiff, the other as defendant--represented by a Tory counsel, in the Four Courts in Dublin, before a member of a foreign judiciary, which on their fundamental axiom should be taboo. The reason is to be found, perhaps, in the fact that they have not yet devised a means by which attachment and committal for contempt of their proposed amateur tribunals will be made effectual. The method by which the resolutions of the National Council are to be carried into effect has not yet been explained, nor have the means by which they will acquire a sanction in so far as their breach will involve the offender in a punishment. We have yet to learn what guarantee there is that the consuls in foreign parts, whom they propose to establish and maintain by voluntary subscription, will be given any facilities by the countries in which they are stationed, without which their presence in those foreign countries would be of no service whatever.

Half a century ago a great voluntary effort, which may well be called Sinn Fein, was made in the foundation of the Catholic University in Dublin. In spite of the glamour of John Henry Newman's name it was crippled from the fact of the poverty of the country on the voluntary contributions of which it had to depend. One may well ask if the exponents of the new policy have any confidence that the same obstacle will not stand in the way of more than a trivial fraction of their extensive, and as I think Utopian, proposals. The No Rent Manifesto fell flat in the midst of the very bitterest struggle of the land war. Does anyone think it likely that we shall see behind the doctrinaires of the Sinn Fein group a country united in cold blood to repudiate its obligations under the Land Purchase and Labourers' Acts?

The Irish people are under no illusions as to the advocates of Sinn Fein, and will, I am convinced, refuse to judge it on its own valuation. If for no other reason its exponents would be suspect in that they have not scrupled to assure a sympathetic Orange audience of the fact that they are on the point of rending asunder the allegiance of Ireland to the National cause. While protesting aloud their patriotism they have not thought it incompatible with their declarations to flood the columns of the Unionist Press--the most hostile to the democracy of their country--with expositions of their views, coupled with strident denunciations of their Nationalist opponents.

Their tirades have been received with open arms by the Orangemen as affording a weapon in the division of their common enemy, by which may be maintained that *de facto*, if not *de jure*, ascendancy, which in spite of the ballot, the extended franchise, and local government, persists in Ireland. But, on the other hand, as has been well said, the fact is not lost on the great bulk of the Irish people that it is from the Sinn Fein section--the little coterie which professes to stand for every sort of idealism--that all the imputations and innuendoes have come.

This extreme school, of course, will in no sense be pleased by ameliorative legislation as applied by this or any other Government, because the worse England treats Ireland the stronger will be their position, and every concession gained by the country is so much ground cut from under their feet; but the policy of refusing all attempts at piecemeal improvement, on the ground that a complete reversal of the existing system is called for, may be magnificent, and on this there must be two opinions, but it is not practical politics which will commend itself to the ordinary Irishman. "Men," wrote Edmund Burke more than a hundred years ago, "do not live upon blotted paper; the favourable or the unfavourable mind of the rulers is of more consequence to a nation than the black letter of any statute." Irish people are not likely to fail to realise this, and the experience of the past is such as to show that remedial legislation has been powerless to stay the National demand, and concessions, so far from putting a period to the appeals of the people for the control of their own affairs, have rather increased the vehemence of their demand, for with democracy, as with most things, *l'appetit vient en mangeant*.

As against the body which we have been considering one hears people speaking of the liberal school of Unionists--the rise of which is so marked a product of recent years in Ireland--as a body who represent the moderate section of opinion, the demands of which are reasonable and comprise all that the Liberal Party can be expected to concede; and among this section of recent writers on Irish politics three stand out prominently by reason of their position and of their proposals:--Mr. T.W. Russell, in "Ireland and the Empire," preached with cogent force the need for the last step in the expropriation of the Irish landlords, the one great obstacle, in his eyes, to a prosperous and contented Ireland. In the economic field Sir Horace Plunkett has pleaded, in "Ireland in the New Century," for the salvation of the Irish race by the development of industries; while in the political sphere Lord Dunraven, in "The Outlook in Ireland," has urged the pressing need for the closer association of Irishmen with the government of their own country. I am not concerned to deny the remarkable fact which these volumes indicate in the change of view on the part of three representative Protestant and Unionist Irishmen; but in this connection two things, on which sufficient stress has not so far been laid, must be recalled. In the first place the members of what is called the middle party are recruits not from

Nationalism but from Unionism; it is some of the members of the latter party who have abated their vehemence, and not any of those of the former who have altered their orientation in respect of great democratic principles.

To speak of the new school of opinion as a party, moreover, is to overstate the case as to the relative positions of three small groups of Unionist opinion, which have little or nothing in common except a joint denunciation of the present *regime*.

The views of Mr. Russell with regard to compulsory purchase are not, one suspects, those of Lord Dunraven. Lord Dunraven's views as to Devolution, it may be surmised, are too democratic for Sir Horace Plunkett, and are not sufficiently democratic for Mr. Russell. It is impossible to conceive a plan of reform which would enjoy the support of all these three while the ideas of ameliorative work entertained by the body of Orangemen led by Mr. Sloan, who are disgusted by the attitude traditionally attached to their order, would, there is no doubt, differ from those of any others. It would be impossible to find a common denominator between the views of these modern converts from the old Unionism which presented an unbending refusal to every demand for reform and held as sacrosanct the existing state of affairs, constitutional and social.

That the numbers of the moderate Unionists of all sections are at present small is not surprising. The country has too long been governed as a dependency, with the Protestant gentry as the ***oculus reipublicae***, for the "garrison" readily to waive that which they have come to look upon as their inalienable heritage. That the numbers of Orangemen will grow small by degrees as a result of land purchase is the general belief; but it must not be forgotten that the more violent among them, in their efforts to rake the ashes; and blow up the cinders of dead prejudices and extinguished hate, will have the backing of a powerful Press, the eagerness of the greatest organ of which in this matter in the past led to the worst blow its prestige has ever endured. Liberal statesmen during the recent general election were constrained to call attention to the manner in which the power of the Press had been exploited by a few persons who had endeavoured to secure a "corner" in those sources of political education, and the obviousness of the policy, it was admitted, did something to defeat its own ends. Of one thing we may be certain, the Orange drum will be beaten once more, for the old ascendancy spirit will die hard; all the devices of artificial respiration will be called in to prolong its life, and when it does breathe its last one may expect it to do so in the arms of its friends in an attic in Printing House Square.

One can only hope that the "ultras" will pitch their tone too high, and that their efforts to revive the old perverse antipathies will fail, so that Irish Unionists will realise, as some of them are doing already, that patriotism, like charity, begins at home, and that they cannot compound for distrust of their own countrymen by loud-voiced protestations of loyalty to the blessings of British rule.

It was very generally admitted that the logical outcome of Mr. Wyndham's Land Act was an Irish authority to stand between the Irish tenant and the British Exchequer, which, under the Act, is left in the invidious position of an absentee landlord to people who dislike its ascendancy and distrust its administrative methods, while an Irish authority with a direct interest in the transaction would be able to see that payments were punctually made. In the not very likely contingency of failure to do this, under the Act as passed, the remedy which lies, is for the Treasury to stop administrative payments to local bodies, an action which would bring Government to a standstill and plunge the country into disaffection. Mr. T.W. Russell has long advocated the creation at Westminster of a Grand Committee of Irish members to deal with the Estimates and with Irish legislation; and, as if there were not a plethora of proposals for the modification of the present system of Government, the plans of the Irish Reform Association have for the last three years been before the country.

The object of their first proposal is the creation of a Financial Council to which the control of Irish expenditure should be handed by the Treasury with the object of making it interested in economising in finance for Irish purposes.

Their proposal with regard to Private Bill Legislation is merely that the principle adopted in 1899 in the case of Scottish Private Bills should apply to Ireland, and this has not met with much objection. Under it local inquiries, which are at present conducted at Westminster, would be carried out in the localities affected, with much saving of expense; and it is only necessary to add that as long ago as 1881 a Bill was introduced to transfer from Westminster to Ireland the semi-judicial and semi-legislative business entailed in the passage of Private Bills through Parliament.

The statutory administrative council proposed by the Irish Reform Association was to consist of thirteen members, of whom six were to be elected by the County Councils, six were to be the nominees of the Crown, while the Lord Lieutenant, who was to preside as chairman, was to have the right to exercise the privilege of a casting vote. From a democratic point of view such a body would be an assembly *pour rire*, and would only serve to entrench the present bureaucracy more securely by the semblance of representation which it would offer, while retaining the power of the purse in the hands of a body carefully constituted in such a way that the small minority who comprise the ascendancy faction in the country would be permanently maintained in a majority on the council. A great deal more could be said in defence of another proposal which has been mooted--namely, that the principle of proportional representation should be adopted. In a country like Ireland, where the dividing line between the two great parties is unusually wide, with an ordinary system of small constituencies, the men of intermediate views like those of Mr. Sloan or of the members of the Reform Association would, even though they existed in much larger numbers than is the case, not secure any great measure of representation, but in comparatively large constituencies this would not be so.

The attitude of the Nationalists in anticipation of the Government proposal of last session was expressed by Mr. Redmond, speaking on St. Patrick's Day at Bradford:--

"If the scheme gave the Irish people genuine power and control over questions of administration alone, if it left unimpaired the National movement and the National Party, and if it lightened the financial burden under which Ireland staggered, then very possibly Ireland might seriously consider whether such a scheme ought not to be accepted for what it was worth."

The Irish Council Bill, as all the world knows, proposed to set up in Dublin an administrative Council, consisting of 82 elected, 24 nominated, members, with the Under Secretary to the Lord Lieutenant as an *ex officio* member. This body was to have control over eight of the forty-five departments which constitute "Dublin Castle"--namely, those relating to Local Government, Public Works, National Education, Intermediate Education, the Registrar-General's Office, Public Works, the Department of Agriculture and Technical Instruction, Congested Districts, and Reformatory Schools. The nature of the departments excluded from its jurisdiction is of more consequence, including as they do the Supreme Court of Judicature, the

Royal Irish Constabulary, the Dublin Metropolitan Police, the Land Commission, and the Prisons' Board.

The Bill proposed that the Council should be elected triennially on the same franchise as that on which local authorities are at present elected, and its powers were to be exercised by four Committees--of Local Government, Finance, Education, and Public Works--the decisions of which were to come up before the Council as a whole, for alteration or approval. The Bill proposed to constitute an Irish Treasury with an Irish fund of L4,000,000, made up of the moneys at present voted to the departments concerned, together with an additional L650,000. The sums paid into this fund were to be fixed by the Imperial Parliament every five years. Finally, the resolutions of the Council, by Clause 3 of the Bill, were subject to the confirmation of the Lord Lieutenant, who, by the same clause, was to be empowered to reserve such resolutions for his own consideration, to remit them for further consideration by the Council, or, lastly, "if in the opinion of the Lord Lieutenant immediate action is necessary with respect to the matter to which the resolution relates, in order to preserve the efficiency of the service, or to prevent public or private injury, the Lord Lieutenant may make such order with respect to the matter as in his opinion the necessity of the case requires, and any order so made shall have the same effect and operate in the same manner as if it were the resolution of the Irish Council."

These were the provisions of the measure which the Liberals introduced to the disappointment of their Unionist opponents, who had foretold that it would be a Home Rule Bill under some form of alias, intended to dupe the predominant partner. It is to be noted that in 1885 Mr. Chamberlain made a proposal which was on the same lines as this, but went further in one respect--that there was no nominated element on the Board which he proposed to create, and furthermore, the powers of the departments would under it have been transferred to a single elective Board, whereas under the Council Bill the departments were to be suffered to continue, albeit under control. Lord Randolph Churchill was prepared at the time of Mr. Chamberlain's proposal to give even more than the latter wished to concede, but both proposals were forgotten on the announcement by Mr. Gladstone of his intention to legislate on a comprehensive basis.

The attitude of Mr. Redmond on the first reading of the Bill has been so grossly misrepresented by the English Press, both Liberal and Conservative, which published only carefully-prepared epitomes of his speech, that it is necessary that one should devote some attention to what he actually said. After asserting that no one could expect him or his colleagues--until they had the actual Bill in their hand and had time to consider every portion of the scheme, and to elicit Irish public opinion with reference to it--to offer a deliberate or final judgment, Mr. Redmond went on to reaffirm what the Irish people have long considered the minimum demand which can satisfy their aspirations, and declared that since the measure was introduced as neither a substitute nor an alternative for Home Rule, he would proceed to consider its terms. "Does the scheme," the Irish leader went on to ask, "give a genuine and effective control to Irish public opinion over those matters of administration referred to the Council? If not the scheme is worse than useless." After protesting strongly against the nominated element in the Council as being undemocratic, Mr. Redmond went on to express his willingness "to accept it or any other safeguard that the wit of man could devise, consistent with the ordinary principles of representative government, which is necessary to show the minority in Ireland that their fears are groundless." He then proceeded strongly to criticise the power of the Lord Lieutenant under Clause 3--a power not confined to a mere exercise of veto such as is possessed by a colonial governor, but something much more than this--"a power on the part of the Lord Lieutenant to interfere with and thwart every single act, so that a hostile Lord Lieutenant might stop the whole machine. If that was the intention of the Government it destroyed the valuable and genuine character of the power given to the Council." Having protested against the proposal that the Chairmen of Committees were to be the nominees of the Lord Lieutenant, and, therefore, not necessarily in sympathy with the majority of the Council, Mr. Redmond went on to say:--"The whole question hinges on whether the finance is adequate. The money grant is ludicrously inadequate. I fear that the L650,000 would be mortgaged from the day the measure passed, and that it would be impossible with such an amount to work the scheme."

Mr. Redmond then concluded his speech with the paragraph to which most prominence was given in the English Press, with a view to suggest that he accepted, with only minor reservations, the proposals of the Government. I quote it *in extenso* to show how slender is the ground for this imputation:--

"I am most anxious to find, if I can, in this scheme an instrument which, while admittedly it will not solve the Irish problem, will, at any rate, remove some of the most glaring and palpable causes which keep Ireland poverty-stricken and Irishmen hopeless and disaffected. It is in that spirit that my colleagues and I will address ourselves to the Bill. We shrink from the responsibility of rejecting anything which after the full consideration which this Bill will secure, seems to our deliberate judgment calculated to ease the suffering of Ireland, and hasten the day of full convalescence."[27]

No one can suggest, in view of these words, that Mr. Redmond committed himself or his colleagues to anything further than to consider the Bill in a critical but not a hostile spirit. As to the suggestion that a vote for the first reading and the printing of the Bill in any sense involved the party in even a modified acceptance of the measure, in doing so the Irish members were acting in fulfilment of a pledge given by Mr. Redmond six months before, when, speaking on September 23rd, he said:--

"When the scheme is produced it will be anxiously and carefully examined. It will be submitted to the judgment of the Irish people, and no decision will be come to, whether by me or by the Irish Party, until the whole question has been submitted to a National Convention. When the hour of that Convention comes any influence which I possess with my fellow-countrymen will be used to induce them firmly to reject any proposal, no matter how plausible, which, in my judgment, may be calculated to injure the prestige of the Irish Party and disrupt the National movement, because my first and my greatest policy, which overshadows everything else, is to preserve a united National Party in Parliament, and a United powerful organisation in Ireland, until we have achieved the full measure of National freedom to which we are entitled."

If the Irish Party had not voted for the first reading we should have been told by their critics that their action was a despotic attempt to override and smother the freely-expressed opinions of the Irish people, but it must not be forgotten that it is due to Mr. Redmond's own initiative that in the case of this Bill, as in the case of the Land Bill of 1903, the final decision has rested, not, as in the case of the Home Rule Bills of 1886 and 1893, with the members of the Parliamentary Party, but, by a sort of referendum, with a National Convention containing representative Irishmen elected for the purpose from every part of the country in the most democratic manner. It is worthy of attention that the very people who five years ago were declaring in Great Britain that Home Rule was dead and damned were those who were loudest during the general election in the attempt to raise latent prejudice on that score, and to bring it to pass that the condition of things existing twenty years ago was repeated when, as Lord Salisbury declared in a speech to the National Conservative Club, "all the politics of the moment are summarised in the one word--Ireland."

In spite of these facts, Mr. Balfour, speaking on the first reading of the Council Bill, was constrained to admit that it bore no resemblance to any plan which the Irish people had ever advocated, and he went on to declare his inability to see how by any process of development it was capable of being turned into anything which the Nationalists ever contemplated. The unanimity with which the Bill was repudiated by Nationalist public opinion in Ireland is to be seen from the fact that not a single voice was raised on its behalf at the National Convention, comprising 3,000 delegates, which was the most representative meeting of any kind which has ever been held in Ireland. The reasons for its rejection are to be read in the light of the repeatedly expressed opinions of the more radical section of the Ministerial Party, to the effect that a bolder and more comprehensive scheme might have been well introduced without any infringement of the election pledges of the Government. Under Clause 3 the Lord Lieutenant, an officer under the new *regime*, as now, of a British Ministry, would have been empowered to act in defiance of the opinion of the Council either by modifying their resolutions as to Executive action or by overriding them by orders of his own, or rather of the Ministry of which he was a member. On points such as this dealing with the constitution of the assembly, Mr. Redmond was able to inform the Convention that no amendments would be accepted by the Government, and experience has taught Irishmen that although these powers might generally, under a Liberal Government, be exercised in a legitimate manner, under a Unionist Lord Lieutenant they would be exercised in a despotic fashion, just as, in the words of the Estates Commissioners themselves, the instructions issued by the Lord Lieutenant in February, 1905, were designed "seriously to impede the expeditious working of the Land Act of 1903." Great objection was taken to the fact that the resources of the Council would be such as to effect little administrative improvement, since the departments under its control were the very bodies which demanded increased expenditure, while it left untouched the Police, the Prisons' Board, and the Judiciary, the reckless extravagance of which afforded obvious sources from which, by modification of their wasteful expense, one could make large economies for the benefit of those portions of the Irish service which at the present moment are starved.

Though it may be said that the acceptance of the Bill without prejudice would not have stultified the principles already vindicated in a long struggle by the Irish people, the body as constituted, it was felt, would have served the purpose of the Unionist party by dividing without a sufficient *quid pro quo* the attention of the Irish people from their devotion to the cause for the broad principles of which they have been striving, and there was this further danger that a body so restricted in its scope and anti-democratic in its administration would have broken down in action, and would have in this way provided Unionists with the very strongest possible argument for opposition to a full autonomy.

While a certain proportion of Liberals are prepared to admit that the Bill made havoc of Liberal principles there is a Laodicean section who have greatly blamed Irish Nationalists for having refused what was offered them, when having asked for bread they were given a stone. To such people as I have in mind I should like to quote what Mr. Gladstone wrote to Lord Hartington on November 10th, 1885:--

"If that consummation--the concession to Ireland of full power to manage her own local affairs--is in any way to be contemplated, action at a stroke will be more honourable, less unsafe, less uneasy than the jolting process of a series of partial measures."[28]

The position of that section of Liberals is strange which is represented by the assertion that their party has already made enough sacrifices in regard to Irish affairs, and which is anxious to return to the *laissez faire* policy of their mid-Victorian predecessors. The point I submit is this, either Liberals do or they do not believe in the principle of self-government as applied to Ireland, and if they do adhere to it no effort is too great, no difficulty too extreme, for them to face in the attempt to solve so serious a problem. Those who think that because in 1886, and again in 1893, the Liberals, with Irish support, unsuccessfully attempted to solve the Irish question, they have thereby contracted out of their moral obligation, take a very curious view of the responsibilities of popular government; but it is not so strange as the position of those who hold that because in 1907 the Irish people refused a particular form of change in the methods of government for which they never asked, they have in consequence closed every avenue to constitutional reform which can be opened for many years.

In politics it is often the unexpected that happens, and he would be a bold prophet who should declare it impossible that within a few years Liberals may not return *in toto* to the advocacy of sound principles in regard to Ireland, the abandonment of which is to be traced to the recrudescence of Whiggism after Mr. Gladstone's death and the desire to find some line of policy which might be pilloried as a scapegoat to account for the disgust of the country with a divided party in the years following 1895. Liberalism, for its part, if it is to settle the problem, must fully appreciate the fact that its proposals, if they are to succeed, must be accepted with the full concurrence of the Irish representative majority, and on the part of Irishmen what is demanded is a recognition of the results of the dispensation which has placed the two islands side by side; by these means only can a practicable policy be ensured, but it must be remembered with regard to those in Ireland who hold extreme views, that the continuance of the system of government which holds the field, and the financial burden at the expense of Ireland which it perpetuates, serve increasingly to obscure and at the same time to counteract the advantages accruing from the connection between the two countries, which one may hope would, in happier circumstances, be obvious.

The Irish people still appreciate the force of that maxim of Edmund Burke's, that the things which are not practicable are not desirable. While they claim that as of right they are entitled to demand a separation of the bonds, to the forging of which they were not consenting parties, as practical men they are prepared loyally to abide by a compromise which will maintain the union of the crowns while separating the Legislatures. An international contract leaving them an independent Parliament with an Executive responsible to it, having control over domestic affairs, is their demand. Grattan's constitution comprised a sovereign Parliament with a non-Parliamentary Executive, in so far as the latter was appointed and dismissed by English Ministers. The constitution which is demanded to-day is the same as that enjoyed by such a colony as Victoria, with a non-sovereign Parliament, having, that is, a definite limit to its legislative powers, such as those under the Bill of 1886 referring to Church Establishment and Customs, but having an Executive directly responsible to it.

The case of the Irish people has never been put with more clearness and frankness than it was by Mr. Redmond in the House of Commons two years ago. Having been accused by Unionists of adopting a more extreme line outside Parliament than that which he followed at St. Stephen's, the Irish leader in reply, after declaring that separation from Great Britain would be better than a continuance of the present method of government, and that he should feel bound to recommend armed revolt if there were any chance of its success, went on to say:--

"I am profoundly convinced that by constitutional means, and within the constitution, it is possible to arrive at a compromise based upon the concession of self-government--or, as Mr. Gladstone used to call it, autonomy--to Ireland, which would put an end to this ancient international quarrel upon terms satisfactory and honourable to both nations."

An Orangeman described the late Government as being engaged in the useless task of trying to conciliate those who will not be conciliated. The words of Mr. Redmond indicate the one way in which a *Pacata Hibernia* can be secured within the Empire. It is a compromise, but it has this one virtue which compromises rarely possess--that it will satisfy the great mass of the Irish people, and it concedes, as we hold, no vital principle.

CHAPTER X
CONCLUSION

"Unsettled questions have no pity for the repose of nations."
--EDMUND BURKE.

The position of the mass of the Irish people with regard to the present form of government has nowhere been more cogently expressed than in the chapter on the Union in the "Cambridge Modern History," the writer of which describes it as a settlement by compulsion, not by consent; and the penalty of such methods is, that the instrument possesses no moral validity for those who do not accept the grounds on which it was adopted. If Englishmen get this firmly fixed in their minds they will understand that we regard all Unionist reforms, whether from Liberal or Conservative Governments, as instalments of conscience money, in regard to which, granting our premises, it would be sheer affectation to express surprise or to feign disgust at the lack of effusive gratitude with which we receive them. "Give us back our ancient liberties" has been the cry of the Irish people ever since George III. gave his assent to the Act of Union. The ties of sentiment which bind her colonies so closely to Great Britain are conspicuous by their absence in the case of Ireland. The ties of common interest which are not less strong in the matter of her colonial possessions are, albeit in existence as far as Great Britain and Ireland are concerned, obscured and vitiated by the system of taxation which makes the poorer country contribute to the joint expenses at a rate altogether disproportionate to her means, and which, while making her in this wise pay the piper, in no sense allows her to call the tune.

Never has there been applied in Ireland that doctrine which the *Times* enunciated so sententiously half a century ago in speaking of the Papal States--"The destiny of a nation ought to be determined not by the opinions of other nations but by the opinion of the nation itself. To decide whether they are well governed or not is for those who live under that government." If the *Times* were to apply the wisdom of these words to the situation in Ireland instead of screaming "Separatism" at every breath of a suggestion of the extension of democratic principles in Ireland, it would take steps to secure a condition of things under which the people would not be alienated and would be a source of strength and not of weakness.

Writing in that paper in 1880, at a time when Ireland was seething with lawlessness, Charles Gordon declared--"I must say that the state of our countrymen in the parts I have named is worse than that of any people in the world, let alone Europe. I believe that these people are made as we are, that they are patient beyond belief, loyal but broken-spirited and desperate; lying on the verge of starvation where we would not keep cattle."

On the day after the murder of Mr. Burke in the Phoenix Park a permanent Civil Servant was sent straight from the admiralty to take his place as Under Secretary. Sir Robert Hamilton who served in Dublin in those trying conditions became a convinced Home Ruler, as did his chief, Lord Spencer; and it is generally said to have been Sir Robert who converted Mr. Gladstone to Home Rule. On the return to power of the Conservatives, after the defeat of the Home Rule Bill of 1886, Sir Robert Hamilton was retired, and in his stead Sir Redvers Buller was sent to rule Ireland *manu militari*. This officer, on being examined by Lord Cowper's Commission, expressed his opinion that the National League had been the tenants' best, if not their only, friend. "You have got," he said, "a very ignorant, poor people, and the law should look after them, instead of which it has only looked after the rich." To hold opinions so unconventional in the service of a Unionist Viceroy was impossible, and in a year other fields for Sir Redvers' activities were found. Sir West Ridgeway, who succeeded him, served as Mr. Balfour's lieutenant during the latter's efforts to "kill Home Rule with kindness," and it is significant to find him at this day writing articles in the reviews on the disappearance of Unionism, and pinning his faith to Dunravenism as the next move.

It is assuredly a remarkable fact that the shrewdest of English statesmen have not been able to see the complication with which the Irish problem is entangled.

Macaulay imagined that the religious difficulty was the crux of the Irish question, but Emancipation did not bring the expected peace and contentment in its train. John Bright imagined that the agrarian question was the only obstacle to reconciliation, but a recognition three-quarters of a century after the Union that the laws of tenure are made for man and not man for the laws of tenure, failed to put an end to Irish disaffection. Mr. Gladstone thought in 1870 that the Irish problem was solved. Complicated as the question has been in its various aspects--religious, racial, economic, and agrarian--our demands have too often and too long been met in the spirit of the Levite who passed by on the other side, until violence has forced tardy redress, acquiesced in with reluctance. If the action of Wellington and Peel was pusillanimous in granting Emancipation, for the express purpose of resisting which they were placed in power, backed as they were in their refusal by their allies in Ireland, the next great measures of reform forty years later were admitted by Mr. Gladstone himself to be equally the result of violence and breaches of the law. The Queen's Speech of 1880 contained but a passing reference to Ireland and of the intention of the Government to rule without exceptional legislation; the Queen's Speech of 1881 contained reference to little but Ireland and of the intention of the Government to introduce a Coercion Bill.

In July, 1885, Lord Salisbury's Viceroy, on taking office, deprecated the use of Coercion, but in January, 1886, the same Government introduced a Coercion Bill, though less than six months before they had repudiated it, and had beaten the Liberal Government on this very issue with the aid of the Irish vote. The manner in which both English parties have eaten their words is warranted to inculcate political cynicism. If in 1881 the Liberals are declared to have jettisoned their principles and to have perpetrated that which a few months before they declared would stultify their whole policy, the same damaging admission must be made by the Tories as to their acquiescence in the Franchise Bill of 1884 and their conduct of the Land Bill of 1887.

"Anyone," said Cavour, "can govern in a state of siege," but I do not think Englishmen realise the extent to which the ruling policy has been to accentuate the repressive to the exclusion of the beneficent side of government, and how ready they have been to make the government not one of opinion, as in their own country, but one of force. When Mr. Balfour introduced his perpetual Coercion Bill of 1887 it was estimated that there had been one such measure for every year of the century that was passing.

In the first instance, the institutions of Ireland, being imposed by a conquering country, never earned that measure of respect bred partly of pride which attaches itself to the self-sown customs and processes of nations; but, having introduced her legal system, England superseded it and took steps to rule by a code outside the Common Law, so that respect was, therefore, asked for legal institutions which, on her own showing, and by her own admissions, had proved inadequate. In Ireland Government did not "meet the headlong violence of angry power by covering the accused all over with the armour of the law," as in Erskine's famous phrase it did in England with regard to those imbued with revolutionary principles.

A rusty statute of Edward III., which was devised for the suppression of brigandage, was used to condemn the leaders of the Irish people, unheard, in a court of law. Trial by jury was suspended and the common right of freedom of speech was infringed. In 1901 no less than ten Members of Parliament were imprisoned under the Crimes Act, and it was not until the appointment of Sir Antony MacDonnell to the Under Secretaryship that the proclamation of the Coercion Act was withdrawn.

It is no small matter that Mr. Bryce, when reviewing his period of office, mentioned among the details of his policy that he had set his face against jury-packing, and had allowed juries to be chosen perfectly freely. The suspension of the most cherished Common Law rights of the subject from Habeas Corpus downwards has been the inevitable result of a failure to apply democratic principles of government. Jury-packing, forbidden meetings, summary arrests and prosecutions, and police reporters form a discreditable paraphernalia by which to maintain the conduct of government.

As examples of the differential treatment meted out to Ireland which is not of a nature to impress her with confidence in English methods may be mentioned the fact that the Irish militia are drafted out of the country for their training, that no citizen army of volunteers is permitted, and the desire of one faction to preserve these discriminations is to be seen in the anger with which was greeted the omission the other day of the Irish Arms Act from the Expiring Laws Continuation Bill.

Under every bad government there arise popular organisations bred of the wildness of despair which enjoy the moral sanction which the law has failed to secure "When citizens," said Filangieri long ago, "see the Sword of Justice idle they snatch a dagger." So long as the Government sate on the safety valve, so long did periodic explosions of revolutionary resentment arise, and one must appreciate the fact that in a country so devoutly Catholic as is Ireland the natural conservatism which attachment to an historic Church inculcates, and the direction on its part of anathemas at secret societies and at violence, served to make it more difficult by far to arouse revolutionary reprisals than it would be in similar circumstances in England.

"When bad men combine," wrote Edmund Burke, "the good must associate, else they will fall one by one an unpitied sacrifice in a contemptible struggle." No one can accuse Burke--the apostle of constitutionalism, the arch-enemy of the French revolution--of condoning violence, but even he admitted that there is a limit at which forbearance ceases to be a virtue.

England must blame herself for the war of classes with which the National struggle has been complicated. It was the Act of Union which made the landlord class look to England, and established it in the anomalous position of a body drawing its income from one country and its support from another; by this means it made them a veritable English garrison appealing to England as being the only loyal people. Let us hope it is not true to say at this date that like the Bourbons they have learnt nothing and forgotten nothing. The rich, the proud, and the powerful have had their day, and can one deny that the attempt to govern Ireland in the sole interests of a minority has made Ireland what it is. An unbiased French observer three-quarters of a century ago declared that the cause of Irish distress was its ***mauvaise aristocratic***. It was the interest of this class, as they themselves admit, which was allowed to dominate the policy of the Unionist Party, and to effect this, force was the only available instrument. With the recognition of the fact that the possession of property is no guarantee of intelligence has come the crippling of the policy of ***laissez faire***, supported though it was by the brewers of Dublin and the shipbuilders of Belfast, for this reason--that rich men tend always to rally to the defence of property. The exercise of the duties which property imposes and the responsibility which it entails being the chief advantages of a landed gentry, and their main ***raison d'etre*** as a ruling caste having been conspicuous by its absence, with few exceptions, in Ireland, the passing of the landowner as a social factor is looked upon with complacency.

English statesmen seem to have applied that maxim of Machiavelli--that benefits should be conferred little by little so as to be more fully appreciated. It is hard to realise that little more than thirty years have elapsed since the time when the landed interest was supreme in these islands. Their power was first assailed by the Ballot Act of 1873, and the Corrupt Practices Act of 1884 did much to put a term to a form of intimidation at which Tories did not hold up their hands in horror, while the Franchise Act of 1883 destroyed their power, so that in those years passed away for ever the time when, as Archbishop Croke put it, an Irish borough would elect Barabbas for thirty pieces of silver.

Of one thing, indeed, we may be certain, and that is that we have touched bottom in the matter of Unionist concessions. The manner in which the programme mapped out between Mr. Wyndham and Sir Antony MacDonnell was rendered nugatory is evidence of that. The administration of the Land Act, under the secret instructions issued by Dublin Castle, was such as to cripple the Estates Commissioners in their application of its provisions. The proposals as to the settlement of the University question were nipped in the bud after advances had been made to the Catholic bishops to discover what was the minimum which they would accept, and this was done although Mr. Balfour had declared at Manchester in 1899--"Unless the University question can be settled Unionism is a failure."

Mr. F.H. Dale, an English Inspector of Schools, who, in the last couple of years, has produced two comprehensive blue books on the state of primary and secondary education in Ireland, declared that he found the desire for higher education in Ireland greater than in England; but in spite of this, so far, neither British party has advanced one step in the direction of a permanent solution, pleading as excuse that the fear of strengthening the hands of the priests blocks the way, albeit a university under predominantly lay control is all that even the hierarchy in Ireland demand; while to add to the groundlessness on which intolerance is based the only institution of a satisfactory kind which is endowed by the State is a Jesuit College supported by what one can only call circuitous means.

Mr. Balfour himself has admitted that no Protestant parent could conscientiously send his son to a college which was as Catholic as Trinity is Protestant.

If Oxford and Cambridge had been founded by foreign Catholics for the express purpose of destroying the Protestant religion in England, a thirty years' abolition of tests, which in no sense affected their "atmosphere," would not have overcome the prejudice and scruples persisting against them.

The vicious circles round which Irish questions rotate is nowhere seen more clearly than in this connection. When complaint is made that a disproportionately small number of Catholics hold high appointments in the public offices in Ireland, the reply is made that the number of members of that Church with high educational qualifications is small; when demands are made for facilities for higher education, the reluctance of English people to publicly endow sectarian education is urged as an excuse, although Irishmen have not, since Trinity abolished tests, made any demands for a purely sectarian University or College.

I have shown how, as a result of our aloofness from both English parties, we find ourselves between the upper and the nether millstones, and in what way in regard to the University question the old error which for so long obstructed the land question is at work--mean the error of denying reform for English reasons and endeavouring to force English doctrines into the law and government of Ireland and of suppressing Irish customs and Irish ideas.

On the advent to power of the present Government the heads of the great departments in Whitehall excused their apparent dilatoriness in effecting those administrative changes which the country expected from a Liberal Government, by the fact that after twenty years of Conservative rule the permanent officials were so steeped in the methods of Toryism their habits were to such a degree tinged and coloured by its policy, that there was the greatest possible difficulty in making the necessary alterations. In the case of Ireland this is so to a much greater extent, and one must recognise the truth of that saying of some Irish member to the effect that a new Chief Secretary was like the change of the dial on a clock--the difference was not great, for the works remain the same.

The main arguments against reform are founded on prophetic fears, and if one is impressed by the threats of a *jacquerie* on the part of the Orangemen, led though they may be again, as they were twenty years ago, by a Minister of Cabinet rank, Nationalists, on the other hand, may remind Englishmen that the Irish volcanoes are not yet extinct, and that the history of reform is such as to show the value of violence on the failure of peaceful persuasion--a feature the most lamentable in Irish politics; and in this connection let it never be forgotten that "the warnings of Irish members," as Mr. Morley wrote in the *Pall Mall Gazette* on the introduction of the Coercion Bill which followed the Phoenix Park murders, "have a most unpleasant knack of coming true." When the counsels of prudence coincide with the claims of justice, surely the last word had been said to disarm opposition.

"Old Buckshot," said Parnell grimly enough in 1881, "thinks that by making Ireland a gaol he will settle the Irish question." Throwing over that theory Great Britain decided in 1884--in the phrase then current--that to count heads was better than to break them, but having counted them she ignored their verdict, and has continued so to do for more than twenty years. One would have thought that she would have applied the rigour of her theories and put an end to this travesty by which she has conceded the letter of democracy--a phantom privilege which she has rendered nugatory. It was the impossibility of ignoring the constitutionally-expressed wishes of the Irish people after he had extended the suffrage, which made Mr. Gladstone a Home Ruler, and Englishmen have to remember that this, the only remedy in the whole of their political materia medica which they have not tried, is the one which has effected a cure wherever else it has been applied.

I ask, to what does England look forward in a prolongation of the present conditions? There is no finality in the politics of Ireland any more than in those of other countries. She cannot say to Ireland--"Thus far shalt thou go, and no further." As one burning question is solved another arises to take its place and to demand redress. The battle for the moment may seem to be to the strong, but in the long run might is unable to resist the advances of right. Time, we may well declare, is on our side; but one has to count the cost in the material damage to us, and in the moral damage to Great Britain, in the ultimate concession, perhaps under duress, of so much which has repeatedly been refused. Ever since, in 1881, Mr. Gladstone "banished to Saturn the laws of political economy," strong measures of State socialism have been enacted by both parties. It is not for nothing that the tenants in the West find themselves to-day paying less than half for their holdings of what they paid twenty years ago, and paying it, moreover, not by way of rent but as a terminable annuity. If there is one point which the events of the last generation have established in their eyes it is this--that Parnell was justified in telling them to keep a firm grip of their holdings, and that Great Britain has admitted the justice of the grounds on which their agitation was based, by the revolution in the social fabric which she has set in train by the Land Purchase Acts.

Who was the witty Frenchman who declared that England was an island and that every Englishman was an island? It is not only because of this preoccupation with their own affairs that their ***amour propre*** has been injured by their failure in Ireland. One cannot expect to gather figs from thistles or grapes from thorns, and when Englishmen appreciate to how small an extent the Union has enured to the advantage of Ireland, they will understand the feelings which actuate the desire for self-government. Is there anything which makes Englishmen believe that the extension of Land Purchase or the foundation of a university will make for a permanent settlement? The history of the last half century can scarcely make them sanguine that when the burning questions of to-day have been disposed of they will find in the Imperial Parliament the knowledge, the interest, or the time necessary for dealing with new questions as they arise--for arise they assuredly will.

Great Britain may legislate with lazy, ill-informed, good intentions, as Mr. Gladstone admitted was done in the case of the Encumbered Estates Act, or she may grant concessions piecemeal, and the minority which thereby she maintains will denounce every reform as mere ***panem et circenses*** by which she hopes to keep the majority subdued.

The "loyal minority" have cried "wolf" too often. Nearly forty years ago, when Disestablishment was threatened, the Protestant Archbishop of Dublin said--"You will put to Irish Protestants the choice between apostacy and expatriation, and every man among them who has money or position, when he sees his Church go, will leave the country. If you do that, you will find Ireland so difficult to manage that you will have to depend on the gibbet and the sword."

The twenty-five attempts to settle by legislation the land question were in nearly every instance denounced as spoliation by the House of Lords, which was constrained to let them pass into law. The pages of Hansard are grey with unfulfilled forebodings as to what would be the effect of the extension of the Franchise and of the grant of popular Local Government. The results of the former took the wind out of the sails of those who declared that popular wishes in Ireland were overridden by a political caucus, the success of local government has given Orangemen occasion to blaspheme.

The history of Irish legislation on all these points has been one of belated concession to demands repeatedly made, at first scouted and finally surrendered. And withal, English statesmen have not killed Home Rule with kindness. "Twenty years of resolute government" were confidently expected to give Irish Nationalism its *quietus. E pur si muove.*

NOTES

[1] L. Paul-Dubois. *L'Irlande Contemporaine*, p. 174.
[2] "Life of Lord Randolph Churchill," Vol. II., p. 455.
[3] *L'Irlande Contemporaine*, p. 232.
[4] Hansard, August 1, 1881.
[5] *Ibid.*, September 3, 1886.
[6] *Ibid.*, August 19, 1886.
[7] *Ibid.*, March 22, 1887.
[8] *Ibid.*, April 22, 1887.
[9] *Ibid.*, February 14, 1907.
[10] The statement in the text, written shortly after the prorogation of Parliament, unexpectedly demands modification. Almost all the planters on the Clanricarde estate have expressed their readiness to clear out of the evicted lands and to accept re-settlement elsewhere. The Lords' amendments will in consequence not prove the obstacle which it was feared they would to the exercise of powers of compulsion by the Estates Commissioners against the owner.
[11] "Greville Memoirs," Series I., Vol. III., p. 269.
[12] *Ibid.*, Series II., p. 217, December, 1843.
[13] *Ibid.*, Series II., Vol. II., March, 1846.
[14] Hansard, February, 1848.
[15] *United Irishman*, May 14, 1904.
[16] "Life of Lord Randolph Churchill," Vol. II., p. 4, October 14, 1885.
[17] Hansard, May 20, 1884.
[18] "Life of Lord Randolph Churchill," Vol. II., p. 456, 1892.
[19] "Greville," Series I., Vol. II., p. 76, November, 1830.
[20] "Life of Whately," Vol. II., p. 246, 1852.
[21] "Life of Lord Randolph Churchill," Vol. II., p. 28, December, 1885.
[22] Morley's "Life of Gladstone," Vol. II., Bk. IX., Cap. 4, p. 524.
[23] Hansard, March 6, 1905.

[24] *Times*, January 10, 1906.
[25] Mrs. John Richard Green, *Independent Review*, June, 1905.
[26] "Ireland and the Empire," p. 275.
[27] Hansard, May 7, 1907.
[28] Morley's "Life of Gladstone," Vol. II., Bk. IX., Cap. 1, p. 481.

www.bookjungle.com email: sales@bookjungle.com fax: 630-214-0564 mail: Book Jungle PO Box 2226 Champaign, IL 61825

The Codes Of Hammurabi And Moses
W. W. Davies

The discovery of the Hammurabi Code is one of the greatest achievements of archaeology, and is of paramount interest, not only to the student of the Bible, but also to all those interested in ancient history...

Religion   **ISBN: *1-59462-338-4***   **Pages:132**
QTY
MSRP $12.95

The Theory of Moral Sentiments
Adam Smith

This work from 1749. contains original theories of conscience amd moral judgment and it is the foundation for systemof morals.

Philosophy   ISBN: *1-59462-777-0*   **Pages:536**
QTY
MSRP $19.95

Jessica's First Prayer
Hesba Stretton

In a screened and secluded corner of one of the many railway-bridges which span the streets of London there could be seen a few years ago, from five o'clock every morning until half past eight, a tidily set-out coffee-stall, consisting of a trestle and board, upon which stood two large tin cans, with a small fire of charcoal burning under each so as to keep the coffee boiling during the early hours of the morning when the work-people were thronging into the city on their way to their daily toil...

Childrens   ISBN: *1-59462-373-2*
QTY
Pages:84
MSRP $9.95

My Life and Work
Henry Ford

Henry Ford revolutionized the world with his implementation of mass production for the Model T automobile. Gain valuable business insight into his life and work with his own auto-biography... "We have only started on our development of our country we have not as yet, with all our talk of wonderful progress, done more than scratch the surface. The progress has been wonderful enough but..."

Biographies/   ISBN: *1-59462-198-5*
QTY
Pages:300
MSRP $21.95

www.bookjungle.com email: sales@bookjungle.com fax: 630-214-0564 mail: Book Jungle PO Box 2226 Champaign, IL 61825

The Art of Cross-Examination
Francis Wellman

I presume it is the experience of every author, after his first book is published upon an important subject, to be almost overwhelmed with a wealth of ideas and illustrations which could readily have been included in his book, and which to his own mind, at least, seem to make a second edition inevitable. Such certainly was the case with me; and when the first edition had reached its sixth impression in five months, I rejoiced to learn that it seemed to my publishers that the book had met with a sufficiently favorable reception to justify a second and considerably enlarged edition. ..

QTY

Reference   ISBN: *1-59462-647-2*   Pages:412 MSRP *$19.95*

On the Duty of Civil Disobedience
Henry David Thoreau

Thoreau wrote his famous essay, On the Duty of Civil Disobedience, as a protest against an unjust but popular war and the immoral but popular institution of slave-owning. He did more than write—he declined to pay his taxes, and was hauled off to gaol in consequence. Who can say how much this refusal of his hastened the end of the war and of slavery ?

QTY

Law   ISBN: *1-59462-747-9*   Pages:48 MSRP *$7.45*

Dream Psychology Psychoanalysis for Beginners
Sigmund Freud

Sigmund Freud, born Sigismund Schlomo Freud (May 6, 1856 - September 23, 1939), was a Jewish-Austrian neurologist and psychiatrist who co-founded the psychoanalytic school of psychology. Freud is best known for his theories of the unconscious mind, especially involving the mechanism of repression; his redefinition of sexual desire as mobile and directed towards a wide variety of objects; and his therapeutic techniques, especially his understanding of transference in the therapeutic relationship and the presumed value of dreams as sources of insight into unconscious desires.

QTY

Psychology   ISBN: *1-59462-905-6*   Pages:196 MSRP *$15.45*

The Miracle of Right Thought
Orison Swett Marden

Believe with all of your heart that you will do what you were made to do. When the mind has once formed the habit of holding cheerful, happy, prosperous pictures, it will not be easy to form the opposite habit. It does not matter how improbable or how far away this realization may see, or how dark the prospects may be, if we visualize them as best we can, as vividly as possible, hold tenaciously to them and vigorously struggle to attain them, they will gradually become actualized, realized in the life. But a desire, a longing without endeavor, a yearning abandoned or held indifferently will vanish without realization.

QTY

Self Help   ISBN: *1-59462-644-8*   Pages:360 MSRP *$25.45*

www.bookjungle.com email: sales@bookjungle.com fax: 630-214-0564 mail: Book Jungle PO Box 2226 Champaign, IL 61825

QTY

☐	**The Rosicrucian Cosmo-Conception Mystic Christianity** *by Max Heindel* The Rosicrucian Cosmo-conception is not dogmatic, neither does it appeal to any other authority than the reason of the student. It is: not controversial, but is: sent forth in the, hope that it may help to clear...	ISBN: *1-59462-188-8*	**$38.95** New Age/Religion Pages 646
☐	**Abandonment To Divine Providence** *by Jean-Pierre de Caussade* "The Rev. Jean Pierre de Caussade was one of the most remarkable spiritual writers of the Society of Jesus in France in the 18th Century. His death took place at Toulouse in 1751. His works have gone through many editions and have been republished..."	ISBN: *1-59462-228-0*	**$25.95** Inspirational/Religion Pages 400
☐	**Mental Chemistry** *by Charles Haanel* Mental Chemistry allows the change of material conditions by combining and appropriately utilizing the power of the mind. Much like applied chemistry creates something new and unique out of careful combinations of chemicals the mastery of mental chemistry...	ISBN: *1-59462-192-6*	**$23.95** New Age Pages 354
☐	**The Letters of Robert Browning and Elizabeth Barret Barrett 1845-1846 vol II** *by Robert Browning and Elizabeth Barrett*	ISBN: *1-59462-193-4*	**$35.95** Biographies Pages 596
☐	**Gleanings In Genesis (volume I)** *by Arthur W. Pink* Appropriately has Genesis been termed "the seed plot of the Bible" for in it we have, in germ form, almost all of the great doctrines which are afterwards fully developed in the books of Scripture which follow...	ISBN: *1-59462-130-6*	**$27.45** Religion/Inspirational Pages 420
☐	**The Master Key** *by L. W. de Laurence* In no branch of human knowledge has there been a more lively increase of the spirit of research during the past few years than in the study of Psychology, Concentration and Mental Discipline. The requests for authentic lessons in Thought Control, Mental Discipline and...	ISBN: *1-59462-001-6*	**$30.95** New Age/Business Pages 422
☐	**The Lesser Key Of Solomon Goetia** *by L. W. de Laurence* This translation of the first book of the "Lernegton" which is now for the first time made accessible to students of Talismanic Magic was done, after careful collation and edition, from numerous Ancient Manuscripts in Hebrew, Latin, and French...	ISBN: *1-59462-092-X*	**$9.95** New Age/Occult Pages 92
☐	**Rubaiyat Of Omar Khayyam** *by Edward Fitzgerald* Edward Fitzgerald, whom the world has already learned, in spite of his own efforts to remain within the shadow of anonymity, to look upon as one of the rarest poets of the century, was born at Bredfield, in Suffolk, on the 31st of March, 1809. He was the third son of John Purcell...	ISBN: *1-59462-332-5*	**$13.95** Music Pages 172
☐	**Ancient Law** *by Henry Maine* The chief object of the following pages is to indicate some of the earliest ideas of mankind, as they are reflected in Ancient Law, and to point out the relation of those ideas to modern thought.	ISBN: *1-59462-128-4*	**$29.95** Religion/History Pages 452
☐	**Far-Away Stories** *by William J. Locke* "Good wine needs no bush, but a collection of mixed vintages does. And this book is just such a collection. Some of the stories I do not want to remain buried for ever in the museum files of dead magazine-numbers an author's not unpardonable vanity..."	ISBN: *1-59462-129-2*	**$19.45** Fiction Pages 272
☐	**Life of David Crockett** *by David Crockett* "Colonel David Crockett was one of the most remarkable men of the times in which he lived. Born in humble life, but gifted with a strong will, an indomitable courage, and unremitting perseverance...	ISBN: *1-59462-250-7*	**$27.45** Biographies/New Age Pages 424
☐	**Lip-Reading** *by Edward Nitchie* Edward B. Nitchie, founder of the New York School for the Hard of Hearing, now the Nitchie School of Lip-Reading, Inc, wrote "LIP-READING Principles and Practice". The development and perfecting of this meritorious work on lip-reading was an undertaking...	ISBN: *1-59462-206-X*	**$25.95** How-to Pages 400
☐	**A Handbook of Suggestive Therapeutics, Applied Hypnotism, Psychic Science** *by Henry Munro*	ISBN: *1-59462-214-0*	**$24.95** Health/New Age/Health/Self-help Pages 376
☐	**A Doll's House: and Two Other Plays** *by Henrik Ibsen* Henrik Ibsen created this classic when in revolutionary 1848 Rome. Introducing some striking concepts in playwriting for the realist genre, this play has been studied the world over.	ISBN: *1-59462-112-8*	**$19.95** Fiction/Classics/Plays 308
☐	**The Light of Asia** *by sir Edwin Arnold* In this poetic masterpiece, Edwin Arnold describes the life and teachings of Buddha. The man who was to become known as Buddha to the world was born as Prince Gautama of India but he rejected the worldly riches and abandoned the reigns of power when...	ISBN: *1-59462-204-3*	**$13.95** Religion/History/Biographies Pages 170
☐	**The Complete Works of Guy de Maupassant** *by Guy de Maupassant* "For days and days, nights and nights, I had dreamed of that first kiss which was to consecrate our engagement, and I knew not on what spot I should put my lips..."	ISBN: *1-59462-157-8*	**$16.95** Fiction/Classics Pages 240
☐	**The Art of Cross-Examination** *by Francis L. Wellman* Written by a renowned trial lawyer, Wellman imparts his experience and uses case studies to explain how to use psychology to extract desired information through questioning.	ISBN: *1-59462-309-0*	**$26.95** How-to/Science/Reference Pages 408
☐	**Answered or Unanswered?** *by Louisa Vaughan* Miracles of Faith in China	ISBN: *1-59462-248-5*	**$10.95** Religion Pages 112
☐	**The Edinburgh Lectures on Mental Science (1909)** *by Thomas* This book contains the substance of a course of lectures recently given by the writer in the Queen Street Hall, Edinburgh. Its purpose is to indicate the Natural Principles governing the relation between Mental Action and Material Conditions...	ISBN: *1-59462-008-3*	**$11.95** New Age/Psychology Pages 148
☐	**Ayesha** *by H. Rider Haggard* Verily and indeed it is the unexpected that happens! Probably if there was one person upon the earth from whom the Editor of this, and of a certain previous history, did not expect to hear again...	ISBN: *1-59462-301-5*	**$24.95** Classics Pages 380
☐	**Ayala's Angel** *by Anthony Trollope* The two girls were both pretty, but Lucy who was twenty-one who supposed to be simple and comparatively unattractive, whereas Ayala was credited, as her Bombwhat romantic name might show, with poetic charm and a taste for romance. Ayala when her father died was nineteen...	ISBN: *1-59462-352-X*	**$29.95** Fiction Pages 484
☐	**The American Commonwealth** *by James Bryce* An interpretation of American democratic political theory. It examines political mechanics and society from the perspective of Scotsman James Bryce	ISBN: *1-59462-286-8*	**$34.45** Politics Pages 572
☐	**Stories of the Pilgrims** *by Margaret P. Pumphrey* This book explores pilgrims religious oppression in England as well as their escape to Holland and eventual crossing to America on the Mayflower, and their early days in New England...	ISBN: *1-59462-116-0*	**$17.95** History Pages 268

www.bookjungle.com email: sales@bookjungle.com fax: 630-214-0564 mail: Book Jungle PO Box 2226 Champaign, IL 61825

		QTY
The Fasting Cure *by Sinclair Upton*	ISBN: *1-59462-222-1* $13.95	☐
In the Cosmopolitan Magazine for May, 1910, and in the Contemporary Review (London) for April, 1910, I published an article dealing with my experiences in fasting. I have written a great many magazine articles, but never one which attracted so much attention... New Age/Self Help/Health Pages 164		
Hebrew Astrology *by Sepharial*	ISBN: *1-59462-308-2* $13.45	☐
In these days of advanced thinking it is a matter of common observation that we have left many of the old landmarks behind and that we are now pressing forward to greater heights and to a wider horizon than that which represented the mind-content of our progenitors... Astrology Pages 144		
Thought Vibration or The Law of Attraction in the Thought World	ISBN: *1-59462-127-6* $12.95	☐
by William Walker Atkinson	Psychology/Religion Pages 144	
Optimism *by Helen Keller*	ISBN: *1-59462-108-X* $15.95	☐
Helen Keller was blind, deaf, and mute since 19 months old, yet famously learned how to overcome these handicaps, communicate with the world, and spread her lectures promoting optimism. An inspiring read for everyone... Biographies/Inspirational Pages 84		
Sara Crewe *by Frances Burnett*	ISBN: *1-59462-360-0* $9.45	☐
In the first place, Miss Minchin lived in London. Her home was a large, dull, tall one, in a large, dull square, where all the houses were alike, and all the sparrows were alike, and where all the door-knockers made the same heavy sound... Childrens/Classic Pages 88		
The Autobiography of Benjamin Franklin *by Benjamin Franklin*	ISBN: *1-59462-135-7* $24.95	☐
The Autobiography of Benjamin Franklin has probably been more extensively read than any other American historical work, and no other book of its kind has had such ups and downs of fortune. Franklin lived for many years in England, where he was agent... Biographies/History Pages 332		

Name	
Email	
Telephone	
Address	
City, State ZIP	

☐ Credit Card   ☐ Check / Money Order

Credit Card Number	
Expiration Date	
Signature	

Please Mail to: Book Jungle
PO Box 2226
Champaign, IL 61825
or Fax to: 630-214-0564

ORDERING INFORMATION

web: *www.bookjungle.com*
email: *sales@bookjungle.com*
fax: *630-214-0564*
mail: *Book Jungle PO Box 2226 Champaign, IL 61825*
or PayPal *to sales@bookjungle.com*

Please contact us for bulk discounts

DIRECT-ORDER TERMS

**20% Discount if You Order
Two or More Books**
Free Domestic Shipping!
Accepted: Master Card, Visa,
Discover, American Express

www.ingramcontent.com/pod-product-compliance
Lightning Source LLC
Chambersburg PA
CBHW081836170426
43199CB00017B/2747